GERMAN IDEOLOGY

LOUIS DUMONT

GERMAN
IDEOLOGY

FROM FRANCE TO GERMANY AND BACK

THE UNIVERSITY OF CHICAGO PRESS

Chicago and London

Louis Dumont is *directeur d'études* at the Ecole des Hautes Etudes en Sciences Sociales. He is a member of the British Academy and the American Academy of Arts and Sciences.

The University of Chicago Press, Chicago 60637
The University of Chicago Press, Ltd., London

© 1994 by The University of Chicago
All rights reserved. Published 1994
Printed in the United States of America

03 02 01 00 99 98 97 96 95 94   1 2 3 4 5
ISBN: 0-226-16952-9   (cloth)
        0-226-16953-7   (paper)

An earlier version of this book was published in 1991 by Gallimard, under the title, *Homo Aequalis II: L'Idéologie allemande, France-Allemagne et retour,* © Editions Gallimard, 1991.

Library of Congress Cataloging-in-Publication Data

Dumont, Louis, 1911–
    [Ideologie Allemande. English]
    German ideology : from France to Germany and back / Louis Dumont.
        p.   cm.
    Includes bibliographical references and index.
    1. Social values—Germany—History.   2. Social values—France—History.   3. Ideology—Germany—History.
    4. Ideology—France—History.   5. Individualism.   6. Holism.
    I. Title.
    HM73.D7913   1994
    302.5—dc20   94-12513
                                                       CIP

This book is printed on acid-free paper.

Contents

Preface to the English Edition   A reader unacquainted with my work may find disconcerting the diversity in the titles of my recent books, especially in English. They do not fall uniformly into a single academic category, and they may seem to suggest heterogeneous contents. This slightly confusing situation results from three combined factors: the novelty of the approach, the immense field of inquiry, and the very limited means of the single worker who has decided to tackle it. The object of my study is the set of ideas and values characteristic of modernity—a set that appears more or less neatly opposed to that which analysis had revealed at work in the caste society of India. Since my book on India bore the title *Homo Hierarchicus,* I conceived a study of modernity under the heading of *Homo Aequalis,* and it is to that end that I have conducted my subsequent research. But the object is of such complexity that it has had to be studied along different dimensions. Moreover, the methodological requirements derived from the principles of social anthropology on the one hand and my personal limitations on the other dictated the form of this study in each of those dimensions: a series of limited and penetrating investigations, or soundings, of which the results would be formulated in so many monographs. The needs of research have primacy in all this; those of the readers are not favored, and their occasional dismay is quite understandable.

I cannot here detail the various dimensions of the general work, its elaboration in several books and articles. Instead, I refer readers to *Essays on Individualism: Modern Ideology in Anthropological Perspective* (University of Chicago Press, 1986), especially the Introduction.

To turn to the present book and its context in the whole inquiry, let me first reiterate that it has its roots in anthropology. As a social anthropologist I mean by *ideology* the set of ideas and values, more or less fundamental, held in common in a group of people. When I chose the term, contrary to a still dominant Marxist usage that was just beginning to be questioned by some anthropologists, I justified it as a sociological necessity. *

Having found that a deep-running difference with respect to ideology separates modern societies from all others, I thought it advisable to single out a "modern ideology." Again, within modern ideology, notable differences distinguish, among others, the main nations and languages. Thus the study of the national variants of modern ideology recommends itself. Such

---

*In the very first footnote of *Homo Hierarchicus* (1966), I stated: "The sociologist needs a term to designate the global ideology, and he cannot accept the special usage whereby ideology is limited to social classes and given a purely negative sense, thus discrediting ideas and 'representations' in general for the sake of partisan aims."

a study will be comparative. Now the whole endeavour, beginning with the Indian work, is comparative. It has brought about a strengthening of the comparative method. The best, most rigorous kind of comparison is that between the observer and the observed (cf. *Essays on Individualism,* p. 2). Therefore the study here will consist of singling out one country at a time and comparing it with one's own. I chose Germany to begin with. Like the Indian fieldwork, this comparison is best seen as a journey, this time from France to Germany and back. A most important point here concerns language. The language of the observer is put in question by that of the observed, and modified, and the language thus modified by the confrontation is, in that very measure, a comparative language. This is a point critics very often miss: they present the vocabulary adopted by the inquirer as a result of his arbitrary choice rather than as the precipitate of a comparative experience which has now—if I may say so—come of age. Thus of the archconcept in the present approach, the opposition between individualism and holism: it has by now done good service, it has proved useful in a number of diverse domains, and it is excessive to present it as the gratuitous product of an author's fancy.

Moreover, there is a kind of cumulative effect in this ever renewed test of language through the fire of comparison. Here comparison is present not just between Germany and France, for this confrontation takes place against a background of previous work, ranging from the aspects of history and modernity that I studied previously, whether in *From Mandeville to Marx* or in the different studies contained in the *Essays,* back to my work on Indian society and culture as representative of traditional societies.

The present book is the result of long and absorbing research in German literature, but it does not conform to my original expectation about the end product of that work, in several respects. First, the conclusions are often expressed in a language that at the start was perfectly foreign to the research, and that cannot give a sufficient idea of the material the research has handled. Whereas the object was initially stated to be "the German variant of modern ideology," the reader will now read about the "interaction" between cultures, about "acculturation" and the like. In fact, the body of the research has consisted of a static, morphological, if comparative, study of one German work after another against the background of the usual categories, including, to begin with, my mainly French stereotypes. It is that work that has compelled in the end the researcher to think of the living relation between cultures, of their action upon each other. I had the benefit of previous work on India and its acculturation to modernity, and of a brief incursion in the Russian domain. To state it briefly, the static study of a particular culture has, by itself alone, led me forcefully, I would say inexorably, to see it in the process of its transformation ("acculturation") and, still more remarkably, to descry a general law of the movement of cultures in our times. A sketch of that movement figures here, thanks to its general character, as chapter 1.

The book differs from what was initially intended in another way. What was contemplated was a wide panorama of German thought, in which the use of comparative language would be able to show both its unity and its major characteristics. Some years ago, I realized that I would inevitably have to limit myself. The research had been successful, at least in my perception of it, but the communication of the results, supported as they ought to be by a series of monographs, would demand a long time—more time than I, given my age, could reasonably count upon.

Then came an invitation from the Royal Anthropological Institute in London to give the 1985 T. H. Huxley Memorial Lecture, which is the highest distinction the Institute accords. I could not but seize the occasion to communicate this relatively new development in anthropology by condensing into one lecture the major conclusions of my work, conclusions that were no doubt still provisional but sufficiently tested to be reasonably sure, and allow me to define concisely what had been singled out at the start as "the German variant of modern ideology." The text is no doubt very brief. Yet it represents the true end result of the work, and as such it constitutes the center of the present book as its second chapter.

It was impossible to complete this outline with the general view of German culture initially contemplated. Failing such a complete picture, we needed at least a sufficiently ample illustration. I chose a part of the ideological domain, the set of ideas on *Bildung* or "self-cultivation" (Bruford 1975), which for more than a century represented a true institution for educated Germans. *Bildung* touches on literature and aesthetics, it was one of the last domains I studied, and it is more delicate to grasp for the sociologist than, say, social philosophy, but it is a choice object for study, for it expressed culture for all those who shared in it. It is treated here in five monographs of varied size, which taken together constitute a sort of sounding into one representative aspect of the global culture (chaps. 3 to 7).

Up to this point, it would be fair to conclude that the initial intention of the research and of this book has been only incompletely achieved. Yet this is not all, for a new development—one that was unexpected although not absolutely excluded—has appeared.

During the course of my research, as the lineaments of German ideology took shape, little by little corresponding French features also acquired a certain consistency. Ideally, if a view of Germany emerges here, this figure will appear against the background of a *modified* image of France, which can in its turn be more precisely delineated. Thus, and by making additional use of other examples, it appeared possible, at a given moment, to "turn round the mirror" and offer a comparative view of the political ideology of the French in its global features. That is how we travel back to France. The division between Right and Left issued from the French Revolution, and a century of very troubled political history is notably cleared up once this division is seen in comparison with Germany (and with the United Kingdom as well). Moreover, the study of the French configuration of values demands that the relation between ideology and the experience of war be elucidated. A surprise is waiting for us here (in chap. 8), namely, that it is possible to isolate a parallel between the two countries without neglecting the contrast. On this note of similarity found at the heart of difference the book ends. One has touched here, en passant, on a task that is also prescribed to our research: to throw light on the diseases of modern politics by restoring to ideology the place that it deserves but does not usually get.

•

This book, published in an earlier version in French in 1991, has been a long time in preparation. I shall here single out assistance received in more recent years. In 1977 a promising stay in Göttingen as a guest of Professor Vierhaus and the Max Planck Institut für Geschichte was cut short by the fatal illness of my first wife. Since then I have benefited for short periods from the hospitality and the facilities of the Woodrow Wilson Center in Washington and of the Center for Advanced Studies in the Behavioral Sciences at Stanford. I am most grateful to those institutions, which remind me of the decisive support I received outside France at the very beginning of my career, whether the Sanskrit lessons generously given to a prisoner of war by Professor Walther Schubring in Hamburg or my adoption by Evans-Pritchard at his Institute of Social Anthropology in Oxford in the early fifties.

Two colloquia at Johns Hopkins University in Baltimore in 1984 and 1986 have helped to advance the formulations, and, apart from the Huxley Lecture already mentioned, conferences given mostly at American universities have also been useful.

I could not possibly cite here all those who have encouraged, supported, and helped me in one form or another during this work. I am deeply indebted to them all.

August 1993

PART ONE

Collective

Identity

] 1 [

Introduction:

Collective Identities

and Universalist

Ideology—the

Actual Interplay

Nous n'avons pas à rougir qu'un hasard nous ait fait naître français. (A French historian.) "There is no cause for blushing in having been born a Frenchman, for it is a matter of chance."

Who but a Frenchman can imagine he could possibly have been both himself and other than French? Only ask a Japanese, or an Iranian. These men know that their personal identity is inseparable from a collective identity, from what we shall call here a culture. The above statement confirms what I previously wrote when contrasting the (predominant) French and German views. The one proclaims "I am a man by nature, and a Frenchman by accident," the other confesses: "I am essentially a German, and I am a man through my being a German" (Dumont 1986, p. 131). (This was about the German of yesterday and before; I know nothing about the Germans of the present day.) Now it is obvious that if these two men speak of the diversity of cultures, they actually do not tell the same story, they do not speak on the same level: the German speaks of something essential, the Frenchman about factual but secondary differences. Actually, our Frenchman will, by a reversal that is built-in, unavoidable, naively identify his own particular culture with "civilization," or universal culture. At bottom, he does not acknowledge the existence of cultures different from his own. We may grant him attenuating circumstances. A people whose culture dominated the civilized world as French culture did in the eighteenth century is so reinforced in its ethnocentrism, or let us better say sociocentrism, that even two centuries later, if it sees its main values still honored by others, it will tend to look down upon manners different from its own as bizarre or uncouth if not altogether corrupt. Moreover, if cultures are collective modes of being, and if our French, and generally modern, values—liberty, equality—are individualistic, it is clear that our culture, being universalist in principle, can only inferiorize or underestimate the other collective modes of being it encounters.

We may thus somehow generalize from our Frenchman to international common sense, meaning the set of representations that prevail in our world beyond all boundaries: there too we may expect the human significance of

This chapter was originally presented at a colloquium at Johns Hopkins University, A French-American Colloquium: The Case of the Humanities: Questionable References, 15–16 November 1984. It was first published in *Theory, Culture and Society,* 3, no. 3 (1986).

culture and of the diversity of cultures to be underestimated. Thus everyone knows that there are two kinds of countries, "developed" and "underdeveloped" (etc.) countries, and the days are not yet far from us when "development" was conceived as perfectly univocal and uniform, even though the matter has become considerably less clear-cut and more complicated in the last thirty years. It is true, modern civilization spreads irresistibly everywhere. Its hegemony is evident, it is seen in the increasing uniformization of all societies and cultures, and it leads sometimes to extrapolate and to conceive, through a progressive leveling of all cultures, a final state of complete and fearful uniformity. Actually, the matter is more complex. What can be readily seen today from one end of the planet to the other is a mixture, which varies from place to place, of two sorts of ways or modes of being. There are the new, universal, modes of being that modern technics and perhaps modern ideas impose or carry with them, and there are older modes of being, proper to a population or a region, that manage to survive, more or less lively, more or less weakened or maimed by the presence of the former and their association with them. In that sense the old debate between the advocates of integral modernization and the supporters of tradition or idolizers of the past has been settled. The enemies of modernity must bow to the obvious: nowhere will they be able to find the untouched, unsullied antithesis or antidote of which they dreamt. We are all in the same boat. In a village in Burgundy, in an Indian township, a Japanese city, a Polynesian island, we see essentially the same scene: the autochthonous objects and manners that centuries had polished are joined by the breathless products and the powerful gestures that men have just invented. The spectacle is anything but beautiful, and one can sympathize with a disabused statement heard in Delhi: "We think of combining the old with the new, and actually we just manage to pervert both." Did this judgment express some temporary weariness, or a sort of recoil at the unsuspected strangeness of the result? There remains the fact of the blending, in the first approximation a blending of two cultures.

Before going any further, I must open a parenthesis and confess to some momentary discomfort. I am here making a plea for a true recognition of cultures, beyond mere lip service, as leading to a better understanding of the present world. Yet I must own that it is very difficult to speak of "culture" with some degree of rigor. We somehow manage among specialists to deal with cultures even though books have been written in the United States discussing the question of what is a culture and how we may, or may not, define culture and study it. I suspect we give the word somewhat different meanings according to what our objective is; thus may come into play unsuspected motives and influences from our respective backgrounds, so that a crossing of cultures underlies the very word of "culture."[1] In the past, people wrote of "manners and customs." If, a little more widely, we call culture the entire set of modes of being that are proper to a given society or population, that is to say a collective set of modes of being, such an entity will be hard to circumscribe. It simply does not exist for the nominalist, who knows only individual men. He will tell us that culture is made by men, but in truth men are also, and more importantly, made by their culture, and they do acknowledge it in their collective identity—with the exception of our Frenchman, who finds it in the human species.

Now, culture thus globally defined is actually made up of a number of seemingly heterogeneous things, from religion to technics, and the degree of solidarity of the different regions, domains, or aspects that we distinguish within culture is obviously varied. Holistic analysis starts from the postulate of a general interdependence, and often verifies it the better, the deeper the analysis is. Yet the postulate is also often contradicted, for punctual borrowings unaccompanied by any notable alteration of the set are common. The point is important regarding the interaction between cultures, for two cultures do not come into contact through their whole surface, but on some points or in some regions only. The impact of the one on the other is differential as regards the culture's domains as well as the categories or parts of the population.

All this notwithstanding, a culture exists in and through the people who are its carriers, and perhaps for this reason we will tend to speak of it as a living being, especially if we consider it as a whole in its relation to others. In fact, if we do not witness the birth of cultures, one is tempted to say that some have been seen to die, and certainly some are changing before our eyes. In such changes there is at work, in addition to the resilience we just mentioned, a finality which will lead one to say that cultures "change in order to persevere in their being," as I more or less did when dealing with the "interaction" of India and the West in the nineteenth century (Dumont 1976). Here itself we shall see cultures "busy modernizing" and producing "hybrid forms" in their "interaction." One could almost speak of cultures in terms of "struggle for life," or at any rate of "domination" of some over others. This case will be encountered in what follows, without our being able to decide whether the aspect really belongs to the intercultural relation, or is found close by it. (Here again is the problem of circumscription.)

1. In a recent article on American anthropology, Hervé Varenne (1984) showed how the global or holistic perceptions attained by a few authors like Ruth Benedict or David Schneider were, subsequently, assimilated into the common stock in individualistic style.

I just repeatedly used quotation marks, and I may do so occasionally in the sequence. Those approximate formulations, those stenographic expressions of complex social phenomena apply to actualities that are sorely neglected under the influence of individualism. That is why we shall not be able to do entirely without them. We must only take care not to be deceived by such *à-peu-près* and to reach a more precise grip, a firmer hold of the object.

Let us begin again. Under the impact of modern civilization, some cultures have disappeared, others closed in upon themselves as far as they could, and still others, probably most of them, entered into "interaction" with the dominant civilization, thus undergoing in each case a degree of transformation. Anthropologists have described, as was natural, the reaction of the dominated culture to the impact, domination, or influence it underwent. They described the different forms of what they called "acculturation." Here is how the small ("Seventh Collegiate") Webster defines it:

> a process of intercultural borrowing between diverse peoples resulting in new and hybrid patterns; *especially,* modifications in a primitive culture resulting from contact with an advanced society.

There is some uneasiness in this definition. The words "people" and "society" seem to be used as duplicates to alleviate the burden that would otherwise fall on "culture." What is more, the phenomenon considered is unilateral—the action of the "advanced" on the "primitive"—and yet it is presented as a special case of an ambilateral process. As if modern civilization were at one and the same time a culture like others and a kind of metaculture imposing itself as such. Is this a two-level discourse like that of our Frenchman?

It seems better to scrutinize directly the certainly serious difference to which refers the distinction between "advanced" and "primitive," a distinction that is both sociocentric and euphemistic. By so doing we shall not be able to explain why the peripheral cultures are so powerfully summoned to modernize, but we shall give at least a theoretical expression of the observed dichotomy. The only way to ferret out sociocentrism is to identify our own system of ideas and values, what I call our ideology. It is precisely the endemic underestimation of the ideology that prevents a reciprocal comparison between "civilization" and "culture," the "moderns," i.e., ourselves, and the others.

In previous studies I endeavored to isolate as *characteristic* of modernity a certain configuration of ideas-and-values. Its features taken one by one are more or less familiar. The attempt has been to define them precisely and to assemble them, for they are interlinked and constitute a relatively consistent configuration signaled by the primacy of the individual, which we will therefore call "the individualistic configuration." Without claiming to be exhaustive, we may take as its general features or architectonic elements the following: individualism (as opposed to holism), primacy of the relations of men to things (as against the relations between men), absolute distinction between subject and object (opposed to a merely relative, fluctuating distinction), segregation of values from facts and ideas (opposed to their indistinction or close association), distribution of knowledge into independent, homologous, and homogeneous planes or disciplines.[2]

This configuration of ideas-and-values, or rather the ideology whose skeleton it is, is exceptional in the history of mankind. It directly contradicts the holistic ideology, which is the general type prevailing everywhere else. Considering the society, the relation of these two ideologies to the given social actuality is different. As ideologies, they both assert values, they say what should be. But while holism expresses or justifies the existing society by reference to values, individualism on the contrary posits its values independently from society as it finds it. Once the individualistic configuration is fully developed, as say in the eighteenth century, it sharpens its claims against the contemporary society, and the belief appears, in some countries and certain social environments, that it is possible to realize a society that would entirely conform to individualism. Here two remarks must be made. First, this is an extreme case, and a whole gamut of attitudes of individualism toward the existing society are possible and documented in fact. In general, it applies selectively to some domains of social life—first of all the political—while it accommodates to what is there, or combines with an attachment to tradition, in other domains. Second, such compromises between the individualistic value and social actuality, and eventual failures in the attempts to implement the value, do not in the long run weaken the strength of the ideology. The most striking example in our day is perhaps the ever increasing extension of the equalitarian claim. Or should we recall the series of revolutions of the eighteenth to twentieth centuries, all underpinned in the last analysis by the belief in the social rationality of individualism and of the artificialism that follows from it?

Against such extreme beliefs and exclusive claims, our concern here is to

2. For some details, see *Essays* (Dumont 1986, Glossary and esp. chap. 7, pp. 261 ff). Features like the ideals of liberty and equality, or the idea of nation, or artificialism, which will be encountered later on, belong to the configuration, but they are rather corollaries or applications of the principles enumerated in the text.

come to some reasonable idea about the place or significance of individualism in society, to gauge the extent to which it has really worked, that is to say, to see between which limits it was able to replace holism, or what role it actually played. Our thesis will be not only that individualism is unable to replace holism wholesale and rule everywhere in society, but that in actual fact it was never able to function without an unperceived contribution of holism to its life. A first reason for this is that it developed in societies which did not cease to live as they had hitherto. Individualism was an ideological outgrowth of them which in a first stage drew sustenance from them. As Edward Shils (1982, p. 325) says: "Living on a soil of substantive traditionality, the ideas of the Enlightenment advanced without undoing themselves." Socially speaking, individualism then was a kind of utopian theory sheltered against any contact with actual social life. In a second stage, as we noticed above, the implementation of the ideology was selective, and even the French Revolution, if it transformed or destroyed institutions, did not raze to the ground the traditional society: neither did it give equality to women, nor did it destroy the family (nor did the Russian). All in all, the individualistic principle cohabited with inherited social forms which imply a certain remanence of the holistic modes of thought.

There is a still more cogent demonstration of the limited applicability of the individualistic ideology to social affairs. It is when the effort to implement it produced or resurrected its contrary. This is clear in the economic domain, regarding which we may refer to Karl Polanyi and *The Great Transformation*. Here the individualistic ideology expresses itself directly in economic liberalism, with the condemnation of any intervention of the State, whose only role is to provide the conditions necessary for the free play of economic rationality in the enterprise and the market. However, no sooner is the system completely in force than it results paradoxically in a renewed intervention of the State in almost all the countries in question, nay, in all of them in the end, as even the United States had, starting with Franklin Roosevelt's New Deal, to dilute its liberal wine with water from unnamed socialist springs, so that nobody there, be he Mr. Reagan, would dare today to return to Hoover's liberalism.

According to Polanyi, liberalism once applied on a vast scale revealed its utopian nature. It produced such negative consequences that the governments, whatever their persuasion, felt compelled to step in, to limit or regulate free competition, if not to take the direction of the economy in the name of the society as a whole, in order to avoid social disasters. The fact is that the implementation of the individualistic principle in this domain brings about counteracting measures which, even if they are not holistic in their inspiration, increase the role of the State and the power of the bureaucracy over the individual citizens.

Incidentally, it is somewhat strange that our socialists sometimes present themselves as pure or radical individualists. Actually Karl Polanyi himself did so. It should be obvious, however, that socialism combines in its fashion individualism and holism. Even apart from socialism, such a combination is present as soon as the liberal theory of the "natural harmony of interests" is replaced by the recognition of a distinct "common interest" endowed with primacy over "particular interests." Actually, the contemporary scene in the Western world is quite clear: we live everywhere in what might be called a post-liberal regime (as well as an "organized" or "advanced" capitalism), meaning a limited or transcended liberalism that combines in varied proportions individualism and its contrary, the latter having been reintroduced, however reluctantly, by reason of necessity.

There is a third mode under which the two opposed systems of values come to blend. It springs from the diffusion of the modern culture-civilization among cultures initially peripheral to it. It differs from the first two modes described above in that the process takes place entirely on the ideological level.

Two examples will make the phenomenon clear. First comes Herder. Many things begin with him, which is why I referred to him several times elsewhere (Dumont 1986, chap. 6). In 1774, in *Auch eine Philosophie der Geschichte* (*Another Philosophy of History*), Johann Gottlieb Herder goes to war against the uniform universalism of the Enlightenment in the name of the diversity of cultures. According to him, each cultural community or *Volk*, "people," expresses in its own way an aspect of humanity. The modern example is the Teutonic people, who carry the Western Christian culture. Against the flat rationalism of the Enlightenment, which knows only the human individual and the human species and believes in the unilinear progress of the species, Herder asserts the existence of actually different cultures, a rich variety of cultures whose contrasted interplay makes up the history of mankind. Herder protests indignantly against what appears to him as an unsufferable amputation or impoverishment of the human figure. At the root of that protest there obviously lies a holistic perception of man (I am what my community has made of me) which is unmistakably German and which at the same time will always be found in the reaction of a particular culture to modernity and the individualist creed. Yet, on this deep holistic feeling something else is, as it were, grafted; individualism is not rejected out of hand. For holism implies sociocentrism (better than "ethnocentrism"), it rejects—or inferiorizes—alien cultures, the cultures that are *other* than one's own. In Herder however this attitude is present only with regard to French culture, for him representative of the Enlightenment, which he saw as effete and senile. Otherwise, touching for instance antique times, Herder attains universalism: he grants all cultures equal value in an absolute sense, or let us say *equal rights,* with only this proviso, that every one has its hour of glory. This very notion of equality is obviously borrowed from the Enlightenment: Herder has transferred it from the level of the human individuals to the level of individual cultures or "peoples." Such a combination of holistic and individualistic features is probably characteristic of the adaptation of a culture to "modern" culture.

In the present case, however, we must surmise that the combination was possible and successful because the distance was relatively very small between the subject culture, German culture, and the dominant "modern" culture. For both were located on what we may call the same cultural continent. In actual fact, German culture had already adopted individualism in what I would call here its first or "former" advance, I mean the Lutheran Reformation. The Reformation applied individualism to the religious level, while it left out the sociopolitical level. In eighteenth-century Germany, Lutheran individualism had developed and spread into what is called pietism, a purely internal individualism which left untouched the sentiment of belonging to the global cultural community. In the second half of the century, pietism is confronted with what I would call the second or "latter" wave of individualism, that of the Enlightenment, and later on of the French Revolution. This time individualism applies to the sociopolitical level and transforms ideally the community into a society. Herder's pamphlet is a response to that situation. It is right to say that the Reformation has "immunized" Germany against the Revolution, and Herder's *Auch* may be seen as a counteroffensive of the German community, supported by Luther's individualism, against the "latter" form of individualism. The individualistic principle itself is not questioned, but only one (at least) of its consequences of the moment: the threat to German cultural identity.

We retain for our purpose the following: Herder's affirmation of distinct cultural communities represents an aspect of German acculturation to the developed form of individualism, and it combines a holistic and an individualistic aspect. Subsequently Herder's cultures or "peoples" of equal right became "nations" defined by a common culture. For here is the source of what we currently call the "ethnic theory" of the nation, as distinct from the "elective theory," which derives the nation from the will of the individuals that compose it. The two theories confronted each other as respectively German and French on one historical occasion, namely, regarding

COLLECTIVE IDENTITIES AND UNIVERSALIST IDEOLOGY

Alsace-Lorraine after 1871. Regretfully I must skip a subsequent chapter on how the Nazis succeeded by their odious manipulations in transforming the "ethnic" group into a "will," thus revealing an unsuspected sinister side of Renan's saying that the nation, issuing from the will of its members, was "an everyday plebiscite."

What is important for us here is that the ethnic theory of the nation has become integrated among the major "modern" political ideas and that it figures, by the side of the elective theory, in our political stock-in-trade. Insofar as it refers to a common culture (let us leave aside the perverse transitions in the meaning of "ethnic"), it is sociologically richer than its rival and, perhaps for that reason, more important. Yet, while the sociologists or political scientists who make use of it have no idea of its origin as a hybrid, it is precisely thence that it draws its cogency, for it is only what it contains of a holistic perception that ensures its grip on social reality, whatever systematic incoherence it also introduces—as the nation is seen as made up of individuals.

Without doubt, this hybrid origin also made for its historical fortune, and that of Herder's view, on the occasion of subsequent acculturations, notably of Slavonic peoples: this type of theory represents precisely an adaptation—an actual application—of individualism to nonindividualistic societies confronted with modernity. We might conclude that, when and where individualism manages to get a grip on the actual, it owes it to its contrary. Anyway, here is an example of a conception which is a full-fledged member of the dominant universal culture of our world and which was actually born from the interaction of the two types of cultures. The example shows how that was possible: the Herderian conception is a Janus. On the one hand it is a vindication of Teutonic culture and an application of the holistic perception, on the other it considers the cultures from the vantage point of an individualistic universalism that was simply transposed from one level to another. Through the latter aspect it adheres to individualism and extends it.

A second example will be provided by Lenin and the sort of intensification to which he subjects Marxism in an artificialist direction (Besançon 1977, p. 205).[3] As we said at the beginning, the individualist ideology gives priority to the man-to-things relation. Actually it corresponds to an unprecedented development of artificialism, and it was perhaps inevitable that, sooner or later, this artificialism should be applied to the most complex objects, including society. However, the French Revolutionaries

3. What follows owes much to that book (Besançon 1977).

thought they were only putting an end to a state of things contrary to nature. As to Marx, if his main declared objective was "to change the (social) world," he nevertheless based the proposed intervention to that end on a presumed law of historical development: it was only a matter of midwifing the predestined birth of a superior form of society. With Lenin, the intervention is made infinitely more daring: he pretends to nothing less than overstepping one historical age, precisely the one that according to Marx produced the conditions for intervening. Under Lenin's leadership, the Bolsheviks assumed to lead Russia directly from czarism to socialism without going through a stage of economic development of bourgeois-capitalist form.

Whence can Lenin have possibly drawn the belief in the possibility of such a transition, a belief very strange for an orthodox Marxist whose consequences we know have been disastrous? When I say "we" here, the word must be understood to have a very wide meaning, if it is true that the members of the Academy of Sciences of the USSR generally admit in private that the collectivization of the land has been an irretrievable catastrophe. It is true, Besançon (1977, p. 15) observes rightly that Lenin did not know that he believed but believed that he knew. Then, we should ask, how could Lenin on this point believe that he knew, against the judgment for instance of his master in Marxism, Plekhanov, who quite exactly foresaw that such an attempt would result in a new despotism?

The answer to the question appears as soon as one leaves Marxist theory and looks toward Russia, or more precisely to the reaction of the Russian intelligentsia to the impact of Western civilization, all through the nineteenth century and especially near its end, in the period of Lenin's formation. The intellectual history of Russia in the century of European industrialization is an intense and complex drama. On the level of values, it is the history of people torn between Russian cultural identity and what we have called here the individualistic configuration of the West. Pamphlets and movements, conspirators and propagandists proliferate to an unheard-of degree. Nowhere is the trauma resulting from the confrontation of cultures so luxuriantly documented for us. The traumatism was deep, despite the fact that Christianity in its—very different—Eastern form had been adopted early in Russia.

The acculturation was in a large measure negative, it inclined more to rejection than to adoption, but it combined in some way both attitudes, as happens in general. Even among the tenants of Westernization, positions are not absent that are characteristic of the opposite tendency, that of the Slavophiles in the first phase, of the Populists later on. Liberalism disappears very early. The backwardness of Russia, seen against the depravity and degeneracy of the West, becomes often enough a sort of privilege; the Russian people are seen as the bearer of superior values which invest them with a high, more or less messianic function. Most particularly the rural commune, the *obshchina,* is contrasted with the individualism of the capitalist regime. Capitalism is the object of unmitigated hostility, and the translation of Marx's *Capital* has the effect only of intensifying that feeling, for those of its aspects that Marx singled out as positive are simply not retained. Starting in the seventies, men of Populist persuasion arrive at the conception of an industrial development that would reject the Western model and draw from autochthonous traditions an alternative, socialist, inspiration. As to Lenin, he rejected no doubt the "economic romanticism" of the Populists, but he prided himself to have extracted from it its "democratic kernel." Thus a Polish exegete could recently write that Lenin had taken up for his own account "the Populist dream of a direct transition from the overthrow of the tsarist autocracy to the building of socialism" (Walicki 1981, p. 1333).[4]

Otherwise, everything confirms that Lenin was much more a product of the Russian reaction to the West than of Marxism. True, his role as a "professional revolutionary" was in line with Marx's intended alliance between philosophy and the proletariat. But as a character he was much more the offspring of generations of Russian conspirators and agitators. One could draw a robot picture of him by assembling features taken from Nechaev, Tkachev, and many others. To begin with, he willed himself to incarnate Rakhmetov, the revolutionary hero of Chernyshevsky, an author whose importance in his formation Lenin confessed: "He has ploughed me to the bottom" (Besançon 1977, p. 199). As a matter of fact, Lenin reproduced Rakhmetov in particulars like his self-willed philistinism or his dressing habits. For Chernyshevsky's Russia, and in Lenin's life as well, Marxism came later. Strange as it may appear, it brought only a complement to a model that was already there, and of course a language and an instrument to the "professional revolutionary" and his party. Furthermore, Lenin was very selective, stressing the class struggle and disregarding the theory of the stages of economic development.

It takes some wonder that the cultural confrontation, so obvious and so well documented through the whole century, is not taken into account for the understanding of the Russian Revolution, even though its principal actor so clearly bears witness to it. This is a weighty point, for many peoples,

4. Cited by Joseph Frank, *Times Literary Supplement,* 13 Nov. 1981.

many cultures either have known, or do know at present, or will know in the future a similar situation. And just as Russia borrowed much from Germany, which had acculturated earlier, so Leninist communism must find a favorable ground in every situation similar to the situation it answered in Russia. It is true that Russian literature seems to express a national pride of inordinate strength. But we must be circumspect, for we do not know for sure whether cultural identity is less intense or less sensitive in Japan, China, or India. That sort of thing can hardly be measured, we can only record the encounter between cultures and its consequences.

To sum up our second example, Lenin's artificialism, adopted later on by communist parties the world over, must appear most of the time, to the observer as well as to its tenants, as an extreme modern development, that is to say for us here, an extreme development of the individualistic configuration. Actually we found that it resulted evidently from Russia's acculturation, that it combined tightly an assertion of Russian cultural identity—as holistic as may be imagined—with the predominant individualist universalism. As in the preceding example, the acculturation of a previously peripheral culture has produced a feature that has passed into the dominant culture, thus introducing surreptitiously into it a component contrary to its essence. This contradictory combination produces an *intensification* of the apparent individualism, more distinctly than in the first example. While its results have been disastrous for Russia itself, this intensification has lost nothing of its ideological appeal.

The examples could be multiplied. I selected two of them in order to reach a general statement. Under the impact of modern civilization, a given culture may disappear, or conversely it may, in principle, reject the contact and close in upon itself. Between these two extremes, and most often, it "acculturates," it adapts to the dominant culture-civilization. In so doing, the culture justifies itself in relation to the dominant culture by constructing *ad hoc* representations. Thus did first Germany, and then Russia and India. These representations constitute a sort of synthesis, which may be more radical or less so, a sort of alloy of the two kinds of ideas and values, the ones being of holistic inspiration, and autochtonous, the others being borrowed from the predominant individualistic configuration. These new representations have thus two sides or faces; the one, turned inside, is particularistic, self-justificatory, the other, turned toward the outside, is universalistic. And here is the big fact, hitherto unperceived, brought to light by our analysis: *thanks to their universalistic aspect, such products of the acculturation of a particular culture may enter into the dominant culture, the world culture of the times.* We may add that they are likely to be welcome there because by their very nature they will suitably apply to any sub-sequent situation of acculturation. This is true of the ethnic theory of the nation as it is true of the intensified, anticapitalist artificialism of Lenin.

The above shows that the confrontation of modern civilization with au-tochthonous cultures does not result simply in one-way borrowings. Quite to the contrary, the dominant partner borrows from the dominated not only isolated or special features like the outrigger canoe or African art, but also representations which in all good faith he believes to be his own while in actual fact they result from acculturation and therefore contain an un-suspected holistic component. It is worthy of note that the individualistic representations do not by any means get diluted or become less pungent as they enter into those combinations. Quite to the contrary, they become more adaptable and even stronger through those associations with their contraries. Indeed we can often verify that the new, hybrid representations are *intensified* as compared with the notions from which they proceed. Fur-thermore, such intensifications can succeed each in a cumulative way, as in a series of overbiddings. I sketched an example when dealing with Hitler (Dumont 1986, p. 151). Each actor climbs on the shoulders of the preced-ing one, each transgression becomes the basis of a further transgression. That hubris of modern man is closely linked with the rivalry of cultures, and it should be permissible at the very least to ask whether here is not a necessary condition of totalitarianism.

Still more generally, the complex drama consisting of the interaction of cultures claims our attention if we want to understand the contemporary world. Each culture should be considered in relation to it environment. The culture carries the collective identity of a population, too often considered in exclusively political terms. As such it tends to persevere in its being, whether by dominating other cultures or by struggling against their domi-nation. Hybrid forms are generated in the process. In terms of values, indi-vidualism and holism are interwoven in them, and they are as dangerous as they are intense. The contemporary stage is rich with illustrations.

The above also warrants a brief conclusion as to the place of individual-ism in history. It is our cardinal value, and so it will remain. But one would be grievously mistaken if one surmised, as is often done at least in France, that individualism can suffice to animate a society or a world of societies, that it can rule everywhere, monolithically as it were. The individualistic configuration that we have isolated as characteristic of modernity was, ac-tually, all through its history, combined with more or less contrary notions, values, or institutions. The fact is not due to a legacy of the past; it is endur-ing, permanent, definitive. One of the reasons for this is that the more

modern civilization spreads in the world, the more the individualistic configuration that it carries gets modified through the integration of hybrid
products which make it radiate more powerfully and at the same time modify it insensibly, by blending with it holistic contents.

Rather than a unique and sufficient principle for social life, individualism represents an extremely powerful ferment of change. In future it will of
necessity be associated with its contrary, probably more and more closely.
The association conceals dangers, to which one remedy can be mentioned,
to wit, that cultures and their interaction, or their struggle, should receive
the scholarly attention they deserve—contrary to the superficial universalism which prevails today as it did in the times of Herder—and that the obscure blend of opposite values be thus replaced in the long run by a clear
hierarchy—the only mode under which they can be associated without
peril.

] 2 [

German Ideology:
Cultural Identity
in Interaction

The following is a summary presentation of the results of comparative research on the German system of ideas and values, or German ideology for short, taken methodologically, to begin with, as a national variant, among others, of modern ideology. The reader is asked to take for granted the comparative framework of this research, namely, that there exists something like a modern ideology, as opposed to nonmodern ideologies in general.[1] I shall define only a few operational terms.

My study bore, in the first place, on the extraordinary blossoming of German thought between 1770 and 1830, as being very much the formative period for the nineteenth and twentieth centuries, considered only up to 1933.[2] The focus was on social philosophy, but the study extended to philosophy in general and to literature, as well as to the main lines of subsequent developments, without ignoring the main historical circumstances and sociological conditions. The study went through two turning points. First came the realization that the assumed "national variant" had largely resulted from the interaction of Germany with its environment—that it was a kind of monumental fact of global acculturation to modernity (cf. Dumont 1971). More recently, a second major event in the research has been the emergence of some provisional conclusions, in the shape of a few simple principles, or characteristics, of the movement as a whole, which will be cited hereafter. The reader is asked to excuse the inevitable dryness of the development, as there is no place for either demonstration or even illustration. I can only hope that, apart from the theoretical appeal of the question, the account will be found plausible from what the reader knows of acculturation on the one hand and of Germany on the other.

We need to be clear about a few terms. "Culture" is taken here in its usual sense. I shall call (modern) "civilization" the dominant, modern Western culture which has spread and is spreading, in whole or in part, to the entire world. An ambiguity will remain attached to the words "mod-

T. H. Huxley Memorial Lecture 1985 (London Royal Anthropological Institute), first published as "Are Cultures Living Beings? German Identity in Interaction," *Man*, n.s., 21 (1986): 587–604.

1. See Dumont 1981, reprinted in French in my *Essais sur l'individualisme,* 1983 (see also the Introduction). I shall refer throughout to an enlarged English version of this book (Dumont 1986). For the present point see Introduction and chap. 9.
2. The study terminates with the fall into Nazism (Dumont 1986: chap. 6).

ern" and "modernity." I designate by these words, essentially, the exceptional ideological pattern I have contrasted with the nonmodern, and which I have called the "individualist configuration." Historically, it corresponds best to the Enlightenment. Yet the more current, chronological acceptance of the word "modern" (including what is properly called "contemporary" times) cannot be entirely avoided, although it is evident that much has changed since the eighteenth century, and that our present-day world ideology is a more complicated affair (see chap. 1 above).[3]

•

I assume that the modern nations of Western Europe taken, say, in the nineteenth century, shared a modern ideology and at the same time differed among themselves, so that we can speak of national subcultures or "national variants" of modern ideology. The word "acculturation" is normally used, of course, to describe the interaction between modern civilization and nonmodern cultures. Yet it stands to reason that nonmodern elements coexist with modern ones in the social as well as the ideological makeup of European countries in various ways, and it is well known that change does not proceed at the same pace in all countries and in all domains. On a micro-level as it were, or segmentarily, we may look at the differences *within* modern civilization just as we do at differences between it and nonmodern cultures. Precisely such contrasts within Germany have often been insisted upon, especially that between the most rapid industrial development and the continued existence of archaic features in the society. The long-standing political fragmentation of Germany and its belated national unification are well known, and certainly important.

I am here concerned with ideology, and especially with classic German thought seen in relation to German common representations and institutions. Throughout Christian history, Germany has shared in the common patrimony of western Europe and has contributed to its development. Take, for example, in relation to general ideas in modern times, the immense genius of Leibniz in the seventeenth century, and, at the end of the eighteenth, the towering figure of Kant, to whom it was once again felt apposite to return, as to a sort of beacon. From about 1770 to 1830 there was

---

3. I shall take some liberties with language in what follows. I shall now and then say "the culture does" for "the members or carriers of the culture do," or perhaps "Germany thinks" for "Germans, according to their ideology, think . . ." Such expressions I use as a sort of shorthand because the precise formulations would be too cumbersome when frequently repeated. Yet I hope a close examination would confirm that I have not, for all that, reified or personified the entities in question.

in Germany an extraordinary intellectual and artistic blossoming, which amounted to a mutation establishing German culture, especially German letters and philosophy, on a new basis. At the same time, this very development marked the beginning of a process of estrangement between Germany and its Western neighbors, a process in which the development of ideas and values in Germany diverged from that of the West in a way that has finally appeared fateful to the best observers.[4]

The beginning of the divergence can be traced to the Enlightenment. The great figure of Lessing notwithstanding, the German Enlightenment differed from its Western counterpart in that it was religious. The Enlightenment in the West, and, topping it all, the French Revolution, took a path from which Germany gradually distanced itself. Clearly something had happened in the West that had not happened in Germany and, in retrospect, it looks as if German culture, being outdistanced, had wanted to reassert itself and in so doing had produced in its turn an unheard-of development of the human mind.

A key to understanding the German contrasts that baffled the foreign observer, such as that between individualism and regimentation, was provided by Ernst Troeltsch in 1916, by means of a simple sociological description: the German lives in a community (*Gemeinschaft*) with which he identifies himself. His community is essentially cultural: he is a man through his being a German (cf. Dumont 1983: 130). The German intellectual not only ignores society (*Gesellschaft*) in the narrow sense of the word, but at the same time, in his inner life, he thinks of himself as an individual and devotes all his care to the development of his personality. This is the famous ideal of *Bildung* or "self-cultivation,"[5] so important in German literature from Goethe to Thomas Mann. Here then is a duality which is both characteristic and, at first sight, puzzling. On the one hand, there is a quiet survival, in modern times, of the community, that is to say, of a holistic feeling and orientation, and, in social life in general, the quasi-proverbial proclivity to obey, the spontaneous subordination to political and social authorities. On the other hand, there is a pronounced inner development of

4. Heinrich Heine, who had chosen to act as an interpreter, both ways, between Germany and France, warned the French, as early as 1833, about the dangers of the German future, as he foresaw it (Heine 1979: 180 ff.). I have quoted elsewhere a text of 1922 by Karl Pribram which looks prophetic in retrospect (Dumont 1986: chap. 6), but the clearest diagnosis is probably to be found in a lecture given by Troeltsch in the same year, "Natural Law and Humanity in World Politics" (Troeltsch 1923), which Ernest Barker translated into English and included in 1934 in his translation of Gierke (Gierke 1957).

5. I borrow "self-cultivation" as a translation of *Bildung* from Bruford (1975). Troeltsch's article of 1916, "The German Idea of Liberty," is analyzed hereafter (chap. 3).

individuality, a jealous interiority devotedly attended to. This feature applies especially to intellectuals, but it should not be taken as restricted to them, for *Schwärmerei* (idle dreaming but also enthusiasm) as well as musical practice are widespread. This would, I think, remain incomprehensible, were it not that the origin of the disposition clearly lies with Luther. Luther asserted individualism in the Church alone, and not in the world, because he was interested in God alone. We might say of him in this regard that he returned to the "individual-outside-the-world" of the first Christians (Dumont 1986: chap. 5).

This idiosyncratic formula of German ideology ("Community holism + self-cultivating individualism") enables us to understand the German reaction to the Western developments of the eighteenth century. In the meantime, the Lutheran disposition had become general through the spread of pietism, and pietism everywhere underlay or accompanied the initial stages of the movement we are considering. From 1750 onward, it allowed the Germans to react in their own way to the secular Enlightenment of the West, to the dominant cosmopolitan French culture, and finally to the Revolution. In the words of Thomas Mann and others,[6] the Reformation had immunized Germany against the Revolution. Or, we might say, a first wave of individualism—purely religious at the start, and always confined to the inner man—had enabled the Germans to resist a second, this time sociopolitical, individualistic wave. The Revolution was received *in the mind,* in the pattern set by the Reformation. It gave rise to a prodigious movement of thought, and the result was, under many diverse forms, a synthesis of individualism and holism: now with both principles masterfully balanced and articulated, as with Hegel; now with the two opposites exacerbated and holism forcefully reasserting its primacy, as in romanticism. In the end, as is well known, the Germans had the feeling of having equaled and surpassed in the mind what others had done on the stage of history—while (and this is a fact we shall have to remember) the polity did not appreciably change. They had asserted, as never before, their cultural identity as Germans.

At this point, two remarks may be made. First, this is perhaps the first example of a peripheral culture acculturating to modernity on the ideological level. It is true that German culture was, from the start, very close to the source of novelty, as it shared the same (Christian) basis and had itself produced, with the Reformation, an earlier form of individualism. Perhaps this proximity accounts for the exuberance of the process. The importance of the products is, of course, in no way diminished by the recognition of the

---

6. The reference is to Thomas Mann's *Reflections of a Nonpolitical Man* (English trans., 1983); see below, chap. 4.

sociocultural process from which they resulted, but the recognition of this process may help us to penetrate the more obscure or more debatable aspects of those forms of thought. I shall return to this. Second, as an exceptionally well-documented example of acculturation to modernity on a purely ideological level, the German case should help greatly in defining general patterns of acculturation, despite the fact that it precedes in time the unleashing of technological and economic forces.

Externally, the undisturbed permanence of holism (accompanied by a strong bent to subordination) and, internally, the formative influence of Luther (strengthening Christian individualism but confining it within the person) are two fundamental features that go far to making understandable the interplay of German culture with its environment and its history. These two features are not new, and I have hitherto done no more than systematize existing insights with the help of a comparative, or intercultural, perspective. I think there is a third feature, little perceived until now, which, once added to the previous two, will allow us to round out the picture of the specificity of German culture.

It concerns political ideology, and what it should explain is "pan-Germanism"—the belief that the German state had a vocation to dominate the world or to share in its domination, or at any rate to dominate other peoples. I have already observed that the cultural change that laid the basis for the culture of the last two centuries had left out politics. Political changes came later. They were made "from above," and they belong to a different series.[7] Until then the political constitution of Germany remained what it had been for ages: a largely nominal Empire and, as historians compete to tell us, under the Empire, a multiplicity of states and principalities of very unequal weight. The number of principalities had been greatly reduced and the map simplified as a result of the Napoleonic wars, and one of the states, Prussia, had shown an unrivaled dynamism and reached a unique position. One question that is not asked is what kind of political ideas the people entertained. Did the practical disappearance of the Empire

7. This is not the way the broad relation between culture and politics is seen in current historical accounts. There, it is maintained that there existed a "liberal" movement until 1848—which is true—and that it is only as a result of its final failure and of the subsequent dominance of *national*-liberalism" under Prussian leadership that both the divorce between intellectuals and (internal) politics and their endorsement of pan-Germanism began to develop. Thus summed up, the thesis immediately appears superficial, as neglecting too much the global ideological background and the continuity of the culture in the long run. My account, in its turn, is of necessity very summary and must neglect relatively minor aspects. The basic question is whether one should isolate as "political" a succession of apparent contingencies, or whether there are deep-lying cultural, i.e., global, lines of force to be detected in the historical development.

result in their being solely the subjects of a particular lord? Was that lord for them a real sovereign? If one thing is sure, it is that, as Germans, they no longer had a sovereign. Their collective identity was, on the contrary, strongly emphasized culturally. The young Hegel hoped for a future Theseus who might restore the armed force without which there could be no unity, no Empire worth the name.[8] The decay of the Empire hides the fact that its ideology had not been replaced by another, and that it lingered on in a sort of latent state, ready, like a phoenix, to be born again from its ashes. This may become clear if we consider the idea of sovereignty. According to Sir Henry Sumner Maine, there are three types of sovereignty, two are primitive: tribal sovereignty and universal sovereignty. One is a modern invention: territorial sovereignty.

From the history of France and of England we know something about the transition from universal sovereignty to territorial sovereignty. It was a complicated, spectacular process, perhaps not studied enough as such, but Kantorowic's great book shows, in the works of theologians and jurists, the beginnings of the transition and of the transfer of values from universal religion to the particular state and territory, with the king claiming to be "Emperor in his kingdom."[9] Nothing of the kind ever happened on German land. The "Holy Roman Empire of the German people"[10] had been the expression of universal sovereignty, and this idea of sovereignty had not been replaced by another. When Germany was again united under Prussia (or almost so, Austria being left out) the new German State, called in its turn an Empire, simply inherited the vocation to universal sovereignty which had been that of its ancient forerunner. The continuity is so clear that only the current underestimation of ideology, together with insufficient comparison between Germany and its Western neighbors, can have hidden the fact from us. Universal sovereignty even had its myth in the very popular legend of the old Emperor Frederick Barbarossa, who had been sleeping for centuries under the mountain (*Kyffhäuser*) but would one day awake to restore order in the world. The belief was not contradicted but

---

8. Hegel's study of the German constitution, unpublished in his lifetime, is translated in Hegel 1964.

9. "Emperor in his kingdom": the formula expresses rigorously the transition, or, if we may say so, the territorialization, of sovereignty (Kantorowicz 1957: esp. 207–72 and index s.v. *Rex est imperator in regno suo.*)

10. Literally "the Holy Roman Empire of the German Nation," but "nation" has here its medieval meaning, far removed from the modern one. In modern terms a "nation" cannot claim "Empire," but Germans may have made the confusion and even used it (I am thinking of the Nazis pretending to revive the Empire, see *Neue Brockhaus* 1938, s.v. Reich).

reinforced by the Germans' conviction that their culture was culture *par excellence, Kultur,* and was destined to dominate all others.

This archaism may well appear far-fetched, and even fantastic, to those who are not concerned with understanding pan-Germanism,[11] or more precisely the fact that German intellectuals—those Germans who left written traces of their views—largely subscribed until 1918 to the belief that Germany was called by a sort of birthright to dominate other people. No doubt they were not unanimous but this was the predominant attitude—witness for example Troeltsch (see below, chaps. 3 and 4). And perhaps more important here than the statistical predominance of an attitude is the fact that it is deeply rooted, and is in accordance with other, very general representations. Here is an example, which I think is the more instructive because it is unintended. In an article entitled "Two possibilities of German Form," in which he contrasted Goethe's classicism and what he called Gothic (we might say romantic) form, Oskar Franz Walzel, a literary historian and critic, began by distinguishing two attitudes to the classics as springing from two different political situations. As long as they lived in the State created by Bismarck, we are told, the Germans looked down upon the cosmopolitanism of the classics, for they had the "proud consciousness with which the Roman called himself 'civis romanus.'" But the situation has changed: "Now we are again closer to the feeling of the classics. . . . Not only have we become almost as poor as they were as regards the State, but even the values which could compensate for the absence of a strong and respected German Empire are shattered, above all the happy consciousness of having conquered the leadership of all other peoples in the Empire of the Spirit" (Walzel 1922: 114).

This text is exemplary in several ways, but note especially the phrase "we have become almost as poor as they were as regards the State." This is how the German State was perceived as a cultural fact: the dimension of domination was so prominent that its loss through defeat was tantamount to a transition from something like the Roman Empire to an almost state-

---

11. To prevent misunderstanding, let me make clearer the nature or status of the archaism in question. It is not a matter of the detached survival of a particular idea, that of the Roman-Germanic Empire, but of the presence of a universal attribute in a particular form. Ethnocentrism, or sociocentrism, is universal. All societies take themselves as the hub of the world, and this essentially holistic belief survives elsewhere as well, albeit in a different way. Thus the French are prone to think of themselves as the teachers of mankind (Dumont 1983: 130). The idea of universal sovereignty is simply the translation of that universal belief on the level of politics, in terms of domination. Now, the Germans having in their heritage a particular form of universal sovereignty, namely, the Roman Germanic Empire, it is only natural that they should express their sociocentrism in its terms.

less society. This goes far beyond a purely political attitude. It gives a glimpse of pan-Germanism as rooted in deep and widespread feelings. It also throws light on subsequent history from 1918 to 1933 and beyond, for the loss of the vocation to external domination contributed to the lack of deep adherence of the German people to the State of the Weimar Republic, while its reassertion by the Nazis—even at the price of the actual substitution of "race" for State or nation as the agent of domination—was widely felt as a revival of true Germanism and its Empire (*Reich*). Here lay probably the most decisive—and fateful—archaism of Germany. If I had time I would develop the view that the belief, quite common today (at least on the Continent), that the First World War was a sheer blunder and that millions of Europeans died in vain, is false, because it was not possible to tolerate such an archaism, such a claim to domination by birthright in our world.[12]

•

I have isolated three general features of German ideology: the strong prevalence of holism, the decisive formative influence of the Lutheran Reformation, and the survival into our own times of the idea of universal sovereignty. What is actually observed is the combination of these three traits. Two of them, holism and universal sovereignty, are closely related and found in many societies, while the impact of the Lutheran Reformation on Germany is a more or less unique historical phenomenon which gives the combination its specific stamp. Apart from its role in political history, the belief in universal sovereignty has, strictly speaking, played only a minor role in German cultural history, which was largely shaped by the other two factors. Lutheranism resulted in proximity between the native culture and the environment which later impinged upon it, and thus, most probably, allowed for the elaboration, deftness, and richness of the response. Holism, on the contrary, being widespread elsewhere, allowed for a wide reception of the German response in other lands.

   The deep imprint left on German minds by the Lutheran Reformation provided the channel, or we might say today the operator, through which the external and institutional elements of the Enlightenment and the Revolution could be internalized: German thinkers provided an equivalent, in terms of representations, of what other people had done on the historical

12. It will be objected that Germany was merely compelled by her late coming to proclaim cynically what earlier, established, imperialisms had practised without saying so. Yet a difference must be maintained between *is* and *ought to be*. It is this difference that prepared the way for the end of the established empires, in accordance with their own professed principles.

stage. That, at any rate, is how German intellectuals generally thought of the process and found in it, and in its results, the mark of the superiority of their national culture. This judgment was not purely subjective, for the German mind, unhampered and unsoiled by the factual entanglements to which the French finally succumbed, could take a detached view of the events, see their necessity, and, as it were, go beyond the limitations inherent in the French development—think of Hegel writing on "absolute freedom and terror" in 1807.

If the purely spiritual individualism of Lutheran parentage determined the mode of adaptation of German collective identity to the new developments of individualism, the role of holism, prevalent throughout the society, was quite different. It necessarily resulted in adaptation taking the form of syntheses, i.e., hybrid representations combining holistic and individualistic aspects. Elsewhere (1986: chap. 4) I have shown this to be true of the ethnic theory of the nation that issued from Herder's vindication of German culture against the cosmopolitanism of the Enlightenment. The point is indeed quite general, and the combination is found throughout the whole movement, in very different forms. From this angle one can see the masterly construction of Hegel's system of philosophy. The clash between the two opposed modes of valuation is avoided through the recognition of a hierarchy of levels, with reversals of primacy between levels or sub-levels. Thus, individualism reigns at the topmost level, that of absolute spirit; holism, with the state, dominates on the level of objective spirit, but encompasses in turn the individualism of civil, or bourgeois, society and abstract right.

The combination is often cruder. Immediately after the First World War, Pribram diagnosed what he called pseudo-universalism—we would say pseudo-holism. He meant theories that start from individualist, "nominalist" premises and proceed to the illegitimate assertion of a holistic construct, as in the Marxist "class" and in the "state" of Prussian nationalism (Dumont 1986: chap. 6). So, throughout the German response, individualism and holism are not only empirically present in the society or juxtaposed in the mind, as in Troeltsch's view of German freedom, but mixed up, confused, implicitly identified with each other. The German confrontation with the world centers on this point. It is therefore very tempting for the sociologist to see here the root of the "duality," the "paradox," or "contradiction" that is so often laid at Germany's door. Does this contrast not lie at the core of German culture? Is it not something like its nervous center or DNA, directing, as it were, the ubiquitous reproduction, or recurrence, of contrariety if not of contradiction? German thought came to capitalize on

contradiction, or, in a weaker form, on contrariety. By and large they became tokens of truth, as the adequation of thought to actuality. If I may
make the comparison, they became the emblem of the "thickness" of the
given in Geertz's sense. So, for the romantic political philosopher Adam
Müller, a thinker admittedly much weaker than Hegel, *Gegensatz,* contrariety or contrast, is found in all truly living institutions; to reach it, beyond simple rationality, is a warrant of authenticity, so that the notion is
self-explanatory. We may also recall that contrariety or contradiction is
part and parcel of a proper hierarchical makeup: given the strength of
the holistic feeling of "community"—Toennies gathered the idea of *Gemeinschaft* from Adam Müller and his followers—the erosion of its normal
hierarchical expression may have left the field to contrariety alone.[13]

At the risk of some repetition, I feel I should emphasize at this point that
most of what has been said here is quite general: while dealing with Germany we have dealt with much more than Germany alone. For all the cultures that later came under the impact of modern civilization were, like the
German, essentially holistic, and therefore either had to operate similar re-
sponses to individualism, or found the German recipes ready at hand to
help them. The success of the ethnic theory of the nation is thus no mystery
nor, more specifically, is the reception of Herder among the Slavs of central
Europe, and the respective vogue of Schiller, Schelling, and Hegel in successive phases of Russian intellectual history in the nineteenth century (Koyré
1976; Malia 1961). In a sense, it may be said that the Germans have prepared more digestible versions of the modern innovation for the use of new-
comers. Those versions were so useful that they sometimes superseded the
original ones, and at the same time their logical status is questionable, as
Pribram saw. "Postmodernity" in that sense was introduced by Germany
as early as 1800.

•

I set out to present the history of German thought and literature from 1770
to 1830 as a response to the challenge of the Enlightenment and the Revolution. So far I have tried to characterize the structure of this response by
means of a few basic and/or recurrent features. What about its unfolding in
time, its chronological sequence? Here there is a striking similarity with

13. On the presence of contrariety in hierarchy, see the postface to *Homo hierarchicus*
(1980: 239–45). I believe that a reader alert to the question will sense its unavowed presence
in Thomas Mann's *Reflections of a Nonpolitical Man* (see below, chap. 4), but, after all, the
ghost of hierarchy is probably haunting German thought in general. What is striking is the
intensity of its suppression—a Lutheran legacy?

processes that took place slightly later elsewhere, in Russia and in India, under the impact of Western innovation.[14] We can distinguish a short initial phase, and a more protracted later development. To begin with, the impact of novelty is very intense and the local culture is thrown off guard. A few individual intellectuals or literate persons accept the foreign universalist message. In Tübingen three young theology students are said to have planted a tree of freedom and they surely took a solemn oath. They were Hölderlin, Hegel, and Schelling. In Saint Petersburg, aristocrats converted to liberalism conspired against the czar. In Bengal a few distinguished young men converted to Christianity. At that moment, the pull toward the new ideas would seem to have been irresistible. But, little by little, a native reaction takes place; there develops a defense and illustration of the native culture in terms of the new ideas and values; partial importations combine with the reassertion of old themes in a new form. The movement becomes increasingly assured and radical until in the end the native culture fully reasserts itself in the conviction that it has victoriously answered the challenge. Thus German romanticism outclassed the individualism of the rationalists while apotheosizing holism; Russian populism surpassed Western capitalism and socialism thanks to the perennial virtues of the Russian rural commune; and Vivekananda announced in Chicago that India was the mother of all religions. The variation in the strength of collective identity through time could be figured as a curve beginning with a deep depression and then gradually reaching up to its former level and beyond. What differs in each case is where the stress is put: on religion in India, on the politico-social in Russia, on the inner life and on the genius of the individual in Germany.

What also differs is the wealth, depth, and magnitude of the development. It is not my intention, and it would lie beyond my powers, to give even a general idea of the German movement in all its diversity. Those sixty German years have added a glorious chapter to the history of human thought and creativity. There is not only a succession of phases, but at one and the same time a galaxy of talents and even geniuses developing various tendencies in distinct fields. I must here sacrifice diversity in order to throw into relief the main lines of the global phenomenon as they appear in the present perspective. In a relatively short spell of time, there was an unheard-of effervescence of minds, most apparently connected with the historical situation, as if the circumstances had stirred the deepest energies.

14. On India, see Dumont 1976. On Russia, the standard account is Masaryk 1967, but I have found Koyré 1976, Malia 1961, and Besançon 1977 most useful (on populism and Lenin, see above, chap. 1).

Something similar, after all, to a revolution took place, even if, to begin with, it was confined to some members of the society only. All in all, not only did German collective identity, in the end, find expression in a renewed culture which is a most imposing monument, but through this contribution the shape of our universal civilization as a whole has been decisively modified and enriched.

The most immediate lesson to be drawn from this is that a culture never exists in isolation but should always be seen in relation to its environment. And yet the fact has frequently been overlooked by French (and other) commentators. It happens naturally every time text is piled upon text and author added to author without acknowledging the existence of a sort of collective entity to which they all belong. At most, the environment will figure in such analyses as an external event, or series of events, to which the German authors will be seen to react. This is how the French Revolution figures in Lukács's attempt to trace the pedigree of National-Socialist ideology in his book, *The Destruction of Reason* (1955). As indicated by the subtitle "The Way of Irrationalism from Schelling to Hitler," Lukács looks at the whole German development from the rationalist and universalist standpoint of the Western Enlightenment. He consigns the powerful German reassertion of holism and collective identity to the fires of hell, cuts into two a movement whose essence is precisely the reunion of opposites—a performance that could hardly have been expected from someone who had previously shown a fine perception of German literature—and has the satisfaction of declaring Nazism to be the direct descendant of romanticism. If this has any meaning at all, it is that Nazism occurred in Germany.

Thomas Mann, an author Lukács never ceased to admire, might have opened his eyes. In his *Reflections of a Nonpolitical Man,* written during the First World War, Mann confesses to belonging to the line that Lukács was later to damn, and he acknowledges the duality of German culture and the presence in himself and in his art of something of the "Western" individualism he condemns—or rather the predominance of which he condemns—as an importation. This is an example of how a searching analysis can reveal within a living culture the tokens of its relation to its environment.

I touch here on a fundamental point which has been too rarely grasped. Thomas Mann himself insists on it: the great German author is, in his very being and activity, a *mediator.* He is not just someone who gives expression to what could be isolated as purely and uniquely German, he mediates between that and the outside world. This is so because German collective identity exists essentially in relation to others. (Thus Lukács by suppressing the relation has missed the unity.) The role was all the more important as Germany could have no *political* representative in the given political conditions. The cultural representative was, so to speak, in charge of more than "culture" alone. The encounters, or the parallels, between Napoleon on the one hand, and Goethe, Hegel, or Beethoven on the other, are deeply emblematic. More important for analysis, the thought of the German thinkers focused not on Germany *per se,* on problems internal to Germany, but on topics located in the zone of articulation or interface with the outside. This is not the same as saying (as philosophers would no doubt prefer) that they deal with universal problems, but that some allowance must be made for their German-ness.[15] I hope to show elsewhere that Hegel labored very hard to transform his initial, largely holistic, view of the philosophical problem into an apotheosis of the individual as the Subject of it all. The notion of an "interface" also throws light on the central role played by the model of ancient Greece, especially during the first phases of the movement.

I should like to add a note here about two of the ideological themes that this formative period, 1770–1830, bequeathed to following generations. Many themes were established, many beacons lit in this period, which laid the basis for scholarly developments that filled the century and established German supremacy in the field of the "sciences of the spirit" (*Geisteswissenschaften*). Two very popular themes may be singled out. One is *Bildung,* or the ideal of "self-cultivation," which, in accordance with German spirituality, governed the life of educated individuals. At the opposite pole, as it were, is the theme of the ancient Germans or Teutons, the idealized Germanic people, not only as early representatives of the culture but more or less as the originators and carriers of modern Christian civilization. The need for legendary origins was widespread in Europe. It merely endured here longer than elsewhere, in the form of an intense need, which was to be expected in the circumstances, for Germanic antiquities. For one thing, the peoples speaking Romance languages, collectively called *Welsch,* such as the French among others, were nothing more than culturally bastardized Teutons. For another, the ancient Germans were believed to have been staunch individualists. According to Hegel, for example, modern representative institutions originated with them, and in recent times their religion was typically Lutheran Christianity. Later on, German historical scholarship made much of presumed inborn Germanic characteristics in the shaping of medieval society and polity. To an anthropologist on the outside,

15. As did Martial Guéroult, writing of Fichte (Dumont 1986: 121).

many assumptions of this sort appear as expressions of an uncritically accepted stereotype.

•

So far I have stressed the relations to the environment as essential to the movement of German thought. Let us now look at the pace or gradient of this movement. Just as there is progressive radicalization in a revolution, we can detect here a progressive reassertion of the collective identity through increasingly intense, bold, and extreme combinations of the old with the new.[16] That this aspect was somehow conscious is shown by the wide occurrence of the word *Steigerung,* let us say "intensification," throughout the movement. The word is popular with the romantics, but it is not confined to them, and it is found, always with a positive connotation, even in the classicist Goethe. Indeed *Steigerung* can be taken as the watchword of the whole process: a movement of intensification, of surpassing. Perhaps the clearest and most central example is found in the relation between Kant and his three great successors, Fichte, Schelling, and Hegel. As if by common agreement, they followed him only to outdo him, and the contrast between them and him is indeed staggering. What he had been at pains to distinguish and separate, they were above all keen to unite. The boundaries he had set as definitive they immediately professed to transgress.[17] Thus Kant had written (in his *Critique of Judgment*) of *intellektuelle Auschauung,* "intellectual intuition," as supra-human and reserved to God alone. Now all three of his successors soon pretended to have realized it. The case is typical. What was for Kant a sort of horizon of thought, a "regulating idea," an ideal, something unattainable but needed like a lodestar to orientate one's thought and direct one's efforts, became for his Promethean successors a hard and fast possession, an element in rational constructions. In Kant's language, a cautious "reflexive judgment" became a "determining judgment," a striving became an affirmation. The point is

16. This is not to say, of course, that later products are *ipso facto* more valuable or more lasting than earlier ones.

17. Yet it is also true that Kant had triggered the development while tabooing it, a little like the Lord God of Genesis pointing to the tree of knowledge. He had located the only reality accessible to man within man himself. It was the noumenal man or absolute self, the free subject. Robert Tucker (1967) was no doubt right in seeing here the root of the "self-aggrandizement" which, as he felicitously showed, characterizes the whole subsequent movement. Fichte's *Wissenschaftslehre* of 1794, a "declaration of omnicompetence on behalf of the Kantian moral subject" (Taylor 1975: 36) as well as the correspondence between Schelling and Hegel in 1795 (Tucker 1967: 39; see the letters of 4.2 and 16.4 1795) show how Kant's successors went about developing Kant's principle of (subjective) freedom into the philosophical "self-aggrandizement" which is, after all, a German equivalent of the French Revolution.

important for us, as anthropologists, for the great German idealists have explored territories we cannot quite ignore, and we may benefit from their explorations provided we return to Kant's caution and exigency.[18]

Can the felt need for "surpassing" be followed up, albeit tentatively, in its psychological consequences? I want to suggest that the German situation brought about a change, namely, an increased distance between the author and reader of philosophical works, and that the change, far from remaining confined to Germany, is, in a way, still with us and still contributes to obscurity and to difficulties of communication in such matters. The obscurity of those philosophers will, of course, be attributed in the first place to the boldness of their thought, their expansion of "Reason" as against trivial understanding, their daring to ask—and solve—problems previously considered by Kant and others to lie beyond human powers. This immoderate ambition itself is in all appearance linked to the historical circumstances. Let us then look a little more closely at the linkage.

Several traits go to magnify the role of author: first, his representative function; second, the ideal of self-cultivation or *Bildung,* which favors originality and self-expression—what Charles Taylor called the "expressivism" of the whole climate, as against strict adherence to established canons; in the third place, the background of cultural rivalry with the outside and the bent for *Steigerung,* fostering personal rivalry, as between Fichte, Schelling, and Hegel. Here at least two sociological features should be noticed: the occurrence of epoch-making debates, as the early "quarrel of pantheism" (*Pantheismusstreit*) unleashed by Jacobi about the Spinozism of Lessing; and the importance of intense friendships, as between Goethe and Schiller in Weimar-Jena, or between Schleiermacher and Frederic Schlegel, and among the first romantics, in Berlin.

It is impossible at this point not to mention Goethe. As the representative author *par excellence,* as the founding hero of self-cultivation, a model for all men of letters, he assumed a status towering above that of his readers. Whatever his occasional haughtiness, his later pontificating, Goethe was first of all a poet, and as such he remained supremely humble and devoted in his approach to the supreme object, the unspeakable core of life and the world, which he knew can only be alluded to or wandered around, never directly grasped or conquered. Philosophers did not, and perhaps could not, maintain this discretion. In this respect, he is greater than them all. Goethe's case is exceptional, but other authors, philosophers among them, did become representative in turn and *think of themselves* as

18. See my essay "The Anthropological Community" (1986: 211).

such. Moreover, Goethe's glory reflected in some manner on every distinctive *littérateur* of subsequent generations.

The increased distance between author and reader comes forth clearly
from a fierce diatribe of Schopenhauer's, himself an exceptional figure in
German philosophy, against the "University philosophers" and Hegel in
particular (Schopenhauer 1963). Schopenhauer impugned at one and the
same time their social function and, especially in the case of Hegel, the
inanity of their theories and the obscurity of their writings. It is clear that
Schopenhauer did not accept the transition from Kant, whom he greatly
admired, to the "philosophers of the chair." He sees them as imposing their
fantastic constructions upon the reader through the impenetrability of
their style. If we may isolate for our own use a relatively mild form of the
complaint, Schopenhauer argues in one passage that Hegel fails to comply
with the usual rules of communication by abusively shifting onto the
reader a large part of the work an author has to do in order to make himself
understandable (1963: 200–202). For anyone who has struggled to penetrate Hegel's writings, the stricture makes some sense. It is symptomatic,
incidentally, that there was until recently a sort of taboo on that question
among those who wrote on Hegel's philosophy: Hegel was accepted—and
presumably understood—wholesale, or rejected wholesale. It comes as a
relief to hear from a professional German philosopher that it remains difficult to make out what Hegel was really after.[19] Also, if the obscurity of
these authors is obviously related to the inordinate ambition of their
thought, we may observe that this ambition is especially expressed in their
will to construct a *system*. German idealism is the birthplace of philosophical *systems*.[20] For these philosophers, rationality and system are identical.
Now there is a sociological aspect here. In the system, the thought of the
author closes in upon itself, and its relation to the outside becomes secondary. No wonder then, given the difficulty of the task, if the needs of communication are relatively neglected. Assuming in his person all the claims of
consistency that were previously at least still to some extent on the level of
interpersonal communication, the German thinker aggrandizes himself
immeasurably. He towers above the reader, as we said of Goethe in a quite
different sense. The center of gravity of consistency, of "rationality," has

19. "Whoever wants to understand Hegel is still always by himself alone. He will find no
commentary that would help his reading instead of only wanting to replace it. . . . We know,
that we still cannot say what really happens in Hegel's thinking—the last one that had the
power to be a theory of science, society, consciousness and world all in one. No one doubts its
significance. Its diagnosis is missing" (Henrich 1975: *Vorwort*; my translation).

20. Heidegger develops this point at length in lectures on Schelling's treatise on liberty of
1809 (Heidegger 1977: section A2 ff., 48 ff.).

shifted from the community to the individual. The reader, insofar as he accepts the new relationship, has become an accomplice in the self-aggrandizement of the author. The ground of communication has shifted as if it had become a mere adjunct to individual quasi self-sufficiency, and communication has become more and more insubstantial. I do not need to insist, first, that there is here a significant step forward in modern individualism, which took place in the general situation we have outlined, against a background of intercultural rivalry and of *Steigerung;* second, that the new approach did not, quite naturally, remain confined within Germany but has become a widespread feature of philosophical or quasi-philosophical writing.

Can we draw practical conclusions from this discussion regarding our own attitude toward these famous authors? On the one hand we shall always have much to learn from them. We find in Hegel, for example, irreplaceable sociological insights—call them pre-sociological if you prefer—which we should ignore at our cost. On the other hand it is clear that, in this tremendous release of human "creativity" as it would now be called, some hubris is at work; it is difficult to deny that, in the person of the author, man is somehow lifted up to the status of a God.[21] Thus, beside valuable sociological insights and brilliant intuitions, we should be prepared, apart from fancy or poetry, to encounter unwarranted extrapolations, doubtful transitions, and indifferent fillers, the worst being our difficulty in separating the grain from the chaff and the danger of doing so prematurely. While keeping to Kant's use of the "regulative idea," it is to our advantage, if not our duty, to vindicate as much as we can of empirical insight or rational success. This endless task is forced upon us by the author himself and the historical conditions in which he worked and by our own existential situation. But in the last analysis, and at our own risk, a selective attitude is inevitable. To prevent misunderstanding, I must anticipate a likely objection to the perspective proposed here. Any German work, it will be said, (and especially the more important ones) belongs to the common human patrimony, and thus exists for us on a universal level. Any statement will be true or false, and so on. Either we intend our "cultural" perspective to replace that universal viewpoint—a pretension which should clearly be rejected—or we add nothing valuable to it except perhaps in matters of detail. The answer is that the cultural or intercultural standpoint reveals

21. Obviously, exaggeration is here of the essence. We should be prepared to find it among those who indict the position (Tucker 1972: chap. 1, and passim) as among those who enjoy it (Marquard 1981). It should be needless to recall that, whatever may be said about it, the topic has powerfully intoxicated our intellectuals.

only one of the determinations of German thought. Let us call it, for short, its cultural dimension. It says nothing about the interest of a given work from a universal viewpoint, or of the truth-value of a given statement, as the philosopher is wont to consider them. At the same time it is there, and it would not be difficult to show that the tendency of interpreters to neglect it sometimes led to bad results. For one thing, whenever understanding is difficult and interpretations doubtful, an additional aid should be welcome. Thus, any interpretation of, for example, Marx or Nietzsche that is not consonant with the author's German-ness, in the sense developed here of a living, dynamic dimension, should be suspect and therefore very critically queried. These authors have written as Germans and should be read—not exclusively, but from one angle—as Germans. The obliteration of this dimension may obscure a particular statement, or make it ambiguous, and then what becomes its value? What the present study suggests is a fresh exegesis with the help of an additional tool. In fact, a new, painstaking exegesis has already been in progress for some years now, on both sides of the Rhine. The intercultural view offers this new exegesis merely an additional device. This means putting an end to the "all or nothing" attitude, and having, in the end, to sift the grain from the chaff, as Benedetto Croce began to do long ago (Croce 1915).

Beyond all this, there remains a quite general problem. How, without contradiction, can we acknowledge the diversity of cultures and at the same time maintain the universal idea of truth-value? I think it can be done by resorting to a more complex model than our current one, where truth-value would figure as a "regulative idea," in the Kantian sense, but this discussion cannot be included here.

•

It so happens that what I hope is an anthropological view of German culture has a chance of contributing to a current philosophical debate. For reasons which have to do with recent history, the German philosophical tradition is under a cloud in some quarters. A recent discussion offers a convenient starting point. To put it bluntly, the participants share a feeling that something has gone wrong somewhere.[22] Habermas locates the wrong turn somewhere in Hegel, Lyotard thinks that the very values of the Enlightenment have been falsified in the event, and Rorty declares insignifi-

22. The discussion is found in the pages of the periodical *Critique*. Lyotard criticized Habermas (Lyotard 1982), Richard Rorty reviewed Habermas and Lyotard on modern and postmodern (Rorty 1984), then Lyotard and Rorty took up the discussion again at a Johns Hopkins colloquium (*Critique*, no. 456, May 1985; see Lyotard 1985; Rorty 1985).

cant the whole philosophical development from Descartes onward and proposes to do away with the whole idealist tradition. Regarding Germany in particular, it looks as if there had been a fatal concatenation in the succession of the foremost and most influential thinkers, leading finally to the general collapse.[23]

Now the anthropologist would maintain, first, that it is not possible to separate, as Rorty does, the development of science from that of philosophy, accepting the former and rejecting the latter, and asserting that

> the fact of pursuing from one end to the other the "subjectivity principle" has been only a diversion to which an isolated order of priests devoted themselves for a few centuries, and which has not had much effect on the successes and failures of the European countries regarding the hopes formulated by the Enlightenment. (Rorty 1984: 192; my translation)

What is strange here is the suggestion either that individualism (or "subjectivism") is absent from "the hopes of the Enlightenment" (and implicitly from the development of science)[24] or that the systematic pursuit of the "subjectivity principle" is not part and parcel of the present situation.

A second anthropological remark, bearing on Rorty's general stance, is that our contemporary world ideology, culture, or civilization is among other things the product of the interplay of a number of national traditions. It is made up of different national components all of which we have to assume or take upon ourselves lest we fall back into parochialism (be it American) and obscurantism. With all their faults when looked at from an Anglo-American standpoint, the French Revolution and German philosophy are in some manner part of ourselves, whether we inhabit one part of the world or another. They are implicitly present in the contemporary world's system of ideas and values to which they have contributed, and this universal (by definition and in fact) unit is presupposed in any smaller cultural unit in advanced or developed countries— and, increasingly, in others.

Let me return to the question of the seemingly fatal concatenation in the history of German thought, in order to try and acknowledge fully its uni-

23. The question may seem too crudely or too restrictively put. Yet it weighed heavily on German minds after the rise, and still more so after the collapse, of Nazism. It is how it was put as early as 1935 in a remarkable book by Helmuth Plessner entitled in its later version *Die verspätete Nation (The Belated Nation)* (1959). And it cannot be avoided in the present perspective, which postulates a unity of German culture, although it is true that it has a universal bearing and that Nazism is not the only problematic phenomenon of our contemporary world.

24. Cf. the characterization of what I call the individualistic configuration (above, chap. 1).

versal bearing. Writing first in 1935, Helmuth Plessner saw it as a series of increasingly radical *demystifications,* leading finally to a dead end, namely, a purely biological worldview paving the way for National-Socialism (Plessner 1969). Leaving aside for a moment the political catastrophe, and concentrating on intellectual history, we recall that Robert Tucker saw the same process as a ceaseless and progressive *"self-aggrandizement,"* while here I have taken it as a process of *Steigerung,* intensification, or outbidding-the-last-bidder. Now each of these three formulations obviously highlights an aspect of what actually took place. They are different expressions of the general shape, curve, or gradient of the process. In particular, since everyone here claimed to be rational, and since reason, at least in our days, is electively critical or debunking, the outbidding had to take the form of demystification. It is clear that there was at work a compulsive need to outdo what had been done before, which owed much of its intensity to the general situation of cultural rivalry. It looks very much as if German thought in the period was compelled to move within a constraining framework which largely determined the global shape of its historical sequence, as it determined, on the political level, the final collapse of an archaic, and later grievously misled, collective identity.[25]

This view should allow for a fresh critical interpretation of each individual thinker and for dissociating, in the measure needed, intellectual history from the political bankruptcy. At any rate, such is, I believe, the contribution that an anthropological or intercultural view can bring to the debate mentioned earlier, and it may also, after all, be in keeping with what Charles Andler wrote during the First World War: "German philosophy . . . reflects a living and impassioned experience. We can read from it the whole destiny of the German people, if only we undertake a painstaking and difficult historical commentary" (Andler 1917: iii).

Conversely, the study of German ideology brings forth insights of more than purely academic interest for the understanding of our contemporary world. Cultures, as the expressions of collective identities, must be taken seriously. Moreover the German example, as a signal case of interaction between the world-civilization and a particular culture, offers in an elaborate form, as under a magnifying glass, much that is ubiquitous in our times. What is *prima facie* seen as an attribute of a particular people is, in fact, often the result of such an interaction. For that reason, the conflicting values of holism and individualism combine in problematic ways in the present world as they did in German history.

25. On the latter point, see Dumont 1986: chap. 6.

PART TWO

Bildung
around
1914

] 3 [

The German Idea of Liberty According to Troeltsch

Having chosen to study Bildung as representative of the entirety of German culture, we shall proceed as is our wont through the monographic analysis of a series of texts. These texts or objects of analysis are of varying dimensions, ranging from a simple article by Troeltsch to a full book in the cases of Mann and Goethe, and even to an entire life—that of Wilhelm von Humboldt—which sought its inspiration in the ideal of Bildung.

A word about the order in which these monographs are presented. The reader would perhaps expect a chronological ordering. Instead, heuristic order was preferred. A chronological order befits the recitation of a previously learned lesson, or a causal explanation. It respects and reinforces the conceptual framework within which a problem is ordinarily posed, and consequently it serves only to highlight details within a preexisting framework. It is our aim, on the contrary, to reconsider the framework itself, revealing the global object by placing it in a perspective broadened by a comparative stand. With this objective in mind, we begin by looking at Bildung in its mature state, adult and lived as self-evident, as it had taken form by the beginning of the twentieth century. The First World War provoked among the German intelligentsia a new self-awareness of their existence as a community. An article by Troeltsch and a book by Thomas Mann will introduce us in medias res. Only thereafter may we return into the past and examine the origins of Bildung in the light of what it was subsequently to become.

My discussion of the Troeltsch's article "Die deutsche Idee von der Freiheit," which is the object of this initial chapter, has already appeared in the English edition of the *Essays on Individualism*. It served there, given the depth of Troeltsch's sociological perspective, to strengthen our argument of German identity in preparation for our examination of Nazi totalitarianism. Yet the same article proves even more pregnant in the present context, offering as it does a presentation of our subject so complete and so concise that it will be difficult to find its equal.

With minor changes, this chapter is reproduced from *Essays on Individualism* (Dumont 1986), pp. 133–48. It was first published in French, *Le Débat* 35 (1985): 40–50.

•

In a 1916 text reprinted in 1925,[1] Ernst Troeltsch clearly defined and ex-
plained the German idea of liberty as contrasted with the English and the
French, both similar yet a little different. If a definition is called for,
Troeltsch says toward the end of the study, it will be

> an organized unity of the people based on a rigorous and at the same
> time critical devotion of the individual to the whole, which is completed
> and legitimized by the independence and individuality of the free spiri-
> tual culture [*Bildung*]. (Troeltsch 1925a: 103)

And, if a slogan is needed, with all the risks it suggests: "*state socialism and
culture individualism [Bildungsindividualismus]*" (ibid.).

The first point concerns devotion to the whole. "Germans have in their
blood devotion to a thing, an idea, an institution, a superindividual entity
[*Wesenheit*]" (ibid.: 96). And of course their "organizational strength,"
their "organizability," is more or less legendary. What we first see here is a
form of holism in the sense that such an attitude or tendency supposes that
the whole is valued at the expense of the individual. But Troeltsch, in the
very sentence just quoted, immediately insists that this devotion is "mobile,
lively, full of initiative, persevering, and ingenious." In other words, the
subject subordinates himself spontaneously to the whole; he has no feeling
of alienation in doing so, and therefore all his personal qualities are given
free rein in the fulfillment of his role. We can thus understand how

This is a definition of central importance to us. Moreover, Troeltsch develops it and comments on it throughout his article (especially pp. 94–
107). In what follows we shall take up in detail each of the two elements of
the formula and the relation between them. Unfortunately the long and
complex sentences of Troeltsch are difficult to translate: limiting our citations to fragments of those sentences,[2] we will try to paraphrase the rest as
accurately as possible.

---

1. "Die deutsche Idee von der Freiheit." *Neue Rundschau,* 1916-1, pp. 50–75. The page
references are to Troeltsch 1925a: the collection *Deutscher Geist und Westeuropa,* pp. 80–
107. I cite other articles from the same collection. These texts are naturally inseparable from
the circumstances of the war during which they appeared. German intellectuals of the day
were anxious to respond to the challenge of enemy propaganda, which was considered formidable, but one is struck by the seriousness they brought to the task and the interest that this
wartime literature, including among others Troeltsch's essays, holds for our purpose.

2. There will be some examples below of the difficulties in translation. A literal translation is often useful for grasping a writer's thought without an intermediary, although it may be
inelegant, or, occasionally, hardly correct English.

Troeltsch can speak of "liberty" or of "organic liberty" as when he writes: "The thought of organic liberty poured out into a harmonious and graduated cooperation of enterprises great and small, state-run or private" thanks to "the disciplined sense of the whole and the sentiment of honor in participating in the whole" (ibid.: 97).

This spontaneous adhesion to the social whole is exactly what Toennies called "spontaneous will" (*Naturwille*), for him the characteristic trait of the community or *Gemeinschaft* as opposed to the "arbitrary will" (*Kürwille*) of the individual subject in the society (*Gesellschaft*) (Toennies 1971). As for Troeltsch, he speaks of "liberty" because he wants to counter the enemy propaganda, which capitalizes on liberty or freedom as the monopoly of the Western democracies, by showing that Germany has "its own sense of liberty, which is determined by German history and the German spirit" (94). It is illuminating for us to observe the seriousness and honesty with which Troeltsch as a scholar carries out what he conceives as a counterpropaganda job and what becomes in fact a kind of comparative exercise.

Here "the individuals do not compose the whole, they identify with it. Liberty is not equality but service by the individual at his place in the function allotted to him" (literally an organ position, *Organstellung*) (ibid.: 94), or again, and more completely: "The liberty of the German is willed discipline, advancement and development of one's own self in a whole and for a whole" (97).

Troeltsch knows very well, and he says so, that the French or English tradition—for brevity we shall call it Western, as he does—cannot see liberty in that formulation but only autocracy, slavery, etc. (97). He simply maintains that that is how liberty is according to Hegel, and how it is expressed, one way or another, "in all the great German creations of the century" (94), and in the Socialist party as well as in the army. Troeltsch traces the origin of this disposition back to the seventeenth century (95–96). It results from the transformation of Christian submission to the patriarchal-absolutist State under the influence of the Western spirit of Enlightenment. The State was modified, and "the submissive believer turned into the freely obedient and devoted citizen, who participates in the general will by fulfilling his duty in his place and freely exercising his criticism" (95). German liberty is thus a "secularization of the religious sense of duty and, in particular, its intensification into an activity of creation in common [*mitgestaltend*]" (96). Here we perceive a recognition of acculturation: we are dealing with a traditional holism that was modified or transformed under the influence of "the spirit of liberty and independence [*Mündigkeit*]" (95).[3]

At the same time the basic underlying assumption will be noticed: far from there being incompatibility between individual development and service to the social whole, it is "in and for the whole" that the individual develops. None of these ideas is exclusive to Troeltsch; all are widely encountered in other authors.

There is no unanimity, however, and here we must dare to pose a radical question: Is all of this genuine, or is it simply a construct of patriotic intellectuals, a representation influenced by the speculations of philosophers, doubtless reinforced by the circumstances of war, but little more than a nationalistic myth unmatched by any deep sentiment in the German people itself? There is no shortage of witnesses to support such an accusation. Under admittedly different circumstances, neither the young Hegel nor the young Marx recognized the existence of this fine union of wills. On the contrary, it was the search for such a union that launched them on their careers as innovators. Troeltsch was surely thinking primarily of 1914 and the extraordinary surge of enthusiasm aroused by the declaration of war.[4] But was he not stretching the notion to periods to which it applied less aptly? Could we not argue that the powerful prewar Social Democratic party was evidence of an alienation of the working class? Troeltsch answered this decisively when he applied the formula of German liberty to that party as well as to the army. Given what we know from history, we must admit that only a small minority was truly alienated.

It is also true that such an excellent Germanist as Robert Minder was able to consider those ideas of integral devotion to the community as ideal images formed in the minds of intellectuals, but I believe that on this point he has himself succumbed to an ideal representation—the representation a Frenchman holds of the "real" society (the *Gesellschaft* of Toennies)—and that he has dangerously separated German literature from German life. Certainly Troeltsch's view represents a stereotype held as much by Germans themselves as by foreigners. In our view, however, this stereotype corresponds sufficiently to experience; Troeltsch broadly spoke the truth; and "society" is, or rather was, not exactly the same thing in France and Ger-

3. *Mündigkeit*, lit. "age of majority." This is how Kant designated the Enlightenment (cf. the booklet *Was ist Aufklärung?*).

4. Cf. the article by Troeltsch himself, entitled after Plenge and Kjellen. "Die Ideen von 1914" (The Ideas of 1914): entry into the war created a "spiritual revolution," "the return of the nation to belief in Idea and Spirit" (1925: 33, 37). In his memoirs Meinecke mentions the unforgettable burst of enthusiasm as one of the peaks of his life (quoted in Stern 1965: 256–57, together with Thomas Mann and Adolf Hitler).

many. The difference is perhaps only a matter of the predominance of one
or the other pattern (community or society), but this predominance is precisely what matters.

Incidentally, we might see here a reason for the weakness of the Weimar
Republic: because of its democratic formula itself, the republic was unable
to arouse the "identification with the whole" that Troeltsch stressed, and
could thus be perceived as a foreign importation.

•

Let us return to Troeltsch. Devotion to the State, which makes a supersens-
ible reality of it, has individualism, personal liberty, as its necessary complement, an indispensable counterweight (99). Given the narrowness of
political conditions in Germany, the liberation of the spirit took place "essentially within the soul" (in the form of) "personal liberty, vivacity and
profundity of thought, imagination [*Phantasie*] and poetry" (98). It is a
perfect independence and inner liberty, which gave life first and foremost to
Selbstbildung, that is, self-construction, self-education, or cultivation.
This personal cultivation had to appropriate and elaborate Western culture
and the cultural heritage of Europe, and at least for a time found a support
and a yardstick in antiquity (98). That culture is broadly human or cosmopolitan, but, comparing it with that of England and France, one perceives
that German humanism is basically an enrichment of German inner life in
the image of the spiritual liberty of antiquity, a spiritual liberation and
deepening of the people itself (98–99).

We have here what might be called German individualism, characterized by two very marked traits: on the one hand the closing up of the self
vis-à-vis the external world, and on the other the activity of construction or
education of the self, the famous *Bildung,* which is more or less identical
with culture. Such a pattern is quite foreign to traditional holism, of
course, and such a deepening of the world of interiority cannot simply result from an adaptation or internalization of the ideas of the Enlightenment
or the French Revolution along the lines of presumed Germanic characteristics, as Troeltsch seems to be saying in this text when taken by itself. In
fact, it is impossible not to think of Luther, and we will come back to this.[5]

5. German characteristics are not specified in our text, but in the same collection, and
dealing precisely with education (*Bildung*), Troeltsch accepts Richard Benz's view that "the
essential thing about Gothic man is the infinity and depth of his imagination" (*Phantasie*)
(Troeltsch 1925a: 229). The relatively restricted view Troeltsch proposed here is surprising
when contrasted with the fullness of his considerations of Protestantism and its developments,
including pietism, or when contrasted with his preoccupation with relations between "Protestantism and the modern spirit" (the title of one of his studies). According to the texts I have

Let us light for a moment on what at first sight appears to be a deep separation between externality and internality, but is in fact a very peculiar relation between them. True, the individual is here folded back on himself; yet at the same time he knows he is, and wants to be, a German; his inwardness rests on his belonging and is actually a part of it: in this sense, this purely internal individualism leaves the surrounding holism standing. The German intellectual also turns away from external conditions but on another level, the level of what we are accustomed to call sociopolitical questions. This is seen in the contrast between German and French fiction in the nineteenth century, rightly emphasized by Robert Minder.[6] The matter immediately gets cleared up if we make use of Toennies's categories: paradoxically enough, the individualism of *Bildung* is located on the level of community (*Gemeinschaft*), which is union, cultural belonging, and has nothing to do with the level of society (*Gesellschaft*), which is division, the struggle of particular interests.

The reader unfamiliar with German culture may well feel that we are exaggerating wantonly. Let us therefore take a spectacular though by no means aberrant example. In 1918, Thomas Mann published his *Reflections of a Nonpolitical Man* (Mann 1922), in which, while identifying himself with Germany at war, he proclaimed his belief that it would have been contrary to his vocation as a German writer to interest himself in politics. It would have been something "directly denationalizing," a "falsification of his own being" (see below, chap. 4 and the long quotation at the beginning).

In a comparative sense, then, there would appear to be two modes or formulas of belonging. One, essentially cultural, holistic, traditional even when modified or somewhat transformed by modern influences, is the German formula, both on the level of that devotion to the whole of which Troeltsch spoke and on the level of the individualistic subject and his vocation of *Bildung*. In the other mode, which is modern, universalistic in the French Revolutionary sense, the nation-state is defined not by concrete belonging but by its conformity or faithfulness to the ideal of equality and

---

read, it seems that the discord can be explained thus: Troeltsch in general is interested in the whole movement of ideas—an international set of ideas—except where he specifies national contexts secondarily; in contrast, the 1914–18 war led him or forced him to focus on what was specifically German as opposed to "Western" ideology, and in this matter he left unexpressed the broader context, the historical underpinnings, up to about 1750. However, the idea that Luther is the prototype of the *Bildung* man bursts upon us if we go back to what was said about him in the *Soziallehren*, for example (Troeltsch 1922, English trans., pp. 540–609).

6. Minder 1962: 5–43.

liberty of individuals; one adheres to the group as a citizen, the act of belonging operates on the sociopolitical level: one is a man by nature, and a
Frenchman empirically, as if by accident, while on the other side a person
thinks himself a man to the extent that he is first a German.[7]

Having clarified this point, let us now get back to German individualism
as being essentially inward and keeping its distance from the external
world—a clear-cut and at first sight strange break between the inner life
and society. It is impossible not to see a descendant of Luther in the *Bildung*
intellectual. Not necessarily a follower—he may even be an atheist—but a
descendant. Actually it is only in Luther that we can understand this dichotomy, which would appear incomprehensible if we looked at it, for example, from a medieval viewpoint. As against the Catholic Church of his
day, and the scholastics whose thought nurtured his own, Luther appears
as someone who has gone back to origins and defines himself, in the manner of the early Christians, as an outworldly individual[8]—or almost so. He
reintroduced a gap—we might say a chasm—between the Christian's relation to God on the one hand, and to the world of social reality and of
relationships between men on the other. Faith, and grace, that is, the relationship with God, are of the essence. Once this relationship is assured, it
expresses itself quite naturally though secondarily in the form of love for
one's fellows, and gives value to the Christian's works. The subordination
of the world and the State to inner life is strongly stressed in Luther, quite
explicitly and still more so perhaps implicitly from the fact that he sup-
pressed the extraordinary power of reconciliation of the great mediator between the two, the Church. As for political institutions, they were no doubt
necessary, and Luther boasted that he had exalted them more than anyone
else and had prescribed obedience to the established powers, whether good
or bad. But what scorn for the wielders of power! Whether Christian or
not, they are nothing but rabble, and a good prince is a rare bird indeed.[9]

In more ways than one, Luther is the prototype of the German intellectual. He is so in particular as a writer, in his basic contribution to the development of the German language, but also as the *representative* of the
German people in relation to the Catholic Church and hence on the world
scene, as witnessed by his popularity, which means that to a great extent
the Germans recognized themselves in him. This function of representative

7. On the subject of education in Germany, Troeltsch cites and underlines C. Burdach:
"But we are men and we feel ourselves to be men uniquely in the nature of our particular
hereditary essence, and only because we feel it to be inalienable [imprescriptible?] and legitimate" (1925a: 225).
8. See the first chapter of my *Essays on Individualism* (Dumont 1986).
9. Plass 1959, respectively nos. 1745 ff.; 868, 1796, etc.

or *mediator* between the German people and the "Western" or universal culture passed on to the German writer and thinker. Troeltsch indicates or implies this, and others have noticed it, even Lukács. It comes out clearly from Thomas Mann's analysis in his war book (Mann 1922: 34–73), and the role is essential. If we are to understand it, we must reflect that in a period when there is no political but only cultural unity, the function of representative devolving elsewhere upon a head of state or an ambassador quite naturally falls on a Goethe, a Hegel, or perhaps a Beethoven. Besides, the German themselves are well aware of this when, as so often, they tell us that Germans have achieved in ideas what others have accomplished on the world scene. And so did Marx. We cannot understand German literature and thought if we neglect this role of representative or mediator in the German intellectual at the height of his renown.[10]

Not only does Luther provide us with the archetype of the *Bildung* individualist, but, what is more, the historical transition from the one to the other is richly documented. As Thomas Mann subtly indicated in the passage quoted above, that transition is found primarily in pietism, which on the one hand has spread and democratized what had remained exceptional in Luther's day—the study of the Bible—and on the other, through a complex interaction with the Enlightenment especially from 1750 onward, has assured the passage from Lutheran inwardness to aesthetics, to patriotism, to romanticism. An abundant recent literature shows that pietism is found everywhere at the roots of the literary and philosophical movement near the end of the eighteenth century.[11]

10. It is surprising that such an eminent Germanist as Robert Minder, in his comparison of French and German literature (Minder 1962: 5–43), should have failed to appreciate this double relationship of the German intellectual. Minder sees him as being in touch exclusively with his own culture, his own people, and paints a dramatic picture of his isolation. For a start, isolation is the natural lot of the artist in our societies; it is even connected to his representativeness. It is not isolation but recognition, wherever it occurs, that might need explanation. Now in the German case representativeness has two faces; or, if you prefer, it is from the nature of its circumstances more two-faced than elsewhere; and without wishing to explain the pitiable funerals of Schiller and Mozart by this point, we can see in it the source of a further distancing of the artist or intellectual from his people. There is something similar about the thinkers' choice of problems. We have found (1986, chap. 4) that the development of thought in Fichte and Hegel had been magnetized by the French Revolution, and we have regretted that they did not thematize hierarchy, an idea that would have imposed itself if it had been a matter of the German people alone: there too mediation was foremost: the deeper concern was to articulate one's own culture and contemporary events expressive of another culture (or rather of another variant of the same culture). At the romantic extreme, this same situation resounds in the vogue for *Gegensatz,* contrast or antithesis (notably in politics with Adam Müller).

11. For aesthetics, see for example my study on Moritz (below, chap. 5); on the political plane, Pinson 1934, Kaiser 1973. But pietistic roots can be seen everywhere, as evidenced in a

•

We have now commented separately on the two complementary aspects of German liberty according to Troeltsch, free dedication of self to the whole and *Bildung* individualism. It remains to consider the relation between them. It should be clear by now that the two factors are less discrepant than it may have seemed at first glance, since the German individualist is no stranger to the holism underlying devotion to the State. Viewed from without, individualism lies within this self-dedication; viewed from inside, it very clearly subordinates concrete external circumstances, to the point of despising them, just as Luther's faith subordinated worldly kingdoms.

Troeltsch insists that the two tendencies he has isolated must remain united. To dissociate them would be fatal, leading either to enslavement to the State or to a sort of ethereal individuality (99). He states that the link between the two ideals is felt, and he makes no bones of the tension between them: German liberty is no more immune than its Western counterparts to degeneracy or to excesses: any idea of liberty has its internal contradictions. Yet German thought tends particularly to reconcile or smooth out (*Ausgleichen*) the two conjoint ideals—in truth, and not by superficial compromises.

We will direct two criticisms at Troeltsch. To begin with, he does not ask himself in this text about the nature of the combination he is insisting on (but only about the nature of the two factors). One has the feeling that, as so often with Germans, he is satisfied to end with an antithesis, that the contrariness he has revealed makes him feel that he has reached the actuality of life. Yet some questions arise. Has not German thought itself actually tried to rid itself of that contradiction, or to suppress it? In the course of the preceding argument, the reader may have evoked the classical period, Goethe and Schiller, and asked whether they had not striven toward a universalism without boundaries, beyond any (conscious) German specificity. It cannot be denied that *Bildung*, including its disaffection for contemporary society, then had pride of place. It was in the very process of being born, in the sense of going through its last metamorphosis.

It is noteworthy that Troeltsch's definition uses the word *liberty* in both the senses that are most often opposed to each other: the negative freedom of nonconstraint, independence of the subject; and liberty in its essentially

---

symbolic fact: in what has remained the *Bildungsroman* par excellence, *The Years of Apprenceship of Wilhelm Meister,* Goethe introduced a portrait of a pietist lady, composed from his youthful memories, which forms a long, rather detached chapter entitled "Confessions of a Beautiful Soul" (see below, chap. 7).

German concept as consisting of the acknowledgment of necessity by a rational subject (here, belonging to the whole is felt as vital and therefore accepted willingly). Since this latter sense has sent us back to Toennies's *Naturwille,* we find ourselves asking whether the "acknowledgment of necessity" is not perhaps a form under which the holism of traditional culture is surreptitiously maintained. At the very least, there is an affinity or congruence between the two attitudes.

It turns out that the evolution of Hegel's thought from his youth to maturity provides a kind of parallel to our problem. Young Hegel was looking for a religion, we may say an ideological form, which would reconcile modern individualism with the fine harmony of community as found in the Greek *polis*. Later he came to construct a philosophy that produces this reconciliation by means of levels of reality, which it organizes hierarchically, ascending from subjective spirit to objective spirit (institutions), and from this to absolute spirit (religion, art, philosophy). The latter two levels broadly correspond to the two poles of Troeltsch's formulations. Still, Hegel knew very well that, as distinct from his youthful dream, this philosophy offered reconciliation only for the benefit of educated people, in other words within *Bildung*. There is something aristocratic, or elitist as we would say today, in the result, just as there is, after all, in Troeltsch's presentation: everything indicates that the common man must be content with self-dedication while individualistic culture will be the privilege of the few. Regarding the State, Troeltsch and Hegel are remarkably similar, but Hegel is more complete. With him, individualism is given free rein on the level of civil (or bourgeois) society—which is absent in Troeltsch, while at the higher level civil society and its individualism are encompassed in the holism of the State, with which the individual subject can do no better than identify himself, exactly as in Troeltsch. The question has sometimes been raised whether Hegel, in his *Philosophy of Right,* was guilty of adapting his theory to the Prussian State of the day; he would seem, rather, to have expressed what was going to be the German reality of the matter for a century. Will it be said that the Wilhelmian State, in contrast to the Hegelian, found a place for universal suffrage? It was only a superficial concession to modern democracy, which did not cut into the monarch's prerogatives, and in the final analysis the German State essentially stayed faithful to traditional holism, in conformity with the Hegelian thesis. Here it is worthwhile to contrast the German and the Western—or, let us say, French—formulas of liberty: on the one side is a spiritual liberty going back to Luther, which leaves the political *community* intact; on the other side, another liberty, which, though also of religious origin, through the Enlightenment and the

Revolution extends into the political realm to the point of appearing to be centered on it, and transforms it into a political *society*. Schematically, Luther and the French Revolution provide two variant forms of liberty in the abstract sense of the term. To some extent they are two equivalent variants, since they have managed to impose themselves in lasting fashion in two neighboring countries at the same period and in similar economic circumstances.

Let me observe once more that this trait is recognized—or almost so, we may say implicitly recognized—by German writers themselves when they contrast German inwardness or German thought to the "historical" outwardness of other peoples. Yet they most often attribute the difference to political circumstances, if not to a metaphysical characteristic of the German people, and more rarely mention what we might call the schismatic introversion introduced by Luther and generalized by pietism.

Making this parallel between the Reformation and the Revolution seems to be fundamental for a Franco-German comparison. Thomas Mann, reflecting studiously on what is specific about German culture in his *Reflections of a Nonpolitical Man,* comes back to the point several times (1922: 242, 257, 535–77). He states among other things:

> Out of the liberty and sovereignty of the Germans Luther made something accomplished by turning them inward and thus keeping them forever out of the sphere of political quarrels. Protestantism has deprived politics of its spiritual goad and has made it a practical matter. (1922: 237)

Here, in the author's own language, is a deep insight supported by Hegel and Carlyle. "Hegel said that France would know no rest for lack of a Reformation" (ibid.: 242), and Carlyle saw in the Revolution a "bad substitute" for Reformation (535–37). It is worth trying to grasp the matter more firmly in our own language and to characterize the two contrasting forms of individualism. That of Luther is located on the religious plane. It is directed against the religious division of labor and against the hierarchy: all Christians become priests and retrieve from the Church the responsibility for their own salvation. There results an internalization and the subordination of everything else to the inner life of the Christian. Politics, especially, is subordinated, the State is subordinated, and by the same token it is accepted as life and power, with its division of labor: there are specialists in government because it is of no import.

In contrast, the French Revolution lines up its forces against the sociopolitical hierarchy, against the hereditary division of labor: in the name of the Individual all citizens are equal; each is simultaneously subject and sovereign. The *community* is dissolved and becomes a *society;* we might say that the State, the nation, loses its ontological reality, as the Church did in the other instance. Ontologically there is no longer anything between the individual and the human species, the concrete global society no longer exists, has no will to live, no will toward power. All this is ideologically denied and enjoys only a residual factual existence.

We must also note that the level on which this conquest of the individual occurs, the political level, subordinates the religious level, the inner life. In both cases, that is, *the level on which the individual is emancipated subordinates the others.* There is nothing new about this in the case of the Reformation, since there the absolute continues to subordinate the rest. But it *is* new in the case of the Revolution, for here the traditional level of the absolute, namely religion, becomes subordinated—a fact of huge significance, and yet one which goes more or less unperceived.

If this is so, can we go even further and say, with Thomas Mann, that "the experience of the Reformation *immunized* people [by itself alone] against Revolution" (1922: 535), it being understood that Mann had only the Lutheran Reformation in mind, in other words, Germany? This would be a hasty conclusion, making light of differences in the political constitution itself. Even if Lutheranism has had an effect on the political constitution of Germany, it is not entirely responsible for it. The crucial fact on the ideological level—hitherto not clearly singled out, it seems—is probably the emergence in the West of the modern type of sovereignty—*territorial sovereignty*—and its absence in Germany. We shall return to this.

It might be objected here that we have strayed from Troeltsch's thought by omitting from liberty the spontaneous self-dedication to the social and political whole that he wanted to be included in it. We omitted it because, as soon as we isolate the political plane, to call liberty Toennies's "spontaneous will" would be to introduce confusion by acknowledging "liberty" in any political regime that is spontaneously accepted by those subjected to it. In fact—and that is our second criticism—we can reproach Troeltsch for having left out of his discussion the nature of the State to which the Germans were spontaneously devoting themselves, especially in 1914. However useful his analysis is, it remains fragmentary from this angle. He has taken us as far as he could, it is for us to take up the baton.

Now the State in question is a pan-Germanist State. At that time the will to dominate others was an integral part of the German conception of the State. The fact may take us by surprise, but it is there, and contemporary writings by Troeltsch himself make it clear: they suppose or imply a State which at the least should play a part in world domination, a "world power" (*Weltmacht*): this is what was at stake in the war according to him.[12] Thomas Mann too is quite explicit on the point (1922: 179, 326–29).

Against the background of this vocation of domination of the German State, the German formula of liberty according to Troeltsch, "self-dedication + *Bildung*," assumes a new meaning. Not only does politics fall outside of education and culture,[13] so that the State is left to itself and accepted in whatever form it wishes to take, but self-dedication is directed to an entity that is destined to dominate non-Germans. The political domain, finding itself here protected institutionally from the individualistic critique which has elsewhere dismantled the absolute monarchy, shelters traditions and survivals. I once wrote that traditional ethnocentrism or, better, sociocentrism survived in the modern era under different guises: universalism, naive or mystifying, on the French side, pan-Germanism, forthright or brutal, on the German side (see Dumont 1986, end of chap. 4), but perhaps in this latter case there is one more survival. In the course of centuries—and Troeltsch alluded to this—the German State also had been transformed, or rather had adapted itself to modern conditions. The Holy Roman–Germanic Empire was finally succeeded by the Prussian State, and then the German State. And everything looks as if the faithful subjects, comforted to see it always referred to by the same term, *Reich* or Empire, had noticed no change and had continued to give to the latter State the sort of allegiance that the former had received in the name of universal sovereignty.

As with everything touching on the political constitution of Germany in the broadest sense of the term, things are obscured in the current accounts of historians because of their underestimation of ideology in general and, in this case, their neglect of the ideological aspect of sovereignty. Such is, at least, the provisional conclusion I have reached. The point is very important for comparison, it demands an ample discussion, but for the moment

12. In the "Ideas of 1914" we read, "It was a matter of power and life" (Troeltsch 1925a: 31); and at the end of this text the construction of a Central European bloc is mentioned (ibid.: 52–53). In 1919 Troeltsch wrote: "Today the Reich [of Bismarck] has toppled over, and all that remains for us is the spirit and the work" (1925a: 210). As if the nation were no longer herself, once deprived of her dimension of domination!

13. In contemporary articles brought together in the same collection, Troeltsch is quite categorical in the matter of primary education: "Education has nothing to do with intensification of national feeling or with the awakening of political awareness" (1925a: 177); and similarly for secondary education (ibid.: 220–21). Here, though contrary opinion and even practice exist, Troeltsch maintains that the school must restrict itself to the spiritual, inner development of the free man, and asks only that a German humanism—however difficult to pinpoint—should supersede the exclusively classical humanism that has held sway up to this time.

it can only be briefly mentioned. We are told constantly about the political fragmentation of Germany, which was provoked or aggravated by the Lutheran Reformation, the treaties of Westphalia, etc. The *material fact* is obvious, but its interpretation calls for caution. Very generally we are told that Germany passed in this way to a territorial political organization, and it is implied—not explicitly stated—that Germany thus achieved the same transition from universal sovereignty to territorial sovereignty that France and England had gone through. Now this is to forget the fact that this transition represents a radical transformation including an essential ideological aspect that is not found in the German case.[14] It is to forget the survival of the Empire. No doubt it had become more and more powerless, but on the *ideological level* it was in no way replaced by the particular territorial identity. Political Germany led a quartered existence between territorial belonging as a fact and universal sovereignty as a principle right down to the battle of Sadowa (1866). In my view, we have here a major fact that has hitherto been concealed by the overestimation of material aspects and the neglect of the ideological dimension, together with insufficient comparison with the Western neighbors. It follows that Germany, once unified by Prussia, was Janus-headed: on the international level it was a national or territorial State among others, while at the level of internal representation it was a resurgence of universal sovereignty. Such is perhaps the deepest explanation for the will to dominate inherent in this "Empire" or, in other words, for pan-Germanism as a concomitant of the German idea of liberty as defined by Troeltsch in 1916.

14. It should be recalled here that according to Sir Henry Sumner Maine there are only two types of primitive or traditional sovereignty—tribal and universal sovereignty. The third type, territorial sovereignty, is a modern innovation (Maine 1887: 103 ff.). This distinction is a fundamental one, and territoriality in this sense is quite obviously a major characteristic of modern ideology (Dumont 1980, App. D, sec. 3).

] 4 [

"Unpolitical" Individualism: German Culture in Thomas Mann's Reflections

The long wartime reflection of Thomas Mann confirms in essentials the idea of *Bildung* that we gathered out of the article by Troeltsch in chapter 3. The two authors, who wrote in different terms at the same period, bear one another out with respect to the idea of an individualism purely internal to the subject which does not affect his membership in the national *community*—i.e., the traditional holism—including its expansionist aims, but which excludes the idea of *society* as composed of individuals and resultant sociopolitical questions. Moreover, a concomitant element of the ideology is confirmed here, concerning the hitherto unnoticed fact that Germany had not developed the—modern—idea of *territorial* or national sovereignty and remained wedded to the traditional idea of *universal* sovereignty embodied in the Holy Roman Empire in the Middle Ages. This explains the vocation to external domination that both our authors attribute to Germany during the 1914–18 war.

We cannot improve on Thomas Mann's own summary of the central thesis of his *Reflections of a Nonpolitical Man (Betrachtungen eines Unpolitischen)* in a lecture he gave a few years later. The book was written during the 1914–18 war. The lecture was given in 1923. Thomas Mann's views had undergone a change after the German defeat, and in speaking to republican students at Munich, he described his own wartime ideas from the outside, as it were:

> The finest characteristic of the typical German, the best-known and also the most flattering to his self-esteem, is his inwardness. It is no accident that it was the Germans who gave to the world the intellectually stimulating and very humane literary form, which we call the novel of personal cultivation [*Bildung*] and development.[1] Western Europe has its novel of social criticism, to which the Germans regard this other type as their own special counterpart; it is at the same time an autobiography, a confession. The inwardness, the culture [*Bildung*] of a German

This text was originally presented at a colloquium in Royaumont, October 1985. English translation by Sybil Wolfram first published in *International Journal of Moral and Social Studies* 1, no. 2 (Summer 1986).

1. This passage is not the only one in which Mann prefers to expand the usual formula of the *Bildungsroman*.

implies introspectiveness [*Versenkung*]; an individualistic cultural conscience; consideration for the careful tending, the shaping [*Formung*], deepening and perfecting of one's own personality or, in religious terms, for the salvation and justification of one's own life; subjectivism in the things of the mind, therefore, a type of culture that might be called pietistic, given to autobiographical confession and deeply personal, one in which the world of the *objective,* the political world, is felt to be profane and is thrust aside with indifference, "because," as Luther says, "this external order is of no consequence [*an dieser aüsserlichen Ordnung nichts gelegen ist*]." What I mean by all this is that the idea of a republic meets with resistance in Germany chiefly because the ordinary middle-class man here, if he ever thought about culture [*Bildung*],[2] never considered politics to be part of it, and still does not do so today. To ask him to transfer his allegiance from inwardness to the objective, to politics, to what the peoples of Europe call *freedom,* would seem to him to amount to a demand [*Aufforderung*] that he should do violence to his own nature, and in fact give up his sense of national identity. (Mann 1965, 2:54–5, trans. Bruford 1975: vii)[3]

The clear line of descent which links the man of *Bildung* to pietism and Luther explains the connection between inwardness and contempt for the political dimension. This is quite undoubtedly what is most valuable to us in the text. At the same time, in the realm of literary history, Mann replied in advance to Minder's surprise at the absence or relative weakness of the social novel in Germany (Minder 1962: 5–43): while French tradition following from the Enlightenment writers and the Revolution devoted itself to the novel of social criticism, German tradition following from Luther developed the *Bildungsroman.* In *Reflections* Thomas Mann several times touches on the parallel and contrast between Lutheran Reformation and French Revolution. These are mutually exclusive, after all, as two variants of individualism: "The experience of the Reformation *immunizes* against the [French] revolution" (Mann 1983: 377; cf. also 188). The point is so important that I already had to make it explicit in the study on Troeltsch, and I shall not return to it here.

The principal interest of the *Reflections* for us arises from the fact that in it Thomas Mann was led to make explicit, or rather found himself constrained to establish, the incompatibility between *Bildung* and Politics. Otherwise it is a strange book, and startling in the novelist's work.[4] A so-

2. Troeltsch tells us the same thing (see chap. 3).
3. This quotation features on the very first page of Bruford's *The German Tradition of Self-Cultivation* (Bruford 1975; vii).
4. Thus Bruford has judged it in devoting the last chapter of his book on *Bildung* to

phisticated aesthete stooped to polemics and lost himself in a reassessment of his values, authorities, and models. But for this very reason, for the sincerity and depth of this "absorption in self," it is an invaluable book in relation to an understanding of German culture. The author himself, in the preface, tried to explain the strangeness of his product, "the work of an artist" which was not a work of art, "something intermediate between work and effusion, composition and hackwork" (Mann 1983: 2), the remainder or remnant of a painful crisis (ibid.: 1). Not without affectation, and a certain complacency of the renowned author—a feature which is not foreign to the cult of *Bildung*—he strove to justify himself, to show how circumstances had forced him away from his creative writing and obliged him to make an unprecedented attempt at elucidation. Thomas Mann never agreed to disown this book in later years, even when he had abandoned and condemned its major theses. It remained for him the residue of an important experience.

Reflections is a war book. In August 1914 a wave of enthusiasm swept German intellectuals (above, chap. 3, & n. 4). Thomas Mann was carried away too; he was torn from his exclusively artistic concerns and became intensely conscious of his national identity, previously subordinate to his personal life. Then, a little later when the initial impetus of the German army to the west had been halted, and the horrors and miseries of war had closed in, Thomas's own elder brother and literary rival, Heinrich Mann, who was both very close to and very different from him, dissociated himself from Germany at war and proclaimed his international pacificism, antinational in Thomas's eyes. Worse, he accused the other side of being conformist intellectuals and aesthete patriots, and all this in a book in honor of Zola, the champion of Dreyfus. In the meantime, Thomas had, as he thought discreetly, extolled Frederick II's courage. He felt personally attacked. He was wounded to the core, in his calling, his faith as a German writer. Unable to pursue his creative writing, he prepared a reply and found himself led to reflect on himself, his art, and his national culture. A work of polemical fratricide and a painful self-examination, *Reflections* occupied him throughout the war years.[5] The big book was to see the light of day

Thomas Mann (Bruford 1975; chap. 11). For my own part, I am grateful to my friend Joseph Frank for drawing my attention to the value of this work for my researches. The references which follow are to the English translation of Mann's *Betrachtungen eines Unpolitischen* (1918): *Reflections of a Nonpolitical Man* (1983), translated by W. D. Morris. All direct quotation is from Morris's translation.

5. Klaus Mann, then a boy of ten, recounted later on that he had been struck by the tense seriousness of his father absorbed in his work during this period (1984: 80–82).

only at the time of the defeat, which destroyed the author's patriotic hopes and justified his brother and antagonist.

One could follow Erich Heller in contrasting Heinrich's moral courage in its flat progressivism to the sharp and often profound views which Thomas brought to the service of an "indefensible cause."[6] But passing over some unfortunate comments in which Thomas espoused his country's most brutal acts of war,[7] the polemics, which are frequently tedious and sometimes difficult, are of no interest to us here. To take their true measure at this distance of time, it is more to the point to note at once that the future was to reconcile the two brothers. When Germany was defeated, Thomas joined the Weimar Republic, and did in fact accept the democracy he had declared hateful. But for all that Heinrich did not triumph. It was now his turn to recognize that the Republic was not what he had dreamed of, that the problem was not so simple as he had supposed. So the two brothers found themselves together again, at a common remove, one might say, from the democracy as it was (cf. Hamilton 1978).

Now the fact is that this future reconciliation can be said to be virtually present in the pages of *Reflections*. This is the essence of the book, the reason for which it proved such a difficulty to the author, for its complexity and internal tension: in the end the analysis isolates, and illuminates, what the feuding brothers, the two sorts of German writer, had in common. Apart from the fact that one may here see the triumph of the integrity of the artist—and of the brother's honesty—even more than his perspicacity, here is a definition of a national artistic culture which is of the utmost value to us. We can easily understand why the author was forever to refuse to disclaim this book, however obsolete it became in other respects. As George Lukács always paid tribute to Thomas Mann, it seems permissible to oppose to his brutal dichotomy of German culture the grasp of it as a whole exhibited by the great writer even when he took the side Lukács was to condemn as reactionary and anti-rational (Lukács 1955). This said in passing, the contrast is instructive: if there are national cultures or, better, national subcultures of modern European culture, they will escape, and German culture itself will necessarily escape anyone who tries to remain narrowly faithful to the naive belief in progress of the Enlightenment—whether

6. Erich Heller in *The Ironic German* (1958), quoted by Enright 1983.
7. In a rather confused review of *Reflections*, D. J. Enright (1983: 825) on the contrary highlights these passages. This seems the more inappropriate today as they occupy relatively little space in the book. What is striking is rather the seriousness of the quest for truth provoked by the war.

through Marxism or otherwise—and whatever aesthetic sensitivity he may otherwise have shown.

•

After this, our path is clear. We shall begin by characterizing in broad terms the ideological conflict, starting from the accusations Thomas brought against his brother. Then we shall follow him through into the picture that he gives of Germany and German cultural unity. It is easy, to begin with, to see in the polemic the play of several fundamental contrasts familiar to students of German culture.

Thomas never named his brother, even though he quoted him several times. He waged war on what he called "the literary man of civilization,"[8] an expression that could equally well apply to Romain Rolland, whom he criticized at length. "Civilization's literary man" is universalist and pacificist, and an advocate of democracy, that is, politics, for "there is only one politics: democracy."

"Civilization," that thing of the West, is contrasted to *Kultur,* which characterizes Germany. This was a hackneyed theme that became general at the period, as the principal slogan by which Germany replied to enemy propaganda. On this level civilization was essentially material progress, by definition common to all and international (Mann 1983: 174), while Germany was the repository of spiritual values, of *Kultur,* which was peculiar to her. However, this was not all, and at this point Thomas Mann recalled that he had long criticized the inadequacy of this view:

> I said to myself that civilization was not only just as spiritual, but that it was even *spirit itself*—spirit in the sense of reason, of morality, of doubt, of enlightenment, and finally, of *dissolution,* while culture on the other hand meant the principle of artistic organization and formation, of the life-preserving, life-glorifying, principle. (ibid.: 121–22, in the discussion of Romain Rolland)

Let us not dwell on the contrast between "disintegration" or atomization and "organization" or organism. To glorify "life," Mann went so far as to oppose it to "spirit" (*Geist*). A sign of the times, certainly. Lukács castigated the vogue for a "philosophy of life" as a betrayal of reason. Mann was referring to Nietzsche rather than to Dilthey, and we shall reencounter "life" as characterizing Germany.

8. The convention in English translations of rendering the phrase "Civilization's literary man" has been adhered to in the rest of this paper. (Trans. note)

It is easy to see that what is being attacked here as "civilization" is what I have elsewhere called the individualism of the French Revolution, an individualism which was applied to social institutions and which was also the carrier of material progress and thus suspect as "materialism." All this was in opposition to inward individualism, which was spiritual, at the least tinged with religion, left the milieu's holism unaffected, and partook of the organic. Let us observe also that what was actually objected to here was the modern attribution of *primacy* to the relation to things. For moderate intellectuals this was a matter only of ranking. It did not prevent Germany from rivaling the West, indeed surpassing it, in the technical field.

"Civilization's literary man" was unfaithful to German values under the guise of a cosmopolitan humanitarianism which was itself superficial and false. He played the enemy's game. Germany was a community, and Western values, which recognize only the individual and the species, threatened German identity. A whole series of terms thus designated the enemy's attributes: civilization, democracy, politics, internationalism. Literature itself must be added, in a sense I shall explain in a moment, so that the phrase "Civilization's literary man" has a powerful polemical redundancy. The opposition here is between community and society, or holism and individualism. We see here a reappearance of Herder's protest against the cosmopolitanism of the Enlightenment, but in a different form, with an anti-democratic emphasis.

Is this an example of the disowning of the Enlightenment, of that betrayal of the values of the great classics, of which, according to Lukács, the German intellectuals were guilty? In fact, Lukács totally failed to identify the great historical phenomenon in question. It is clearly revealed only when we look at it from an intercultural perspective. I can make no more than a brief allusion to this here, but it is necessary to mention it in passing, however crudely. On the one hand, Herder's holism was already basically incompatible with democracy, and the Germans from the start emphasized a distance from the French Revolution—or in any case they implied it, as Fichte witnesses.[9] On the other hand, to the extent that there was in effect a subsequent development, it was that of a culture which succeeded in its adaptation or acculturation to the dominant culture—by means of a minimum of change—and which reaffirmed itself in its originality. One can take as paradigm of this movement Hegel's Philosophy of Right, which appears in that light to have been truly prophetic: individualism is there rele-

9. See my study in Dumont 1986, chap. 4.

gated to the level of civil society, itself encompassed, that is both contained and contradicted, or contained in both senses of the term, in and by the holism of the State.

Thomas Mann himself did not quite understand the matter, but he had some sense of it. On the one hand, he regarded himself as essentially a nineteenth-century man, the century Nietzsche called "honest but gloomy" (Mann 1983: 11), which was more or less positivist, unlike the eighteenth (or the twentieth) century, more ambitious, humanitarian, reforming. On the other hand, he noted that in the first half of the nineteenth century it was still possible to be both a democrat and a patriot, like Uhland and Storm. This was indeed the period when "liberalism" had not yet given way to "national-liberalism," when State unity had not yet stifled democratic hopes.

But what is Germany, in what exactly does this *Kultur* consist which, by his brother's showing, was betrayed by "Civilization's literary man"? The picture of Germany as Thomas Mann saw it in this book is not a simple one, and we shall succeed in getting an idea of it, even schematically, only in two stages.

First of all, one can readily cull numerous characteristics from the *Reflections*. Some of them are familiar. Troeltsch has given us the key to a formula like "Freedom, duty, and freedom again, that is Germany" (Mann 1983: 202). One is first a German, then and thereby a man, as Dostoevsky saw (ibid.: 324). While "to liberate" is the *idée fixe* of democracy, for the German it is perhaps more important to bind oneself (376), and there is a "proud obedience" (355); service and human dignity are not incompatible (354). An authoritarian state (*Obrigkeitsstaat*), a State the principle of which is authority, is, by contrast to a democratic state, that which suits the German people.

It is clear that for the author Germany's unity, or that of the German "people," is essentially cultural. He called it somewhat metaphysical to indicate a sphere superior to the social and political (179). Thus classical literature helped to form the nation. By turning his back on politics and "progress" Goethe paved the way for the "day of glory" of national assertion—and, here as elsewhere, Goethe is clearly the model venerated by the artist.

All the same, Mann avoided borrowing the glory of the nation by mingling with it. "Propriety, pride and modesty" (110) demand "individual distancing" of "the *I* from the whole" (110). As Dostoevsky said, it is "the moral idea" which forms a nation's character (386), and Mann strives to bring out this national "moral idea." Perhaps it was the idea of life. The German people are anti-radical and aliterary, or, to put the same thing in positive terms, "it is the nation of life" (58):

> The *life concept,* this conservative concept, deeply German, Goethean, and, in the highest sense, religious concept, is the one Nietzsche imbued with new feeling, . . . elevated to the highest rank, to universal sovereignty. (my trans.)

It is in the same sense that Kant's practical reason was opposed to "theoretical, radical philosophy" (136) and to the intellectualism of Western civilization (125). "It is German to relegate radicalism to the intellect and to act in a practical-ethical, antiradical manner towards life" (136). And *Bildung,* the Goethean development of the spirit, rests on "reverence for life" (372).

The crucial question is what one is, not what one's volitions and opinions are (60). Freedom, according to Schopenhauer, does not lie in the *operari,* but in the *esse* (94).

At the level of the nation or state, this means that "affirmation of self and expansion . . . cannot be differentiated." Thomas Mann not only believed in victory, at least in the early years of the war. Like Troeltsch and unlike his brother, he also believed that Germany had a vocation for power. External politics are by definition power politics. There was a deep-seated accord between Germany and her leaders (245–46), and she had shown by her exploits that she had a right to the "management of the earth" (147 ff., 245). On a page where he was concerned to justify German exactions, Mann even wrote: "The world people [*Weltvolk*] of the spirit . . . wanted to become a world people . . . *the* world people of reality—if necessary . . . by means of a violent breakthrough" (246).[10]

In the interests of power, one can even consent to some democratization (177–78). However, I shall leave on one side the author's efforts in this direction (189 ff.), and his borrowings from Lagarde (199) and the school of "the politics of cultural despair," as Fritz Stern called this line of thinking (Stern 1965).

Two points emerge. First, Thomas Mann here shared the general representations of his country, his *milieu.* As we saw in connection with Troeltsch, German patriotism expressed itself in a will for power. The pan-Germanist dimension, or external domination, was an integral part of the

10. Morris translates *Weltvolk* as "nation," a word that has no place here. "World people" shows the survival of the idea of universal sovereignty (that of the Holy Roman Empire), as mentioned above in chap. 2. It is relatively secondary after this that Germany, in contrast to her enemies, was reputed to be without hate.

idea that German intellectuals had of their State. But, secondly, this desire for power was not linked in depth to the whole set of our author's representations, or at any rate not to the same degree as other characteristics we shall meet presently. Basically it assorted badly with his low opinion of politics in general, and it did not, for example, prevent him from being full of distrust of the instrument or even the subject of this power, that is, the State (180).

So one can understand that Thomas Mann was able, much later it is true, at the moment of the wreck of Nazism—against which he had fought valiantly—expressly to reject as inept the very dream of domination. He had long admitted that the nation could rest only on inward liberty, and he could then declare that the German people, vowed to inwardness, had shown itself inept at politics both in its rejection of democracy and in its "medieval dreams," as we could well put it, of universal sovereignty (Mann 1965, 2:13–15; Mann 1976: 313–32, cf. 324–25).

Indeed, doubts about ultimate victory crept in and increased from 1917 onward. They were aroused by the development of the war, and even more by the fact that, as the quarrel between the two brothers demonstrated, Germany was divided (Mann 1983: 135) and weak in the face of enemy propaganda. The trouble was that the German people were a "problem" people, a contradictory people, so that in one passage Thomas Mann came to ask himself whether their vocation was not rather to be the ferment of Europe than to dominate it (373, trans. modified). We thus return from the level of "reality" to that of the spirit, and we are on the threshold of the profound idea Thomas Mann had of his country in relation to his art and himself.

On this point, it is convenient to look for the essentials in some rather brief chapters at the beginning of the book. In his attempt to define Germany, Thomas Mann first resorted to Dostoevsky: Germany is Protest (25–30), the millennial protest against Roman civilization. It is therefore the "unliterary country" (31–33). For, according to Rome, human dignity is indissolubly linked to literature—and not to music or poetry (32). The legacy of Rome, the Latin character, is "the beautiful, heart-stirring phrase that is worthy of a human being" (32–33). It is the literary man, the lawyer, the Enlightenment, progress, philosophy (33). It culminated in the French Revolution to congeal into pedantry, and become a bourgeois affair, the imperialism of civilization, the last form of Roman unity to which Germany, as always in the past, had no words to oppose but only its courage (32). For Germany has no voice and no hate.

But look at "Civilization's literary man": with their country at war, some Germans appealed to a universalism that was essentially Western. These were the literary men in an unliterary country, the protesters against protest (56). Yet the author refrained from calling these people un-German (37). The very brother who made himself the mouthpiece of the foreigner was a German too. The truth was that Germany was contradictory to the core. No doubt all European countries had their internal contrasts, but the spiritual antitheses were greater in Germany than elsewhere (36). The proof of this could be found in the author himself. He had remained faithful to the German cause. Yet he found in himself traces of what he condemned elsewhere as unpatriotic. Here is the point where the drama of the *Reflections* unfolds, and we arrive, with the "abyss" (37) of German-ness, at the profound analysis which foreshadowed the union of the two brothers.

Thomas Mann had just arraigned "cosmopolitan radicalism" when he exclaimed "Oh well, yes, I share it." This is the opening of a chapter called "Soul-Searching" (*Einkehr*) 4: 34) and of a subtle analysis of the cosmopolitan or "Western" aspects found in the author himself—wasn't he, for a start, given to a not quite German literary genre, the "social novel" (36)?— and in the tradition of the masters he claims as his own. For simplicity and brevity, I shall mention only a few features of these predecessors.

"A tendency toward . . . cosmopolitanism . . . is inseparable from the essence of German nationality" (48). There are traces of it even in Goethe. And what about Schiller? These two names mentioned in this context make one think furtively of Thomas and Heinrich. Lukács wrote, using later texts of Thomas Mann's:

> [Goethe is] fundamentally German and fundamentally unpatriotic,
> while Schiller is an international patriot. He represents the bourgeois
> ideal in the political and democratic sense; Goethe, on the other hand,
> in the intellectual and cultural one. (Lukács 1964: 147)[11]

In our text, Thomas Mann made a fundamental distinction between the German *Bürger,* the main carrier of German culture, and the democratic and "international" French bourgeois (96 ff.). He could have said that Goethe was a *Bürger* and not a bourgeois. However, the incompatibility between German-ness and politics, displayed by Goethe in 1813, reappeared in Schopenhauer in 1848 and Nietzsche in 1871.

The three names which were at the basis of his intellectual and artistic development, according to Thomas Mann, designate "events that are not

---

11. Quotation from Thomas Mann taken from a collection in German of 1934, called *Sufferings and Greatness of the Masters.*

intimately German, but European: Schopenhauer, Nietzsche and Wagner"
(49). Schopenhauer, the only German philosopher who was a great writer,
seems to have written first in Latin and thus gained "an immortal precision" (49). As for Nietzsche, dressing the German idea of life up in
Frenchifying prose, "an antiradical, antinihilistic, antiliterary, most highly
German idea" (58), "with his Europeanism, [he] has contributed more
than anyone else to Germany's education in criticism, to her intellectualiz-
ation, psychologization, radicalization, or, not to shun the political word,
to her democratization" (60). Note that Mann spoke of the influence exerted by Nietzsche, and scarcely at all of foreign influences on him, or,
more accurately, of what he had found outside Germany.

A marginal comment suggests itself. It arises from what has been said
here about *Bildung*. Mann says somewhere, without mentioning Nietzsche, that Germany scarcely believes in the "possibility of a synthesis of
power and intellect" (184). In the perspective of German tradition it might
be said that everything happened as if Nietzsche had perceived the crisis of
Bildung, the tearing apart of Germany between inwardness and Etatisme,
and had sought—among other things, but notably—to transcend and replace *Bildung* both in its relation to the global society and in itself. From
this point of view, the "will to power" might well appear as the crucible
meant for the transmutation of both "will" and "power."

What Thomas Mann says about Wagner is particularly striking. He borrows from a Swedish critic. Wagner's art is finally more outward than inward, more national than folk in origin, unlike that of Schumann,
Schubert, or Brahms. Wagner's music "admittedly had many characteristics that *foreigners especially* would find German, but at the same time it
had unmistakably cosmopolitan cachet" (52). It was rather like a "theatrical presentation" of "the German essence." It could reach the point where
it became grotesque, became a parody, or "to put it very crudely," as if it
was intended for tourists, for making an *Entente* audience exclaim "Ah ça,
c'est bien allemand par exemple."[12] However deeply German it was, Wagner's art was above all European, and critical. Nietzsche and Wagner were
the two great critics of German-ness. Wagner intellectualized it: "he glori-
fies [it] in a critical-decorative way" (53). Mann gives a dramatic turn to an
open-air concert at Rome as a "supra-German intellectual experience"
(56)—and perhaps the recent history of Bayreuth does not contradict this
view.

The case seems to me exemplary. In the person of Wagner, one fully

12. I.e., "Ah now, that is truly German."

grasps the *representative* role of the great German artist, his function as a *mediator* between German culture and the surrounding culture, European or universal. One could say as much of Nietzsche or Goethe. But to say this is thereby to recognize the presence of an element defined as foreign, non-German, cosmopolitan, in the author's masters. This is indeed what he intended. It was his justification for pursuing the same enquiry with respect to his own work, which he did with subtlety if not without some complacency.

This brings us to a conclusion which Thomas Mann apparently never drew explicitly. What he condemned about Heinrich was not the presence of a cosmopolitan component, but only the predominance, or exclusive role, accorded to this component at the cost of the "Germanic" component. The war obliged the patriot to assert the latter unequivocally, and unless he was an artist, without any admixture.

Thus, the German author was aware of two components in German culture. One he felt to be autochthonous and called "Germanic." The other he analyzed as essentially foreign. We can relate it to the cultural environment, to European or universal culture. This enables us to get a clearer understanding of what we have already been told or are still to find elsewhere in the book of spiritual antagonisms within Germany. Germany was not a nation. It was a meeting place of European antagonisms, the "quintessence of Europe" (Hamilton 1978: 176). Germany, and every German's soul, was the battlefield of Europe. German-ness was an abyss.

So now Germany was no longer defined simply as "Protest," but by the contradiction which consisted of recognizing that she also had within herself to some degree, at any given time, that against which she was protesting. Thus, if Germany was eminently Lutheran Protestant, she was also Catholic. The contradiction was between what was specific to German culture and the surrounding "civilization," in which it participated willy-nilly. The contradiction was rooted in *relation,* in the fact that Germany was not the world; it was structural. More than "Protest," there was interaction, there was a complex dialogue, sometimes dramatic, but necessary. Thomas Mann recognized this throughout his analysis and when he declared that "perhaps without some foreign admixture, no higher German character is possible" (48; cf. 111–12). Only the words "perhaps," and, strictly speaking, even "higher" are superfluous here.[13] One could say as much of every other national subculture of European culture: this is just one particular

13. This is what on his side Thorstein Veblen caricatured in his malicious pamphlet of 1915, *Imperial Germany,* where he claims that since prehistoric times the savages of the Baltic shores were never able to invent, but only to copy.

case of a sociological law which is easy to grasp and verify (Dumont 1980: Postface). Pan-Germanism itself was after all a particular manner of recognizing the necessity of the relation.

The best example of the need for a foreign support is perhaps the fascination which the Greece idealized by Winckelmann exercised on German classics. This influence was so great that one has to understand its necessity. Its fruitfulness can be gauged from one fact alone, namely that, most especially through Goethe, it was a component of *Bildung*, which, although less radical than the pietism of Lutheran descent, played an indispensable role precisely in the secularization or laicization of inward individualism (thus, Mann 1983: 202). We are reminded of the passage in Troeltsch where he recognized that German culture found a support "at least for a time"[14] in classical antiquity, even if ultimately the result was "a deepening of the German essence."

Perhaps I have reduced an iridescent and subtle work to a skeletal schema. Yet I hope I have isolated, with the moral beauty that comes forth when a deepened national awareness is wrested from a grievous quarrel, and beyond the incompatibility of *Bildung* and Politics, a major lesson which makes *Reflections of a Nonpolitical Man* a fundamental book for the comparison of national forms or subdivisions of modern culture: a definition of German culture as a *unity-in-relation*, with, as a corollary, the role of the writer or artist as a representative or mediator that is characteristic of Germany.

14. Troeltsch also objected vigorously to Cassirer, who limited German liberty to classical rationalism (Troeltsch 1925*a*, 4:696–98).

PART THREE

The
Dawn
of
Bildung

] 5 [

From Pietism to Aesthetics: Totality and Hierarchy in the Aesthetics of Karl Philipp Moritz

This study is dedicated to the memory of André Schaeffner, a scholar who, while he was a Germanist, united in his person aesthetics and anthropology.

Our intention is to widen in some measure a recent interpretation of the aesthetics of Karl Philipp Moritz by insisting on two points: first, the idea of the work of art as a totality; and second, the intimate relationship between this aesthetic and the religion from which it originated, inasmuch as the religion accounts for the internal structure of the aesthetic.

Tzvetan Todorov has called attention to Moritz in his book *Les Théories du symbole (The Theories of the Symbol)* and has brought back to light this little-known author by showing that he presents "in germinal form the entire aesthetic doctrine of [German] romanticism" (1977: 179). The choice of Moritz is obviously judicious, but whatever the merits of the semiological approach applied by Todorov to the study of aesthetics, the twenty pages he devotes to Moritz, and in which he quotes him at length, leave something to be desired for the informed reader, and one of Todorov's conclusions actually raises doubts. After checking the quoted passages—and with the help of an admirable book by Robert Minder on Moritz's religious development as evidenced in his autobiographical writings (a book not mentioned by Todorov)—it seems clear that a wider view will be useful for delineating the exemplary figure of Moritz and his place in the history of ideas in Germany and in the genesis of modern aesthetics.

"The central concept of Moritz's aesthetics," Todorov tells us, "is in fact totality" (1977: 187). We shall therefore in turn organize our discussion of the two texts on aesthetics quoted most often by Todorov around the concept of totality. In so doing, we will reach a rather dissimilar interpretation from Todorov's. Our intention is not polemical, and we will therefore not stress every divergence between the two interpretations, only the more notable ones.

Moritz was genuinely concerned with the definition and the implications of the notion of whole. This is to his credit, since the notion is not as

First published in "Hommage à André Schaeffner," Special issue of the *Revue de Musicologie* 68, nos. 1–2 (1982): 64–76. Translated by Christophe Robert and revised by the author.

clear in modern culture as one might wish. Even German thought in its great period, between 1770 and 1830, is not entirely satisfactory on this point. Although the notion of whole or wholes was an important concern at the time, the category as such was not treated thematically. Perhaps it was mostly the aesthetic dimension that aroused interest in the category of totality. Lessing, Herder, Goethe, and Schiller are more explicit on this theme than Kant, Fichte, or Hegel. Reflections on the work of art must somehow directly raise the question of the relationship of the parts to each other and to the whole. Moritz is thus part of a tradition; nevertheless we shall see that his approach is quite original.

Let us first take the very concise text dedicated to Moses Mendelssohn, entitled "Essay at a Reunion of the Arts and Sciences of the Beautiful under the Concept of the Accomplished-in-Itself" (Moritz 1962: 3–9).[1] This 1785 text dates from before Moritz's meeting with Goethe (1786–87) and belongs to the period in his thought that can be labeled rationalistic (we shall come back to this point). The work of art is here defined as "accomplished-in-itself" (we could also say perfect or complete, *vollendete*), that is, explains Moritz, it "constitutes a whole in itself." As such, it is the opposite of a useful object, and the whole development of his argument follows from this distinction.

A useful object is not something that is accomplished-in-itself: I use it, which is to say that it complements me. The work of art, on the contrary, is self-sufficient. We could say that it becomes complete through the *disinterested* pleasure it provides me. In other words, the end of the useful object is external while that of the work of art is internal. For the work of art, "the absence of external finality has to be replaced by an internal finality" (Moritz 1962: 6; cf. Todorov 1977: 190). In order to pass from the useful to the beautiful I must displace the end out of myself, as it were, and transfer it to the object itself (literally: roll back, *zurückwälzen*, the end into the object). Here already is a hierarchical perception: the center of gravity lies sometimes within the subject (for the useful object) and sometimes within the object (for the work of art). In the relationship of usefulness, the object is subordinate to the subject; in the relationship of beauty, the subject subordinates itself to the work—and this is valid, as we shall see, for the creator of the work as well as for the art lover.

This is an important point and should be stressed. Moritz, for instance, writes:

1. In a 1757 text Mendelssohn had made the distinction between "sciences" (such as painting or music), which use natural signs, and "arts" (such as poetry), which use arbitrary signs. See Cassirer 1922: 139–40.

. . . the sweet wonder, the *pleasant abandon of ourselves* in the contemplation of a work of art is proof that our pleasure is something which is here subordinate, that we willingly let ourselves be determined by the beautiful, to which we grant, for a while, a sort of dominion [*Obergewalt*] over our emotions. . . . At that moment, we sacrifice our limited individual existence to a higher one. (1962: 5)

Herein lies what we usually call the enjoyment of a work of art. As for its "creation," Moritz is just as explicit. In the six-page text of 1785, we find this passage among others:

[For the true artist as for the sage], the purest blissfulness itself should be encountered [*mitgenommen*] on the way to perfection and should not be the object of a quest. The line of felicity only runs parallel to the line of perfection: if felicity becomes the goal, the line of perfection necessarily assumes entirely false directions. A series of actions tending to pleasure only will no doubt take on a semblance of finality, but will fail to build up an ordered and harmonious whole. The same holds true for the arts when the concept of perfection, or of the accomplished-in-itself, is subordinate to the concept of pleasure. (1962: 8)

These two passages call for a dual remark. It is not a coincidence that they both contain the word *subordinate*. The notion is constantly present in Moritz, in this text as well as in the better known and more complete 1788 text, "On the Formative Imitation of the Beautiful." Moreover, it is revealing that the second quotation intimately links the notion of whole with that of subordination. In order for the work of art to constitute a whole, man has to subordinate himself to it, or, better, he has to subordinate all his feelings to the feeling of beauty evoked or provided by the work. Moritz seems nowhere to directly set forth the notion of hierarchy as subordination of the part to the whole, and yet he closely links the two notions of totality and of subordination. This is perhaps because he is concerned with the relationship of man to the work of art. He invites us, as it were, to construct a concept that encompasses the work of art on the one hand, and the human actions and feelings that create it and through which it lives on the other.[2] Within this concept of the work-as-experienced, so to speak, the rule is the subordination of man to the work in the narrow sense of the word. It is between these two elements of the work-as-experienced that there is subordination, or hierarchy.

2. "The beautiful needs us to be acknowledged" . . . "works of art cannot really last as such without our consideration" . . . "we consider them for themselves in order to give them, as it were, their genuine and complete existence by our attention" (Moritz 1962: 4).

The fact remains that it is not a proper assessment of Moritz's aesthetics to say that, for him, "all creation may and should be the object of enjoyment" (Todorov 1977: 188), and that in his thought all subordination has disappeared.

•

We have seen that the work of art is characterized by the fact that its end is internal rather than external to it. This also implies a necessary relationship between its parts, since an arbitrary relationship would point to the presence of an external factor. According to Moritz, internal coherence is therefore a corollary of internal finality (and not "another idea," as Todorov seems to suggest [1977: 189]).

> Where an object lacks utility or an external end, these must be sought in the object itself, if this object is to arouse pleasure in me; that is, I must find *so much finality in the separate [einzelne] parts of this object that I forget to ask: but what purpose is the whole?* (Moritz 1962: 6; cf. Todorov 1977: 189)

Inasmuch as the work of art constitutes a whole, Moritz perceives it as having a privileged relationship with the great Whole of nature. Todorov strongly emphasizes, justifiably so, the profound change in the notion of imitation: instead of the work imitating nature (*natura naturata*), it is henceforth the artist who imitates nature as creator (*natura naturans*). Starting with the title itself of his 1788 essay, "On the Formative [*bildende*] Imitation of the Beautiful" (1962: 63–93), Moritz is careful to specify the constructive or formative aspect of this imitation.

> Any beautiful totality born of the hands of the artist which forms it is therefore an imprint of the supreme beauty found in the great totality of nature [1962: 73]. The active force [*Thatkraft*][3] . . . grasps the dependence within things, and with what it has taken from nature itself, forms a whole existing for itself by its own strength. (1962: 74; Todorov 1977: 186, with a few changes)

More precisely, we once again encounter finality here. To use parts of another quotation from Todorov:

> The artist must seek to replace (roll back, *zurückwälzen*) the end, which in nature is always exterior to the object, within the object itself, to make it accomplished-in-itself. Then we see a whole where before we

3. Since Leibniz and on through Herder, the word *Kraft*, "force," has represented the dynamic unity of any being, or entelechy. *Tatkraft* almost sounds like Fichte, by anticipation, but the emphasis on the act or the "doing" is general, and found in Goethe as well.

only saw parts with divergent purposes. (1962: 153, from the text entitled "The Metaphysical Line of Beauty;" quoted in Todorov 1977: 190)

Here again is an expression already encountered in the discussion on the
useful. In both cases the end that is external to the object must be "rolled
back" into it so that the object can gain access to beauty.[4] We notice that
some characteristics that we often observe correspond, materially and psy-
chologically, to Moritz's concerns. In a painting, for instance, the relation
to the frame or boundaries and the various courses, attractions, or gradua-
tions offered to the eye of the spectator in order to bring his attention back
from the periphery to the focal points are evocative of a kind of rolling back
upon itself of the painting.

It is understandable that Tzvetan Todorov was impressed by the aspect
of immanence present in the self-teleology of the work of art, "the conversion of external to internal finality" (1977: 191). The work of art differs
from all the objects we use, and from all natural objects; it is similar only to
the great Whole of nature. This is an extraordinary privilege that makes it
the equal of Nature and makes the Beautiful the equal of or, better, the substitute for God. The Beautiful, or the work of art, becomes something akin
to a supreme entity. That the supreme entity is located not in the hereafter
anymore but on earth, that it is in some way a human production, is, to be
sure, a revolution announcing developments of which we are well aware. If
this were the only relevant feature, we could conclude with Todorov that,
already in Moritz, immanence has replaced transcendence. But there is another fundamental aspect in Moritz's aesthetics: the subordination of man
to the work of art. Undoubtedly, this second characteristic is not homologous with the first; it can even appear to be its opposite, which is perhaps
why Todorov did not mention it. It is this second aspect that prevents us
from seeing in the fact that the work of art is self-sufficient "a privilege of
man over nature" (1977: 191). It also prevents us from agreeing with
Todorov when he passes directly from the "formative imitation" of the Creator (or rather of nature) by the artist to the exaltation of man, as well as
when he portrays Moritz as the opposite of Saint Augustine and concludes:

> To be, intransitively, becomes a supreme value for Moritz, and he ends
> his treatise *on the formative imitation of the Beautiful* with these excla-
> mations: "That we ourselves *are*, this is our highest and noblest thought.

4. The formula used by Moritz seems remarkably clear and precise compared to that of
others. Let us mention Goethe, for whom perfection in the arts ("style") rests on an intuition
of the deep nature of the object that is represented, or Hölderlin, who transforms the artistic
matter into a whole by introducing a foundation (*Grund*) with the use of metaphor; cf. Ryan
1962: 55.

No more sublime word on *the beautiful* can escape from mortal lips
than this: *It is!*" (1977: 189)

However, it already appears that the affirmation "we are" is not independent from "it is," and this is absolutely clear when one reads what precedes
it in Moritz's text. Here is a literal translation of the entire paragraph:

> Death and destruction themselves are lost in the concept of the *eter-
> nally formative* [bildende] *imitation of the beautiful, itself elevated
> above formation* [Bildung], and which can only be imitated as *a being*
> [Dasein] *which ceaselessly rejuvenates itself.*
>
> It is through this ceaselessly self-rejuvenating being that *we ourselves
> are.*
>
> That we ourselves *are,* here is our highest and noblest thought.
>
> And mortal lips cannot utter anything more sublime about the beau-
> tiful than: *It is.*
> (1962: 93)

We have read correctly: it is through the beautiful, "this being which
ceaselessly rejuvenates itself . . . that *we ourselves* [in spite of our being
mortal] *are.*" It is therefore clear that the "supreme value" is here invested
in the beautiful and not in the supposedly intransitive being of man. We see
from this phrase, once again, that man is transcended in the beautiful,
which contains and transcends "death and destruction," and which, by
"ceaselessly rejuvenating itself," provides man with his being. At first
glance, the God of Saint Augustine seems to have become the Beautiful of
Moritz. Moritz has not replaced "submission by equality" (Todorov 1977:
188). If it is true in a way that the transcendental instance has come down
to earth from the sky, it has, however, not disappeared, and Moritz is not
Picasso. It is true that Moritz does exalt man, that is, man including his
relation to the work of art, which comprises his subordination, as we have
seen. If there is in Moritz something more than this aesthetic exaltation, it
is in a sense that will become clear only later.

For the present, we must return to the previous quotation and attempt
to understand the solemn affirmation with which Moritz begins the conclusion of his essay: "Death and destruction themselves are lost. . . ."
These words actually echo and summarize a long development in the essay.
This dense thirty-page essay is a surprising and difficult text, a philosophical rhapsody of sorts, both discursive and incantatory, somewhat reminiscent of *The Letters on the Aesthetic Education of Man,* except that Moritz
does not possess the supreme glow through which Schiller achieves his in-
imitable alloy of reason and sensitivity. We shall not attempt here to sum-

marize Moritz's essay; we will only isolate a theme that accompanies the previously mentioned distinction between the beautiful and the useful and that, after a short appearance (1962: 83), takes up the last pages of the essay (1962: 86 ff.). If the beautiful is easily distinguishable from the useful, it also, paradoxically, has an intimate relationship with the harmful. Let us reflect on this: to say that "we sacrifice our existence to a higher one" is to say that the beautiful is harmful to our existence in the narrower sense of the word. Only by positing that *the superior realizes the inferior by destroying it* can we manage to escape this conclusion. Therefore, the inferior, the less perfect, can be harmful to the more perfect, the superior, but the reverse does not hold: there is an ascending law for living beings that governs their annihilation in the name of higher forms. The hierarchy has a destructive face; the great chain of being is a chain of destruction while simultaneously being one of fulfillment. At the top is man, and above man is sacrifice, beauty, love, and metaphysical nostalgia (if I can thus render *Sehnsucht*). "There seems to exist nothing greater to which sacrifice itself should be sacrificed" (1962: 80, line 30). This dramatic theodicy calls to mind not only Schiller's "Die and Become" but precisely Hegel's *Aufhebung* and the Hegelian sentiment of reality. Let us state the supreme transition that interests us, that from man to the beautiful. Moritz quite logically puts the beautiful, as "appearance" (*Erscheinung*), above common or real humanity and above "reality" (*Wirklichkeit*). Reality is on the level of the *individual,* while appearance and the beautiful work of art are on the level of the *human species* (*Gattung*).[5] The work of art is part of the patrimony of the species, or, as Moritz phrases it, the misfortunes of the Trojan War become, thanks to Homer, a treasure for posterity. Individual or real man has to suffer or endure (*dulden*) in order to make this transition, and, as we grasp better now, he must rid himself of all personal or egoistical aspects when working at the beautiful, not only in the sense that the beautiful is accomplished-in-itself but also in the sense that the work must take its place at the level of the human species.

This is approximately what echoes in the reader's mind when Moritz concludes: "Death and destruction themselves are lost in the concept of the formative imitation of the beautiful." Undoubtedly Moritz exalts man, whose capacity to reflect the universe in himself has placed him at the top of the chain of being—the Leibnizian monad even if Leibniz is not mentioned—but in the end this capacity orders man to place his product

5. One inevitably thinks of Kant: "In man . . . those natural capacities which are directed to the use of his reason are to be fully developed only in the species, not in the individual" ("Idea for a Universal History . . . ," Kant 1965: 28).

outside of himself, in the work of art. For us, (although these expressions are not found in Moritz), man must reach beyond himself in the work of art. The work of art is the redemption of reality, of the individual, on the level of the beautiful appearance, which belongs to the species.

•

Religion has been encountered too often in the preceding pages for us to be able to avoid considering the relationship between Moritz's aesthetics and religion in more detail, as well as the role played by religion in the constitution of his ideas. It so happens that Robert Minder has analyzed Moritz's autobiographical writings in a masterly work (Minder 1936)[6] in which he painstakingly described Moritz's complex transition from the quietism-influenced pietism of his youth to the aesthetic theory of his thirties. Nothing is better established today than the deep and substantial contribution made by pietism to the constitution of classical German culture and philosophy in the most diverse realms. Its decisive influence on the elaboration of romantic aesthetics is thrown into relief by the case of Karl Philipp Moritz.

Since we cannot here follow Minder's precise and subtle analyses, especially concerning the complex religiosity emanating from Moritz's family and milieu, we shall merely point out the outlines of Moritz's evolution and then characterize his aesthetics both in contrast to the initial phase and in continuity with it.

Minder shows the general parallelism between Moritz's personal evolution and that of the dominant German ideology during the eighteenth century, especially the succession of literary movements and trends, from *Sturm und Drang* to romanticism. What one witnesses on the level of global ideology is a gradual secularization. Minder is careful to underline the fact that pietism, which dominates in the first half of the century, is itself already a secularized form of Protestantism: dogma and symbolism are absent; it is an internalized religion in which the believer facing his God is alone. Pietism opens the way, on the one hand, through its tendency to fade into an ethics, to the religion of reason, and on the other hand, through the place it gives to individual sentiments, to the development of sensitivity in literature (*Empfindsamkeit*) and later, in philosophical thought, to the rehabilitation of sensitivity which is so important in the successors of Kant.

6. As a French complementary doctoral thesis, it was written in German (Minder 1936).

Minder convinces us that there is an homology between Moritz's personal experiences and the general evolution of pietism in the second half of the century under the influence of the rationalism of the Enlightenment, leading to its eventual transformation into a mysticism principally grounded in aesthetics.

Moritz depicted himself as dissatisfied, from an early age and in spite of his efforts, with the religion of his milieu, a pietism and a quietism that confined and isolated the individual (Minder 1936: 250). Pietism teaches self-hatred (ibid., 33), and the quietism inspired by Madame Guyon goes so far as to require a kind of self-destruction. The worshiper encounters only a faceless beyond (248), the wasteland of the metaphysical infinite. The young Moritz suffocates; he is "oppressed" (166) by the pietist obsession with self-contempt.[7] But whereas renouncing the world is thus a failure for Moritz, it is the awakening of understanding that opens the world to Anton Reiser, his autobiographical alter ego. Moritz explains that understanding and writing gave him or restored in him the notion of the Whole and allowed him to "enjoy the profound delight [*Wonne*] of thinking" as early as sixteen (Minder 1936: 135). From then on, his motto will be "never in the individual [or separate, *Einzelne*] to lose sight of the whole." Instead of facing God alone, he is now a member of the human community again; instead of despising himself, he has learned to be reasonably satisfied with himself.

It is not surprising therefore, that after a tumultuous adolescence, Moritz became a Freemason at the age of twenty-two in Berlin. It is his conversion to rationalism that, contrary to the religion that preceded it, allows "activity" (*Tätigkeit*), an activity in relation to the human community. Minder notes, however, that this desire and need for activity will lead Moritz neither to rebellion nor to social or political activism (249). Activity remains largely internal, since the fundamental trait, the main concern with internal perfection, has survived this conversion and accounts for the original combination of traits that characterizes Moritz, when we compare him with more simplistic or fanatical rationalists (162). Let us therefore note that Moritz belongs to the common and general line of German writers and thinkers for whom a concern with internal perfection and education of the self outweighs other concerns, to the point of excluding them.[8] Moritz

7. This summary is unavoidably sketchy. I have used Minder's expressions as much as possible. Rather than pietism in general, we encounter here the pietism current in this given environment. Moreover, Moritz writes in a rationalist vein that sharpens the criticism.

8. On the primacy of *Bildung* in this sense, cf. Minder 1962: 5–43; and Bruford 1975.

will later be able to come back to mysticism, although under a different form, without ever renouncing reason.

•

If we now compare the configuration of value-ideas and of feelings expressed in Moritz's aesthetics as outlined above with the corresponding configuration from which it originated (the pietism tinged with quietism of his family and youth), we notice a deep transformation from the one to the other, but also a continuation of the initial disposition in its fundamental structure.

The transformation is considerable, since the "faceless beyond," the "wasteland of the metaphysical infinite," has been replaced by the great Whole of nature and by the work of art, which is accessible to the subject both at the level of feeling (*Empfindungsfähigkeit*) and, if only he is capable of it, at the level of the formative or creative force (*Bildungskraft*). The beautiful therefore allows activity (*Tätigkeit*), which the unattainable God seemed to preclude. So to speak, we are now free to act here on earth.

Simultaneously, however, one notices the permanence of the same psychological disposition or configuration throughout the transformation taking place. First, for man as an individual it is clear that the beautiful replaces God as transcendence. We subordinate ourselves or we "sacrifice" ourselves to a higher existence in order to attain beauty, just as we used to do with the divine in religion. For the art lover and even more for the artist, the work of art is a beyond, or as Minder puts it, "at this immanent level, the pietist background reappears" (1936: 248): aesthetic unselfishness requires the same abandon toward the beautiful that pietism required toward God. Possibly, even the self-annihilation, or "destruction," against which Moritz balked when he was younger is found again both in the general hierarchy of beings and in artistic creation, which requires that the artist renounce his individuality to establish, *outside of himself,* the work of art by which the human moves from the level of reality, that is to say, of the individual, to the level of appearance, that is, of the species. Even the pleasure, sweetness, or delight that we feel when creating or admiring a work of art, as well as in religion, is subordinated to the self-denial required by the transcendence of the higher level over the lower one.

E. Lehmann wrote that the eighteenth century thus prolongs, at the level of clear understanding, what pietism had started at the level of belief.[9] To

9. "*Die Humanität und Pädagogik* des 18. Jahrhunderts ist das Durchführen dessen mit klarem *Verstand,* was der *Pietismus* im *Glauben* begonnen hatte" (Lehmann, quoted in Minder 1936: 168).

sum up, Moritz's aesthetics offers a synthesis, an original combination of rationalism and mysticism.[10]

This synthesis is fascinating, and by looking more closely one realizes that this quality stems from the fact that it is in itself contradictory. The incomplete interpretation offered by Todorov already alerts us to this fact: if we want to render immanence absolute, as posterity has attempted ever since Moritz, we have to abandon man's subordination to the work. Conversely, the chain of subordination on which Moritz insists, and the hierarchical perspective implied by it, cannot without contradiction culminate in the artificial withdrawal of the work of art into itself. There is a contradiction between two conceptions of the "whole" used by Moritz, one of which is clearly stated while the other is present indirectly, as a necessary assumption. To show this, we have to make Moritz's presuppositions explicit.

The question concerns the nature of the internal cohesiveness that distinguishes a whole from a simple aggregate. On the one hand Moritz states that the work of art is "a self-sufficient whole," its coherence coming from the fact that instead of having an external finality, which would subordinate it to something else, its ends have been "rolled back" into it in order to give it an "internal finality." On the other hand this autonomy, or rather this self-teleology of the work, has for its prerequisite the subordination of man to the work. Not only is this subordination vigorously marked, but it also replicates a general tendency of nature, seen as a chain of hierarchical levels, in which each level finds its finality in the level immediately above. We have seen Moritz express this in a dramatic form as the destruction of each level by the one above it—whereas it is obvious that the Beautiful "destroys" man's individual reality only in a partial and very limited way. What should hold our attention is the fact that the self-sufficient work represents an exception, a ceiling or a consummation—in other words, a halt in this chain of subordination. We are now concerned with the legitimacy of this halt.

In order to better grasp the logic of Moritz's hierarchical chain, we can use a text by Arthur Koestler:

> Organisms and societies are multi-leveled hierarchies of semi-
> autonomous sub-wholes branching into sub-wholes of a lower order
> and so on. The term "holons" has been introduced to refer to these in-
> termediate entities, which *relative to their subordinates* in the hierarchy

10. Fritz Brüggemann concluded that Moritz was torn between the world of ideas and reality, and by his concern with offering a critical analysis of the two in relation to each other (1976: 344).

function as self-contained wholes; *relative to their superordinates* as dependent parts. (1967: 58, italics are mine; let us add that for each level
subordination to the level above takes precedence over its own
integration)[11]

It is clear that we are now at the diametrical opposite of self-sufficient entities; here are only subwholes, and each one, or "holon," is part of a dual
relationship linking its coherence and its subordination, which are both
relative. It is obvious that Moritz has perceived some of this. At the same
time, however, he extended the image of the great Whole of nature to the
work of art. We are now at the crux of the problem: is there not, we wonder,
a Whole of wholes, a total whole, which alone would deserve the name,
since there would be nothing outside it or above it, and to which Koestler's
definition would not apply? Our answer will be twofold: either we define
this Whole in a purely external or mechanical fashion as something that
does not leave anything external, and we then cannot affirm its coherence
since it is only an exhaustive aggregate of what exists; or it is a whole similar to any other, and its coherence is guaranteed by something that transcends it. Given that this is the last stage of experience, experience needs a
beyond to escape incoherence.

We know that the traditional religious view found assurance of the coherence of reality in divine perfection, goodness, or will. God functioned
precisely as the beyond invested with the necessary properties, and divine
warrant was inseparable from the initial assumptions of the various attempts to discover order in nature and in history. The same relationship
was present, though reversed, in the teleological proof of the existence of
God, which concluded that the order found in nature was the manifestation of a transcendental will. From this point of view, we do not know what,
for Moritz, resulted of his conversion to rationalism. At any rate, it is clear
that the great Whole of nature in itself does not allow the absolute withdrawal of the work of art into itself.

The subwholes which we are able to isolate or construct in nature are
always dependent upon a whole of a higher order. We are well aware that
the work of art does not cease to locate itself within a larger framework. Its
radiance, its multivalent perfection, allows it to span centuries and cultural
boundaries, but whoever wishes to analyze it more adequately must *locate*
it. The hierarchical perspective Moritz resorted to in part allows for a final
stage only beyond experience. This may be the Beautiful but it cannot be

11. On the last point, cf. Dumont 1980, end of postscript.

the work of art, which abusively claims for itself the prerogative of the beyond.

It is striking to note that on this point Moritz's aesthetics clearly differs from that of his closest contemporaries, and even an author as keen as Cassirer seems to have missed this divergence. Writing about Schiller in *Liberty and Form*, Cassirer acknowledges Moritz[12] and quotes two of Schiller's letters to his friend Körner in which Schiller tells of his high esteem for Moritz and the "many points of contact" he feels they have in common; Cassirer also mentions Kant's *Critique of Judgment*, which was written after the *Formative Imitation*. But in Schiller's *Letters on Aesthetic Education*, as in Kant, the analogy is between the work of art and the living organism—not nature as a whole. The atmosphere is thus more frankly Leibnizian than in Moritz: the fact that the monad, be it the work of art or the living organism, possesses its own internal law by no means excludes the implicit hierarchical ordering of the set and does not prevent the submission to the "pure law of the whole" (Cassirer 1922: 438). The same is obviously also true of Goethe, be it for art or natural science, so much so that Moritz appears singular for his quasi-mystical stress on hierarchy as well as for his absolutizing of the work of art. We can perhaps discern a relic of religious demand here, in particular since he assigns the actual place of God to the work of art and seems obsessed with destruction. Could it be precisely at this junction that Moritz foreshadows romanticism? Moritz has revived and sometimes even exaggerated the notion of hierarchy in order to open the way for the self-realization of man on earth and obtain a precise theory of the work of art as a totality, while simultaneously contradicting it in favor of the absolute immanence of the work of art.

12. Cassirer 1922: 438–41. The same source (437) also brought to mind the reference to the teleological proof found above.

6

Wilhelm von Humboldt, or *Bildung* Alive

INTRODUCTION: BIRTH OF *BILDUNG*

A conceptual transformation takes place at the end of the eighteenth century in Germany: it is nothing less than the birth of a value-idea, expressed by the word *Bildung*. Before investigating this conception in Wilhelm von Humboldt, we need to familiarize ourselves with the notion and briefly consider the event of its birth. Let us say, to begin with, that the word designates here education, especially and preeminently self-education. Rudolf Vierhaus, in a long encyclopedic article on the history of the concept, has brilliantly traced its genesis (Vierhaus 1972). The word itself is not new, but in the eighteenth century its meaning broadens and is transformed and elevated; it now signals a major idea that eclipses similar conceptions and assumes a fundamental value. Whereas *Bildung* was previously a synonym for *Erziehung* (from *erziehen*, to educate, to bring up [a child]) and was related to Enlightenment (*Aufklärung*), the idea now encompasses all this and is elevated into the region of *Kultur* and *Humanität*. This change takes place in the last quarter of the century and is characteristic of the so-called classical literary period that follows the *Sturm und Drang*, in Wieland and especially in Herder and Goethe as well as in the writings, still mostly confidential, of Humboldt.

In a remarkable study, E. L. Stahl has traced the evolution of this whole complex of ideas and shown how the necessary conditions for the birth of a new ideal were realized (Stahl 1934). From *Bild*, "picture," and *bilden*, "to represent or form," the idea of form has always been essential to the word. *Bildung* had meant "form" or "formation" in a religious sense since the mystics of the late Middle Ages. The two moments of this "formation" were the opening to the divine grace, followed by its action on the worshiper, whose one and only model, *Vorbild*, is Jesus Christ. We note that pietism strongly stressed subjectivity, although essentially in order to destroy it (*Entselbstung*).[1] There is a blatant discontinuity between this religious idea of *Bildung* and the one that is our concern here. We have to do

Translated by Christophe Robert and revised by the author.

1. Note the strange parallel with the renouncer in India, about whom I wrote: "In leaving the world he finds himself invested with an individuality which he apparently finds uncomfortable since all his efforts tend to its extinction or its transcendence" (Dumont 1980: 274–75). Moreover, there are various tendencies within pietism.

with what Stahl, following Spranger, calls the "philosophy of humanity" (Spranger 1909). It is here a pantheism, or rather a panentheism; each individual, each creature, is original (*eigentümlich*) and unique, each "exhibits dispositions that are its own and have never previously existed under that form" (Stahl 1934: 27):

> The idea of *Bildung* according to the philosophy of humanity requires that these capacities be harmoniously developed and set forth in their particularity [*Eigentümlichkeit*], as well as in their totality. The important factor here is that particularity must be preserved, that there is no supreme law valid for all. There is to be sure something that is common, namely, the natural force present in all of us. But it assumes the most varied shapes and must also appear in its diversity. (ibid.)

The matter is even more complex than it appears so far. To begin with, it is of course impossible not to think of Leibniz. Stahl notes that the individual here is not that of the Renaissance, a microcosm of totality, nor that of the *Sturm und Drang,* who struggles with the whole world. In Goethe, the contrast between Werther and Wilhelm Meister, the *Bildung* hero, is clear. Meister in the *Apprenticeship,* and Goethe in his autobiography, *Poetry and Truth,* form themselves in interaction with the milieu—we have therefore gone beyond Leibniz. The subject is a particular totality whose development rests, as for plants, on the reciprocal interplay between innate capacities and the influence of the milieu. Stahl, who calls these two components formation by development and formation by adaptation (*Ausbildung* and *Anbildung*), shows that this combination rests on the drawn out conflict between preformationism (Leibniz) and creationism, and on Tetens's synthesis, the so-called epigenesis by evolution, in which, remarkably, the milieu's action completely replaces the divine intervention of earlier ages. We see that, far from being a purely human matter, *Bildung* entails a complete rearrangement of creation.

Let us come back to the transition from a monotheistic to a panentheistic creed. We could see it as a qualitative jump from a transcendental to an immanent conception of the divine, and think that, as such, it was arduous or required a considerable amount of time. But if Protestantism from Luther onward removed God from the world, the traditional monotheistic creed combined immanence and transcendence in such a way that the distance between the two was perhaps less than one would assume. Stahl mentions an admirable insight of Giordano Bruno's, who, although he was a heretic, probably kept something of the common creed on this point. For Bruno, the Soul of the world which emanates from a transcendent God is both transcendent and immanent, it acts as external "cause" on the one hand and as "principle" internal to matter on the other; it animates while it forms and guides while it governs (Stahl 1934: 76–77).

At any rate, Stahl demonstrates precisely how the transition occurs in the space of a few years in a single man, namely in Herder, the main inventor of *Bildung*. Stahl follows in detail the evolution of Herder's ideas, from his sermons in Riga—Herder was a pastor, famous for his eloquence—to the texts that followed his journey to France, in which he adopted pantheism. Let us note in passing that Spinoza's influence is general in the milieu, after Jacobi has revealed Lessing's Spinozism.

We need to broaden our perspective here, since it was during this same period that Herder asserted the diversity of cultures in the face of the universalism of the Enlightenment in a pamphlet entitled, precisely, "Another Philosophy of History for the *Bildung* of Humanity," whose importance we have insisted on elsewhere (Dumont 1986: chap. 4). It is important to note this synchronism in Herder between his protest against the idea of a uniform human culture and the disappearance of the single model of Christ for individual (self-)formation. Simultaneously, each human subject, and each culture or people (*Volk*), carries an irreplaceable originality, and henceforth *Bildung* in Herder will always have to be understood at both the individual and the collective levels: there is a *Bildung* of communities as well as of individuals. This stands as a warning for us: throughout our study we shall have to keep in mind this parallelism and osmosis between the conceptions of individual man and of collective man, which are linked within the idea of *Bildung* itself. Weintraub, an author of German tradition, in an attempt to demonstrate how the autobiographical genre culminates in Goethe, states that the individual is deemed singular when, the milieu being apprehended in its historical particularity, he considers it a secondary, though active, component in the development of his personality (Weintraub 1978). There is a close connection between the consecration of individual particularity and the birth of historicism (cf. Meinecke 1965).

Having chosen to study *Bildung* in one of its heroes, we want to establish a rough background of generalities and antecedents before introducing him. We will set aside for later consideration a trait that will find its place better in Humboldt than anywhere else, that is, the tendency of the Germans to find in the ancient Greeks the precedent and the guarantee for their notion of *Bildung*. This preliminary discussion should also help make it clear why we will give up any attempt to translate the word *Bildung* in what follows. Let us be clear: we can use approximate equivalents or circumlocutions, or allude to the idea and speak of (self-)education, self-formation, self-development or self-improvement, etc., as did the excellent English exegete who entitled his book *The German Tradition of Self-Cultivation* (Bruford 1975). But translating the German concept itself is another matter altogether. Let us beware, for it is a genuine *institution*. As Fauconnet and Mauss wrote in their definition of sociology in 1901 (*Grande Encyclopédie,* s.v. "*Sociologie*"), we do not have to reserve the use of the word institution for "political constitutions" or "main juridical organizations." "For what is an institution if not a set of actions and ideas, already in place, that individuals encounter, and that more or less imposes itself on them?" (reprinted in Mauss 1968–69, 3:150). No reader of our chapter on Thomas Mann (chap. 4), and of this book in general, should doubt that the set of representations condensed or implied in the word *Bildung* is as important sociologically as that on which any of our public establishments is founded. Moreover, throughout its existence *Bildung* is part of a constellation comprising external or even material elements; from Humboldt to Thomas Mann, we see it interact and engage in a dialogue with political institutions in the usual sense of the word.

The expedient of translating such an important idea, which is so constitutive of a culture, by a different term according to context would dismember what is a living entity, a cardinal value for our authors, and would brush aside the innumerable implied notions and harmonics that resonate in the German word. It would be contrary to the very goal of our investigation, which is to grasp the German notion in its ramified unity and not to substitute our own semantic categories for it. Actually, we are touching here on the relationship between language and culture: we cannot translate the word because we must *learn the culture* through the language. In order to even out typography and facilitate reading, we shall from now on drop even the italics and use the word as a common noun: Bildung.

BIOGRAPHICAL OUTLINE

> In every man . . . there is one part which concerns only himself and his contingent existence, is properly unknown to anybody else and dies with him. And there is another part through which he holds to an idea which is expressed through him with an eminent clarity, and of which he is the symbol (Humboldt, "Autobiographical Fragment," 1816, *GS*, 15:452.)

Where Herder, who had been his student as a youth, affirmed himself in parallel with the older Kant of the great works—the disagreement between them appearing only discreetly on occasion—Humboldt, twenty-three years younger, belonged to the generation who matured in the shadow of the *Critiques*. Thus Bildung is characterized in Humboldt as a personal and universal imperative, which differentiates him from Herder on the one hand and from Goethe on the other. Viewing Bildung as the great affair of any man, he made it his own, and he never ceased to develop its problematic and to cast all things in its light. Posterity, which for a long time knew only part of his thought, since most of his works remained unpublished until the beginning of this century, has recognized this: "The name of Wilhelm von Humboldt is inseparably connected with the growth of the German ideas about Bildung" (Bruford 1975: 1).

However, the renewed interest in Humboldt shown in recent publications tends to focus on other aspects of his work, perhaps considered to be of more current interest, especially the theory of language (Humboldt 1974; Aarsleff 1982) and the reflection on history (Humboldt 1985; Quillien 1983). In fact, just as Humboldt's life exhibits a succession of distinct phases and types of activity, his writings belong to different disciplines, from aesthetics and literary criticism, to political philosophy and history, to comparative anthropology and linguistics. Nevertheless, even though the differentiation of specialities has accelerated since 1800 or even 1830, diversity is to be found here more in the object studied than in the mode of approach and the spirit of the study, as Humboldt himself will tell us. Let us for the moment simply make a general observation. Humboldt asserted that external diversity was a necessary condition for the development of the human subject's own dispositions, that is to say, Bildung itself. If he appears to evade our usual classifications, it is simply because they would isolate the various facets of a single major preoccupation.

Therefore, and as a result of the author's diffuse mode of expression, a study of the conception of Bildung and of its implications in Humboldt would in principle require the study of a considerable quantity of writings: in all, seventeen volumes of complete works, (*Gesammelte Schriften,* referred to hereafter as *GS*), which are often difficult to read, along with an incredible number of letters—seven volumes for his correspondence with his wife alone. Being unable to pay close attention to all of this, I have resorted to secondary sources, which are fortunately excellent. In particular, the biography by Leroux ending with the year 1794 (Leroux 1932) and the more recent monumental biography by Sweet (1978–80) help follow Humboldt's intellectual evolution in relation to the circumstances of his life. The bibliographic and general discussion Flitner provides in his edition of chosen extracts is also very useful (Humboldt 1956). Bruford made a detailed study of Bildung in Humboldt's correspondence in two articles that are marked by sound judgment (Bruford 1959, 1962). Thanks to these authors, and to others we will mention on the way, it was possible to limit the breadth of the inquiry into Humboldt's own texts.[2]

Our intention is to show the unity of Humboldt's thought by starting from his conception of Bildung as a value. We therefore shall have to reduce the apparent discontinuities in his writings by using this fundamental conception. In order to do so, after a brief biographical reminder, we shall first examine, following Leroux, the thought of the young Humboldt until the time of his meeting with Schiller in Jena in 1794. The idea of Bildung directly inspires all the writings of this period, and we will also include what proceeds directly from Bildung in subsequent works. We shall then have to show how the apparently disparate scholarly concerns that animate Humboldt's studies and permeate his writings until the end of his life—dealing mostly with the comparative understanding of cultures and languages— are tied to what came before. In order to do so, we shall isolate two successive stages in the transition: the 1795–97 project of a comparative anthropology, and the assertion of the primacy of languages from 1800 onward. At this point we shall see that the content of the activity, its final object and goal, remained unchanged: change is found first in the passage from a subjective reference to an objective point of view, and then in the almost complete transition from the individualism of Bildung to the holism imposed by the comparison of languages.

The distinction made by Humboldt in the epigraph to this section may, rightly or wrongly, seem obsolete today, but it also contains the requirement expressed more explicitly in a passage translated by Leroux: ". . . in order to guess someone's essential character, we shall have to identify its best and greatest productions, and group these higher manifestations into a totality which we shall consider to be his proper and essential structure [*eigentliche und wesentliche Beschaffenheit*], and it is in relation to this totality that we shall take as fortuitous all traits which are foreign to it" (Leroux 1958: 54).[3] We cannot entirely subscribe to the distinction be-

2. We have to acknowledge that our usual method is here stretched to its limits, given the breadth of the field of inquiry, if not of the field of analysis, since the principle of a monographic analysis of a text or of a circumscribed set of texts can only be applied according to a more or less arbitrary selection. The matter is further complicated by Humboldt's very peculiar mode of exposition. He manages to be pedantic without being truly systematic. Bildung itself is never fully defined; one or another of its characteristics surface more clearly in one text or another according to the objective of the moment, at years of interval, and we would run the risk of being misled if we followed one version exclusively, whereas the intention becomes clear when versions are juxtaposed, as we shall soon find.

3. Apart from the biography mentioned above (Leroux 1932), Leroux is the author of three other studies, on Humboldt's sexed metaphysics and aesthetics (1945, 1948), and on his comparative anthropology, quoted here (1958).

tween "higher" and "fortuitous"—we shall have ample opportunity to
come back to this point—but we hope that the path we have taken below
satisfies the requirement of essential unity posited here.

•

Wilhelm von Humboldt (1767–1835) was born to a recently ennobled
family in the service of the royal house of Prussia. His younger brother, Alexander (1769–1859), an encyclopedic mind and a great traveler and natu-
ralist, was considered a genius and attained fame during his lifetime.
Thanks to carefully chosen tutors, the two brothers had an impeccable education, but Wilhelm felt oppressed and later complained of his lonesome
and joyless childhood (Bruford 1959: 19). Early on, he adopted a moral
attitude that he cultivated throughout his life. Self-control, distance vis-
à-vis the external world, and independence from it were values Humboldt
seems, as far as we can tell from his correspondence, to have cherished even
in the midst of political struggles or diplomatic intricacies. This is, properly
speaking, a stoic attitude; Humboldt reveals in a relatively late autobiographical fragment that he adopted it in his twelfth year, prompted
both by his own impulse and by the example of the Stoics.[4]

This biographical trait deserves a moment of attention. The spontaneous adaptation to the world, the naive identification with it, is here replaced by the subordination of the world to the subject, and as a result,
worldly activity is subordinated to the subject's inner activity. Youthful detachment was the primer or the seed of the activity of self-formation or self-
education, i.e., of Bildung, which will be Humboldt's great preoccupation.
This sheds light on the epigraph. It is obvious that Humboldt has willed
himself to be the man of Bildung. At most, it may be that some developments implicit in this "idea" only progressively became obvious to him.
Our study of his life is therefore facilitated: without confining ourselves to
it completely, we shall have to privilege Humboldt as he willed himself, as
he constructed himself, as against the man he may otherwise have been.
There is no need to erase the disparities that some critics saw in him, or to
bridge the gap that some witnesses noted between the actual man and his
theoretical or educational views.[5] The essential does not lie there. In his
biography of Humboldt, Sweet quotes from a letter by one of his acquain-
tances at the time, Friedrich Gentz—someone who was not easily fooled—
an impressive portrait of Humboldt as a young man of twenty-four: for

4. "Bruchstück einer Selbsbiographie," dated 1816, in GS 15:451–54.
5. On critics, cf. Flitner (Humboldt 1956), pp. 147–48; Bruford 1959: 28, 31; Sweet
1978–80, 2:489. Sweet quotes the witness Varnhagen von Ense (2:485–86).

him, "fate is not relevant . . . he can rise above any event . . . life's goal is
to raise one's and others' vital energy to the highest degree . . . . One cannot be sure whether he has any tempers, since for him it is child's play to
master them."[6]

From early on, the young Wilhelm frequents intellectual circles in Berlin. He contracts an intimate association with Henriette Hertz, a remarkable woman soon to be famous for her salon, and a few other friends of
both sexes. That is called a league of virtue (*Tugendbund*) or of (mutual)
ennobling (*Veredelungsbund*). Other examples are known of such confidential grouping in which members freely pour out their feelings to each
other. This is the beginning of a series of friendships with women that will
play a substantial role in Humboldt's life and in the orientation of his
thought. He rebels rather quickly against the platonic character Henriette
Hertz chooses to maintain in their privileged relationship: for him, to pretend to throttle the senses is to go against the harmonious development of
the personality and of the higher faculties themselves. We note here the
presence, on the level of intimate experience, of the need to reintegrate sensitivity with reason, which is one of the lines of force of the post-Kantian
generation, except for Fichte. At the same time, the "league of virtue" is a
clear milestone toward the elaboration of a moral theory of self-education,
which Humboldt will express a little later on. As we shall see, he will conceive this education as an enrichment that supposes a multiplicity of relationships and experiences.

A brief university stint, at Göttingen mostly, widens Humboldt's circle
of friends, including notably Georg Forster and his wife, Therese, and he
adds Jacobi a little later. This helps distance him from the Enlightenment of
Berlin and from utilitarianism and reinforces his bent for inwardness.

Shortly thereafter Humboldt travels to Paris, where he stays in August
1789.[7] The extent of his private, and later official, travels in Europe will
distinguish the aristocratic Humboldt among the German intellectuals of
the classical period.

Upon his return, Humboldt, who is about to marry, obtains an appointment as a magistrate. He relinquishes the position the following year to
retire to his estate and devote himself to self-improvement. A period of intense reflection follows, during which Humboldt, with a remarkable independence of mind, defines his own path in the light of contemporary events.

During the spring of 1794, the Humboldts settle in Jena, close to the

6. Letter of 19 April 1791 from Gentz to Garve, in Sweet 1978–80, 1:91–92.
7. Humboldt's Paris journal was recently translated into French by Marianne Schaub
(Humboldt 1986).

Schillers and not far from Goethe. Their stay will last little more than a year, but it is the beginning of a close association between Humboldt and Schiller, to which their correspondence testifies. Furthermore, the confident exchanges with the two literary glories of the time were bound to influence Humboldt. We shall later insist, more than is usual, on Humboldt's growing concern with the written word, which inflected his central preoccupations from then on.

We will not dwell on the details of the remaining biography. First come years of travels, to Paris, Spain, and the Basque region. Then Humboldt is again a civil servant for the Prussian State, from 1802 to 1819, first as Resident at the Vatican. This is a relatively quiet appointment, and his stay in Rome allows Humboldt, like Goethe before him, to immerse himself in classical antiquity. The Eternal City does more for him, teaching him how to overcome the pain of his oldest son's death, and of Schiller's death a while later, in the kind of serenity that knows how to make a place for death in life.[8] In 1809–10, during the space of a few months, as a second-rank minister, he reforms public education and creates the University of Berlin in accordance with his personal ideas. As an ambassador in Vienna, and later as a plenipotentiary minister, he takes part in the victorious struggle against Napoleon and the subsequent lengthy peace negotiations, in which he represents Prussia's hard line. He ends his political career in 1819, following persistent disagreements with the old chancellor Hardenberg and the government's antiliberal orientation, and retires to his castle in Tegel, close to Berlin, where he essentially devotes himself to comparative linguistics until his death in 1835. In order to reduce the apparent discontinuity of this career, we shall later show that serving the State at the higher echelons is not incompatible with the ideal of self-cultivation. For the time being, let us merely stress that while Humboldt was extremely active and productive in his official functions, particularly during diplomatic conferences, his correspondence shows that he never abandoned his stoic detachment. We would be willing to suppose that this inability to engage himself fully contributed to his eventual lack of political success, and it is plausible that he retired from public life in 1819, as in 1791, after having weighed the relative merits of both ways of life under the given circumstances.

YOUTH: BILDUNG

Apart from examining his correspondence (as Bruford [1959, 1962] has done), we can best study Humboldt's idea of Bildung by looking at the

---

8. Letter of 8 June 1805 to Körner, in Sweet 1978–80, 2:272–73.

texts preceding his meeting with Schiller in Jena in 1794. During this period, Humboldt defined himself in terms of self-development and self-improvement, while also reacting to political events. He wrote a protest, unpublished at the time, against the Wöllner edicts of 1788—under which we know that Kant suffered—by which the Prussian State claimed to rule over religion, including thought insofar as it pertained to religion. An article of Humboldt's on the new French constitution criticizes neither the change in government nor the principles themselves, but the pretension to erect a State entirely from the principles of reason without taking into account the inevitable reaction of the existing contingent elements. In sum, he condemns artificiality in the name of historical continuity, which imposes itself whatever changes may be made.

Finally, a long theoretical study, the *Essay on the Limits of State Action,* argues from Bildung to limit the functions of the State to a minimum. Posing individual liberty as a principle, and unhindered self-development, i.e., Bildung, as a duty for everyone, Humboldt concludes that the role of the State must simply be to ensure the security of its subjects. Conversely, it is clear for us that the despotism of Frederick William II on the one hand and the French Revolution on the other led the twenty-five-year-old Humboldt to specify and articulate his conception of Bildung in itself and in its implications. We shall come back to the political aspect proper.

We have seen Humboldt give preeminence to Bildung in his own life, for instance when he renounced a judiciary career he had just happily begun. In a letter to his wife he justifies his decision by saying that the most useful thing a man can do for others is to work at his own improvement. Here is a remarkable statement. It is probable, as Flitner mentions (Humboldt 1956: 134–35), that in fact Humboldt weighed the circumstances and that the government's despotic orientation at the time, and possibly somewhat of an aversion for the career of a magistrate, tipped the scale. But the judgment remains, in which we can see the emergence of a kind of faith.

As soon as he is free from his obligations, Humboldt immerses himself in an intensive reading of his beloved Greek classics (Sweet 1978–80, 1:123). In so doing, he gives a first answer to the question his faith in Bildung poses for us. Actually the model of Bildung is the Greek *paideia,* as Humboldt tells us: "It is the undeniable contribution of the Germans to have been the first to truly comprehend the nature of the Greek Bildung" (*GS* 2:184, quoted in Sweet 1978–80, 1:52). In fact, Wieland had written precisely that "the Greeks thought that a man was only a kind of embryo at birth, and that it had to develop [*ausbilden*] into a man" (quoted in Vierhaus 1972: 518). Let us compare this with what Henri Irénée Marrou tells us concerning the Hellenistic ideal of *paideia* in his classic *History of Education in Antiquity:*

> To make oneself; to produce from the child that one has been at first, from the imperfectly formed creature one may so easily remain, the man who is fully a man, of whose ideal figure one can just catch a glimpse, that is the work of the entire life, the one work worthy of a lifetime's devotion. (Marrou 1981: 352; quoted in Bruford 1959: 32)

Here is precisely the ideal Humboldt subscribed to, and tried to specify and articulate for himself. Pierre Hadot has recently reminded us, in line with this idea, that Greek philosophy, as opposed to modern philosophy, was not a doctrinal exposé but a preparation of man for the truth (Hadot 1981). From a similar vantage point Humboldt considers current philosophy as one speciality among others and subordinates it to the great undertaking of self-development and self-improvement (GS 1:282–83). Assuming we saw Humboldt as a philosopher, it would be in the ancient, and not the modern, acceptation of the term. We see here not only an understanding but a genuine borrowing of the philosophical attitude of the Greeks. But this itself poses a problem for us.

We know that on the level of cultures, borrowing never simply stems from the chance of an external encounter but entails an inner predisposition. The borrowed trait must correspond to a need, there has to be a convergence of need and event, and what is borrowed is usually modified as a result. In the present case, we know today that the idealization of Greece by German classical writers involved a specific interpretation. We ourselves would suppose that they needed an alternative model that would weaken the hold of the cosmopolitan individualism of the Enlightenment, but obviously we cannot demonstrate this here. At any rate, the case that occupies us is different, for it is a singular and genuine borrowing.

Therefore, the question we shall ask, if one allows us a brief and hypothetical digression, is: What is it that impelled the Germans to perceive individual man as embryonic or amorphous and made them wish to form or transform him, that is, to subscribe to the Bildung ideal? In the perspective adopted here, the reason is to be found in the relationship between the holistic foundations of German culture and the individualism of the Enlightenment. The individual of the Enlightenment is obviously present in Germany, as elsewhere, but to some, and notably to Herder, he appears abstract and lifeless. He therefore has to be transformed, which is possible only by enriching him with everything that was until then posited in the holistic mode, namely, organism, totality, and perfection. Vierhaus told us that when the ideological process is completed, Bildung is raised from the general level of education and the Enlightenment to one where it neighbors *Kultur* and *Humanität*. *Humanität* is the very notion Herder despaired of defining in his *Ideen*, precisely because he had poured the two opposites into it and attempted to include social man as a whole in the individual. At this last stage, with the trilogy of concepts, *Bildung, Kultur, Humanität*— and regardless of subsequent modifications—we truly witness a re-created Germany, which has answered the challenge of Western Enlightenment and has in some way incorporated it. Naturally, we shall have to see whether this process can be detected in Humboldt himself.

At the onset of a study of the ideal of self-formation in Humboldt, we should perhaps point out that he often refers to it without specifically using the word Bildung—as we shall do for convenience, thus following his successors in this intellectual tradition. Flitner notes (Humboldt 1956: 140) that the concept is still in the process of maturing in Humboldt, yet he uses the word on occasion, as we saw above in the quotation about the Greeks. It is true, Bildung is sometimes supplemented by an adjective, and it is perhaps characteristic that, in the essay on religion for instance, Bildung is taken both absolutely and in the moral aspect corresponding to the context, at a one-page interval (*GS* 1:69–70). We can neglect the historical nuance by which the verb (*bilden, sich bilden*) is used instead of the substantive form. As to the aesthetic aspect, which is part and parcel of the concept in Humboldt and in the intellectual tradition we mentioned, it does not matter here that it is no longer commonly present today.

As we mentioned previously, Bildung is never defined once and for all. We shall therefore start from two main formulas, which are often repeated under varying forms, in order to set forth the notion and gather remarks bearing successively on Bildung's very pronounced imperative aspect, on its relation to aesthetics, and finally on the coming into play of the notion of totality. In a relatively brief excerpt from 1793 entitled by the editor "Theory of Bildung," we read this:

> *A*
> The ultimate task of our existence is to provide as large as possible a
> content to the concept of humanity in our person during our lifetime, as
> well as beyond through the traces of living activity we leave behind us.
> This task can only be accomplished by binding our self to the world for
> the most generalized, lively, and free reciprocal action possible. (*GS*
> 1:238, translated literally)[9]

9. In the event that one would object to the roughness of our translations here and elsewhere, we shall repeat that literalness is essential. Moreover, Humboldt's readers admit that

Let us add a later variant:

> *A'*
> He who can say to himself as he dies "I have seized as much of the world
> as I could and I have changed it into my humanity," has reached his tar-
> get . . . he has achieved what is called living in the highest sense of the
> word.[10]

(The signs *A*, *A'*, etc., in front of our quotes will be used to refer to them
throughout this section.)

This text clarifies the previous one by setting up a hierarchy between the
subject and the world; as Stahl said, the essential lies in the subject's activity, but his development (*Ausbildung*) is possible only thanks to the presence of the milieu and his adaptation to it (*Anbildung*).

We may be struck by the exaggeration in the reference to humanity and
to the "concept of humanity in our person." Further on, Humboldt answers the charge of hyperbole by stating that his formula conforms to reality (*GS* 1:284). To comment: there is the individual on the one hand and
the human species on the other. We are at the level of individualism pure
and simple, facing a corollary supposedly derived from the categorical imperative; the same holds for the decision to retire from public service in
order to be more useful to mankind. But is this solemn universality not connected somehow to the French Revolution?

We know that Humboldt visited Paris in August 1789; contrary to his
fellow traveler, his former tutor Campe, he immediately distanced himself
from the event (Sweet 1978–80, 1:60–62). However, his political writings
are related to this experience: the *Essay on the Limits of State Action*
makes the State, as we have just seen, dependent on Bildung, and there is
obviously a connection between the subordination of the State to Bildung
and the 1790–91 decision to retire from civil service.

After an introduction in which he evokes in passing the drawbacks of a
revolution compared to reform from above, the second section of the *Essay*
opens with a succinct definition of Bildung:

> *B*
> The true aim of man, prescribed to him, not by a changing inclination,
> but by eternally immutable reason, is the highest and most proportioned
> formation [*Bildung*] of his strengths into a whole. (*GS* 1:106)

---

his style leaves much to be desired, even in published texts. For an unpublished excerpt, it
matters little if the translation increases the awkwardness of the original.

10. Letter from Humboldt to his wife, from Rome, in Bruford 1959: 41.

The author immediately adds that this Bildung presupposes the reunion of two conditions, namely, liberty on the one hand, and the diversity of situations on the other (once again we encounter the subject and the milieu; other texts explain that this diversity is necessary for the enrichment of the personality).

The solemn assertion in [B] requires an exegesis. We shall try to show that it posits Bildung as an implicit counterpoint to the French Revolution, since both have something in common while also being opposites. Both claim to be rooted in reason, posit liberty, and strive for man's exaltation. But the Revolution is in fact unfaithful to its rational principle: it gives way to the disorderly movement of the "masses" (the word is used in GS 1:101, 1.21), and therefore to "changing inclination"—which is after all characteristic of the French in general (cf. below).[11]

In contrast, not only is Bildung immutably faithful to reason, but—an important point—it allows for an intensification of the feeling of liberty, in two ways. First, it withdraws into the individual and ignores external actions and constraints, drawing its sustenance only from the milieu. It also subordinates itself to its own obligation, i.e., the exaltation of man. This last point, which may seem obscure, is capital and probably underlies the entire German reaction to the French Revolution. Liberty intensifies by drawing an obligation from itself; Kantian moralism therefore absolves Germans from any suspicion of halfheartedness or selfishness toward the French Revolution.

If our interpretation is well founded, it helps explain why Humboldt used the overstated expressions that stopped us in the previous quotations, [A] and [A'], i.e., the reference to the self as humanity and the "concept of humanity in our person." These expressions may be compared with the emphasis of the French revolutionaries. Bildung does not lag behind in terms of Man and Humanity.

This analysis is corroborated by Humboldt's political reflection on the French Revolution in his *Essay,* whose exact title was "Ideas for an Essay [*Versuch*] to determine the limits of the actions of the State." Concerning this work, we have at our disposal the large study by Ulrich Muhlack on the politics of Humboldt throughout his career (Muhlack 1967). Muhlack's point is precisely to show that Humboldt built his theoretical and practical politics entirely as a counterpoint to the theory and practice of the French Revolution and its Napoleonic sequel. It is particularly important to find here the interaction between cultures recognized in its fullest extent, in this

---

11. One may say that my interpretation rests too much on this isolated expression, but how else could we explain its presence, in contrast with reason, which is "immutable"?

particular case and for the topic under consideration. Let us therefore say plainly that Muhlack's analysis represents a noticeable improvement over earlier authors (Meinecke 1965, Kaehler 1927), who, without being able to ignore the relation to France, tended to close off and withdraw the German development into itself, or even to explain Humboldt's politics on the basis of his psychology, presupposed or interpreted to this end. In its major developments, Muhlack's work appears to open a new era, which doesn't mean, of course, that we have to subscribe to all its statements in detail or that we need to discuss them here. With regard to the point that concerns us, it was well known that Humboldt's *Essay* was directed against both despotism and the French Revolution, although Muhlack's vantage point allows him to see it essentially as an answer—for us, a German answer—to the Revolution. At first, Humboldt had admired the enlightened despotism of Frederick II. He then began to develop the corollaries of his idea of Bildung on the level of politics in his 1788 article on religion, in which he still accepted that the State should be involved in its subjects' prosperity. It is only after his trip to France in 1789 that he accepted Dohm's argument, according to which, in the name of individual liberty, the State's only responsibility is to ensure the security of its subjects. The *Essay* originated in discussions with Gentz and Dalberg, until it reached the size of a book, large sections of which were published in Schiller's review and in a Berlin monthly, but which after some delays Humboldt finally refused to publish in toto (cf. Sweet 1978–80, 1:100–102).

For Humboldt, the deep inspiration of the French Revolution, to which one cannot but subscribe, is the assertion of liberty. But the Revolution betrayed it by instituting the political domain as an autonomous sphere that, by its very existence, threatens individual liberty. Here the Revolution returns to what Muhlack calls the "absolutism" against which the *Essay* is directed. We scarcely need to point out that Humboldt thus gave a form to the most common reaction of German intellectuals to the French Revolution: an initial enthusiasm for the idea in principle, followed by reservations and an increasing distancing from its concrete manifestations. We notice—and this is not an isolated case, in Humboldt and elsewhere—that the reference to France remains implicit, as if elided, in the *Essay*. We need to go back to an earlier outline, in a letter to Gentz dated January 1792, to find an explicit reference to the Constituent Assembly (Leitzmann 1935: 56–58). Sweet, who mentions this letter in a separate article (Sweet 1973: 476), notes that in it Humboldt did not simply, as in the *Essay,* discuss the legitimate *ends* of the State but also outlined a discussion of the *means* it would use in which he criticized the Constituent Assembly. In the end

Humboldt left this discussion out of the version that was to be published. The *Essay* thus gained in homogeneity, as a work independent of historical circumstances: it stands not as a theory of politics but as a unilateral discussion. We might misunderstand its dimension, its somewhat pedantic extent, if we did not see it as a German reply to the major contemporary phenomenon. It was perhaps a saving grace for Humboldt that the essay was published only partially. The fact that it survived is definitely a blessing for the historian of ideas.

We can, for instance, isolate two characteristic traits of German ideology in the *Essay*. On the one hand, concerning individual liberty, to choose Bildung rather than the Revolution is to internalize the debate; in other words, individualism is prevented from directly expressing itself on the political level, and the State is left alone. On the other hand, the refusal to constitute politics into an autonomous sphere amounts to accepting that subordination continues to dominate everywhere, as in feudal times (comment by Marx; cf. Dumont 1977: 127–28). Humboldt neglects the French demand for equality.[12] Moreover, he grants the Prussian State the ability to reform itself; he prefers reform from above to Revolution from below. Now, we do not see how an autonomous sphere would possibly restrain its powers on its own volition; we can therefore conclude that for Humboldt the Prussian State is not autonomous but is simply the organ of the national community. This indicates that the individualism of Bildung is complemented on the sociopolitical level by a holistic community characterized by the ubiquity of subordination and by a monarchical power seen as an emanation of the community (as such, it could therefore restrict its own prerogatives).

We know that the formula we can thus extract from Humboldt's thought remained that of Germany until Marx (on the level of thought), and well beyond (on the level of State practice).

What is proper to Humboldt, however, is his conviction that politics must remain subordinate to Bildung. Muhlack is certainly correct when he

12 In the passage on the Constituent Assembly in the letter to Gentz mentioned above (Leitzmann 1935: 57), Humboldt declares that "the Constitution is entirely based on equality, and for the first time certainly, the equality not of citizens but of men." He questions whether equality could, like liberty, be part and parcel of the rights of man. He adds that equality does not guarantee the maintenance of the regime.

In a conversation on 1 November 1789 in Lausanne, Humboldt criticizes the night of 4 August. The numerous arguments he uses show his deep hostility toward the abolition of privileges in the name of the "egalitarian chimera" (Journal, *GS* 14:221). Let us recall that Humboldt was a nobleman and owned large estates. His "liberty," which excludes equality, reminds one of what Tocqueville said about the liberty the French nobles felt they enjoyed under the ancien régime.

states that Humboldt maintained this dependence in his personal practice throughout his entire life. By so doing, he was opposing, in his political activity, what he had perceived about France through the years, in particular during his stay in Paris in the last years of the century. For him, French culture with its autonomy of politics seemed exhausted, up to and including Napoleonic expansionism, and the superiority of German culture was to ensure the supremacy of Germany in the future, assuming that the dependence of politics on culture was maintained. Thus national interest was in keeping with Humboldt's intimate predilection and personal credo.

What in fact was the fate of this conviction? Humboldt enjoyed a period of success when the Prussian State, at the nadir of its existence after Jena, asked him to reorganize public education and allowed him to create the University of Berlin according to his views. But things were different on the political level. After years of distinguished service, Humboldt was sent back to his studies in 1819. The despotic regime thus signified to him that the idea of reform from above was utopian. Humboldt, protected by his imperturbable ethics, does not seem to have recorded this failure as such, nor do historians seem to have weighed it properly.

Like that of the French revolutionaries, the emphasis which tinges the various definitions of Bildung we have encountered could point to a value transfer from religion. Let us recall that Stahl mentioned a kind of religious prehistory of the notion of Bildung, but he was concerned with the word's history more than with the idea's filiation, except perhaps with Herder. Nothing in Humboldt himself, except for a "Leibnizian ecstasy" he is said to have experienced in his youth (Sweet 1978–80, 1:21), evokes such a transfer. A more immediate connection imposes itself between the Bildung ideal and the ideal of the work of art for the artist, as we saw it, emanating from religion, in Moritz. Humboldt exhibits a greater degree of immanence than Moritz: the totality the artist saw in the work of art, and to which he subordinated himself, is now found in the life of the subject; the work of art becomes his life itself. Of course, such a filiation is entirely absent in Humboldt. I have in mind only a logical connection, though a consequential one, for instance concerning Humboldt's friendly and trusting relationship with Schiller and Goethe in Jena.

Moreover, Humboldt felt this likeness between the work of art and the ideal formation of self from very early on. Thus, in his first text on the Greek model, he stresses the similarity between the balance achieved in the beauty of the work of art and that which must characterize the moral man, and he concludes that "one cannot deny that the Greeks had [and he underlines] a strong propensity to develop [*ausbilden*] man in the widest diversity and unity" (*GS* 1:270). Better yet, having in 1830, like Goethe, decided to publish his correspondence with Schiller, he defines Schiller's art by the very formula he had previously used to define Bildung. He writes:

> His life actually consisted in achieving as a poet what he said somewhere about the accomplished man [*idealisch gebildete*]: draw toward oneself as much of the world as one's imagination can embrace, in all the diversity of its manifestations, and mold it into the unity of the work of art [*Kunstform*]. (Seidel 1962, 1:38)

True, this is a later text, but it would be wrong to reject it on that score, since we can read in it, along with a partially involuntary identification of the two friends, the categorical distinction between them, insofar as the one puts form in his art and the other in his life. And except for this distinction, which we repeatedly encounter in the correspondence, the convergence between them is indeed obvious. As early as 1794, thinking in terms of Bildung, Humboldt, who could have read only Schiller's early texts, quite often concurs in writing with what Schiller states in terms of aesthetics. In this sense, their meeting was predestined: This is essentially due to the fact that, while both are imbued with Kantian distinctions, they want to redeem sensitivity and the close link they perceive between aesthetics and ethics. Thus, in the study "On Religion," dated 1788–89, Humboldt conjures up man's ability to "link sensitive representations to extrasensitive ideas." He searches for an appropriate expression to name it, i.e., aesthetic sentiment or imagination [*Einbildungskraft*] (*GS* 1:56). Impossible not to think of the three impulses of Schiller's *Letters on the Aesthetic Education of Man:* the impulses of the senses and of form and, binding them together, the impulse of play, or aesthetics, which Schiller sees as the instrument of a moral progress of humanity. For the 1794–95 period, Leroux showed that we can indeed speak of a mutual influence between the two authors concerning the two articles on sexual differences given by Humboldt to Schiller's review, *The Hours* (Leroux 1948: 269–73).

•

We have related the formulations of Bildung by Humboldt that we isolated in [A], [A'], and [B] with external items such as the French Revolution and aesthetics. It is now time to analyze them in themselves. The two types of formulas, [A] and [B], shed light on each other. Thus, formula [B], "the highest and most proportioned formation of his strengths into a whole," is found time and again in Humboldt, and is probably typical in that he in-

cludes in it what matters to him without undue effort at clarification. Formula [B] is made somewhat clearer by the more primitive formulas [A] and
[A'], in which the subject in his unity has to assimilate as much as possible
of the external diversity. Conversely, [B] demonstrates that [A] does not
mean acquiring and accumulating riches in quasi-economic style.

In [B], the notion of totality inevitably refers one to the Leibnizian
monad, while at the same time going beyond it. Humboldt expressly criticized the monad from this point of view, in the sense that the entity in question is not immaterial and that it is fundamentally *in relation* to the
external world. Leroux is surely right (1932: 79 ff.) to consider Platonism
and the experience of love as the origin of the ideal of a totality to be
reached. Two traits of this conception are profoundly Leibnizian. Let us
note first the feeling, very strong and constant in Humboldt, that this totality always remains particular and limited. Stahl (1934) contrasted the "total," though always particular, individual of the philosophy of humanity,
which concerns us here, with the "universal" individual of the Renaissance. For Humboldt, any spontaneous manifestation, be it of a person, a
historical period, or especially of a work, action, or event, is "unilateral"
(*einseitig*). This holds for the person before the development of Bildung;
hence the necessity of the largest possible number of complements to enrich it and hoist it to the level of a totality. Particularity will not disappear,
but unilaterality will be transformed into "originality" (*Eigentümlichkeit*).
(We know the fortune of this term with the romantics, but here the requirement of unity, order, and "proportion" prevails). We cannot emphasize it
enough: there is in Humboldt a true hunger for diversity, especially in human relations. He erected it into a theory, starting with his first contacts—
with Forster, with Jacobi; these friendships and others nourished him, and
his first texts show traces of these contacts, we might say these influences,
which contributed to the formation of his personality.

It would seem that this set of notions is particular to Humboldt; he at
least distinguishes himself from Goethe in this regard. If we turn to *Poetry
and Truth* (*Dichtung und Wahreit*), we encounter the idea of development
in relation to the milieu, but not the dual insistence on the original defect
and on the diversity that has to be assimilated. Rather, the accent is put on
the individual as unique and incomparable, which conversely is only implied, not accentuated, in Humboldt. As we know, posterity will follow
Goethe on this point. We can perhaps see in the negative value that initially
attaches to particularity in Humboldt and that has to be redeemed later on,
a trace of the strength in him of the universalism of the Enlightenment and

of Kant, which is also expressed in the reference to humanity in [A] and [A'] and, much more deeply, in the normative point of view, apparent in *"the highest and most proportioned formation"* of [B], which will always be paramount for Humboldt.

The metaphor of organic growth naturally imposes itself here as elsewhere, and Kant himself had recognized, among other things, that the organic being "grows by elaborating the substances it receives from the external world" (Leroux 1932: 275–76). We are fortunate that when he writes the *Essay on the Limits of State Action,* Humboldt has already encountered Goethe's *Metamorphosis of Plants,* published in 1790, and refers to it regarding the dialectics of form and matter and of unity and diversity (*GS* 1:108–9). Yet we should point out that Humboldt does not overuse this figure; he does not fall into organicism.

Here also, passing from plant to man, his first word concerns the "energic activity" that man must use to assimilate what he receives. Sensitivity and activity (*Selbsttätigkeit*) interact in the subject thanks to the presence of an external object. Activity or "force" is the second Leibnizian trait we announced: it is common among German authors at the time. For Humboldt, the secret of each being resides in its specific energy, an "internal force" that animates it, in other words an entelechy. This "force" of the living is in close relation to the life of the senses (cf. above), and, conscious that he is innovating, Humboldt resolutely engages in the rehabilitation of the life of the senses—if I can thus render *Sinnlichkeit,* which is something much broader than "sensuality," going from instinctive impulses to the feeling of the beautiful. Following Sweet (1978–80, 1:108–9, and esp. 1973: 478), we have to insist on this point. Humboldt develops this theme in a chapter of the *Essay on Limits* on the "improvement of ethics." Sweet quotes this concise statement from a 1791 letter to Gentz: "Thus the life of the senses and reason are the source of all force and [the source] of all direction of force respectively" (Leitzmann 1935: 52). One thinks of William Blake, who was writing the *Marriage of Heaven and Hell* roughly at the same time: "Energy is the only life and is from the Body and Reason is the bound or outward circonference of Energy" (Blake 1927: 60). It is true that Humboldt leaves more room for reason and sees a creative tension between *Sinnlichkeit* and *Vernunft.*

We are now ready to understand the place of "enjoyment" (*Genuss*) in Humboldt. The supreme bliss in Leibniz, the utmost "enjoyment" in Humboldt, is to be found not in contemplation but in activity. In the *Letters to a Lady Friend* (Sweet 1978–80, 1:51), the end of man lies not in happiness but in fully cultivating oneself. Absolute or highest[13] enjoyment consists, according to the excellent commentary of Leroux, "in the exalting feeling of an internal activity that takes place in the plenitude of its natural differentiated energy" (1958: 54).

This activist or energetic conception of man helps us understand that Bildung is not a goal to be reached, i.e., a whole that would be "the highest and most proportioned formation" in an absolute sense, but rather it consists in the constant effort to increase and better proportion our forces, in short, a process directed toward the ideal. Of course, we would like to know how one can recognize a better proportioned whole or, as is said elsewhere, the "harmonious plenitude" one should strive for. But in this first period of his life, Humboldt is more preoccupied with proclaiming his ideal and applying it than with explaining the content of his judgments, and his subsequent writings on anthropology will shed more light on this (cf. below). We can only say here, by anticipation, that the requirements of universalism are paramount. In the end, particularity remains subordinated to the sovereign judgment of universalism. For instance, originality is reached when a case of unilaterality has passed beyond itself and demonstrates that it is compatible with universalism.

We are left with the emergence of the notion of totality, the belief that self-improvement leads in a way to the constitution of a totality. The work of art provides an analogy, and there is probably an extrapolation here from what nature exhibits on the level of material organisms. But some kind of faith is needed; it is obvious that the accumulation of diversities, even directed by a determined particularity, is one thing, and the realization of an "harmonious plenitude" another. What is the source of such an assurance, in the absence of divine warrant?[14]

The question clears up if we recall that, contrary to most intellectuals with whom he mingles, Humboldt is a nobleman, and if we reflect on the traditional role of the nobility, we immediately remember that it behooves

13. These adjectives are used here not only for clarity's sake, but they are also found in Humboldt's relevant texts, *GS* 1:126 (*Limits of State Action*) and *GS* 1:261 ("On the Study of Antiquity"); cf. the discussion of *Genuss,* literally "enjoyment," by Flitner (Humboldt 1956: 135–37: religious fervor, deep feeling of life) and by Sweet (1978–80, 1:128–29: joy of the highest order, of the being as a whole). The two texts, characteristically, point out that this supreme feeling encompasses its opposites—misfortune, pain, and even the subject's self-destruction; pain is always local, ephemeral. "Whoever observes the whole sees that it raises there what it lowers here" (*GS* 1:261). This is still Leibniz!

14. Spranger, in his very respectful exegesis of Humboldt's Bildung, distinguishes three moments: unilaterality, universality, and totality. He writes that totality is somewhat mysterious, that it rests on the combination or proportion of the first two, and that it is a matter of aesthetics (1909: 14).

the aristocrat, not to work, but simply to live, to be himself. Goethe says precisely this in the very novel of Bildung; in a letter to his brother-in-law, Wilhelm Meister explains that, being a bourgeois by birth, he is forced to exercise one profession or another, whereas in Germany, the nobleman alone has the liberty to be himself. And Goethe adds: "If he knows how to command his demeanor at every moment of his existence, nothing more can ever be demanded of him and anything else he may possess in his person—ability, talent, wealth—appears as a pleasant supplement."[15] Sweet draws a judicious parallel between this passage and the portrait of Humboldt by Gentz that we cited earlier (Sweet 1978–80, 1:115 n. 24). Goethe even says of the nobleman that "he is a public person," an expression that sums up the essential, for, on the level of values, the distinction is between the entire social body and the corresponding function—royalty, aristocracy—on the one hand, and society's particular parts or functions on the other. Here is the raison d'être of the political domain, which is often ignored today under the influence of egalitarianism and economism.[16] Where Goethe says "public person," Hegel speaks of the "universal class" that is in charge of the State, that is to say, of society as a totality (he has in view the landed gentry at first, and later on the body of civil servants). It is important for our discussion that in the king and, therefore, in the nobleman the social totality expresses itself in a person as totality. Here is perhaps the deep reason for Humboldt's assurance when he states that the development of the person has the vocation of harmonious totality. In this system of representations, social or cultural totality and the totality of the person communicate with and echo each other. That fact will help us understand the development of Humboldt's studies, and in this sense we shall have to keep it in mind. At the same time, we touch here on German idiosyncrasy.

To complete the parallel with Wilhelm Meister, his "desire to be a public person" leads him to choose the theater, and we note, although it is not mentioned by Goethe, that as an actor he will in principle be able, like Humboldt, to espouse human diversities.

As for Bildung and Humboldt, our preliminary conclusion is that Hum-

15. *Wilhelm Meisters Lehrjahre*, book 5, chap. 3 (Goethe 1954: 636–37).

16. Authors have searched far and wide in their attempts to define politics as a particular domain within the general social domain, while the logic of hierarchy readily suggests an answer: in a society perceived as multiple, politics occurs as soon as a requirement of unity appears (vis-à-vis the outside world or otherwise), which implies the subordination of multiplicity to unity. In Hegel's *Philosophy of Right*, civil society, made of economic individuals, is encompassed in the State, that is to say, in society conceived as a communal entity, and symbolized by the person of the king.

boldt gave a very specific personal development to ideas that were being formulated at the time by German writers and artists because, as a nobleman, he was not committed to any task or work other than that of being himself, as a living totality more or less in the image of the social totality. The other possibility was to serve the State, which Humboldt will do as an ambassador, or "resident," and as a plenipotentiary, and even, briefly, as a member of the Prussian government in charge of reorganizing education. Moreover, in the first part of his life, he will use his material means and social graces to travel and establish the most diverse contacts among intellectuals and the powerful.

Thus, during his stay in Paris, he becomes acquainted with Destutt de Tracy and other Idéologues; he visits Condorcet's widow and assiduously studies the theater; he has several talks with Sieyès and observes closely the First Consul at the Institut—not to mention an impromptu meeting of the two families at the menagerie of the Jardin des Plantes (GS 14:438).[17]

•

We have studied the idea of Bildung in Humboldt's early writings, but it is obvious that his later works are not independent of it. In particular, it would seem natural to consider his educational reforms and the founding of the University of Berlin in 1809–10. However, although it is closely related to the theoretical views we have just studied, Humboldt's educational reform also presupposes the subsequent development of his thought, to which we are now turning. Thus we shall leave Humboldt's work on public education for a little later.

CONVERSION TO ANTHROPOLOGY

Having chosen to see in Humboldt, as both he himself and his posterity invite us to do, the man of Bildung, we have come to insist on the fact that he was an aristocrat. Only a young aristocrat could have undertaken to make self-education the great affair of his life and to erect it at the same time as the supreme principle of modernity. Moreover, the aristocrat's traditional vocation is to serve the State. It was therefore natural for Wilhelm von Humboldt to represent his country abroad or to become a member of the government. He was innovative in keeping these official functions subordinate in his life, as a result of the primacy of Bildung and of corresponding psychological dispositions. Furthermore, as we have already noticed,

17. We can surmise that Humboldt spoke French fluently. We find a few texts in French in his complete works, apart from reports to the king of Prussia in GS vols. 11 and 13; cf. 3:1 ff., 300 ff.

the two kinds of activity are less disparate than it would seem at first: they are both oriented toward totality; the aristocracy is traditionally devoted to the service of the social totality, while Bildung tends to erect a single subject into a totality.

We have thus resolved a first discontinuity or apparent heterogeneity in our hero's life. However, there remains another one, formidable at first glance. What can we make of the last sixteen years of his life, when, after having relinquished his official functions, he dedicated himself to what we would today call comparative linguistics? Did the cultured nobleman and dilettante really turn into a specialist and a precursor of our human or social sciences?

We propose to show that here again the distance is less than it seems, and that the transition, which was in fact gradual, can be understood from two main observations. First, a change of attitude occurs concerning the place of writing in the subject's life: during the years 1794–97, he deeply experiences the need to be able to express himself in a work to be communicated to others. The fact is abundantly documented, and the circumstances (discussed below) help explain the acuteness of the problem. After reflection—and that is our second point—Humboldt finds that such a work will necessarily fit into the framework of a comparative anthropology, which he immediately attempts to delineate.[18] Why? Simply because such is the projection, in an *objective* perspective, of contents or preoccupations that originally concerned the *subject:* Bildung opens onto the comparison of men, cultures, and even possibly languages. The actual topic of the activity or the inquiry remains the same. This is a privileged case for our study, which focuses on the interplay of individualism and holism in Germany. Our task is therefore to show in detail that there was no discontinuity whatever in the transition for Humboldt himself.

•

In Bildung, as we found it defined by Humboldt for his own use, literary expression is no problem and no consideration. Given that it was posited as the sole objective, self-improvement logically seemed to preclude the production of a work out of the self, insofar as the subject would thereby submit to a totality other than the one to be built within the self: Bildung is one thing and a writing career another.

However, not only is self-cultivation sustained by the existing culture, and especially literature, but it also cannot dispense completely with writ-

18. Much later, in 1816, Humboldt envisages the possibility of an autobiography, but he remains at the level of the "Fragment."

ing. Humboldt never rejected the idea of leaving something for posterity. The first definition [A], cited above, mentions "the traces of living activity we leave behind us"—let us simply note the subordination of the "traces" to life. In a letter to Forster, in which he announces that he is marrying and that he is leaving the magistracy, Humboldt writes that he has opted to live for himself and his family, and perhaps also, with luck, to "contribute somewhat to what the turmoil of the world is only a means to, against its will possibly, that is the enrichment and the rectification of our ideas" (Leitzmann 1936: 74–75).

Above all, writing is indispensable for communication. Self-cultivation, as we have seen, rests on the most numerous, diverse, and intense relations possible with other subjects, i.e., on a multiplicity of dialogues which correspondence prolongs, complements, and perhaps deepens. And as we know, Humboldt's correspondence was quite abundant. We notice that it even finds its way to some extent into the essays themselves: Humboldt's writings prior to 1794, for the most part unpublished during his lifetime, remained limited to communication with friends, and they reflect and prolong exchanges of views with Forster, Dohm, Dalberg, or Gentz.[19]

The *Essay on the Limits of State Action* reached the size of a book probably because it was perceived as a tentative answer on the part of the German intelligentsia to the French Revolution, against which it erected the individualism of Bildung as a supreme principle; but Bildung reigns supreme in all these texts, and writing occupies here an absolutely unproblematic subordinate role.

The sojourn of more than a year in Jena in close contact with Schiller and near Goethe, and the participation in their literary ventures, especially in the review directed by Schiller, *The Hours,* and his *Almanac of the Muses,* would radically modify the place of writing in Humboldt's concerns, in two ways. On the one hand, a kind of emulation will push him to produce literary works in the wider sense of the word. On the other hand, he will become aware, by experience and by comparison, of his limits in this domain, and especially of his inferiority as a writer. This resulted in an acute problem of self-expression that he painfully experienced in the years 1795–97, which were also difficult on a familial level (Sweet 1978–80, 1:172–81).

His own Bildung had of course always involved for Humboldt a certain degree of self-expression. In his first years of leisure, his assiduous study of

19. Even the long review of Jacobi's *Woldemar,* published in September 1794, is a kind of tribute presented to a philosopher who honored Humboldt with his friendship, which explains why the praise may have seemed insincere.

Greek authors led him to form the project of publishing a review devoted to Greece. With the encouragement of his friend the philologist F. A. Wolf he wrote an introduction entitled "On the Study of Antiquity, and of Greek Antiquity in particular," which remained incomplete and was known only to Schiller and a few others, although Wolf used it later. We have noted the parallel development of aesthetic ideas in Humboldt and Schiller. Schiller greatly appreciated Humboldt's conversation, which probably explains how he happened to settle down in Jena precisely at the time when Schiller and Goethe, who lives in nearby Weimar, have become friends, and support and help each other. Here is Humboldt, neither a poet nor a philosopher, only a cultured *homme du monde,* adopted as it were more or less as an equal by the two geniuses of the age. Yet, as early as the study on Jacobi in the summer of 1794, Schiller as well as Humboldt himself entertain no illusions regarding his talent as a writer (Sweet 1978–80, 1:165). He gives to Schiller's *The Hours* two lengthy studies on the different characters of the two sexes in relation to Bildung (excellently summarized in Leroux 1945, 1948). Schiller is convinced that these essays contain important ideas, but, being written in a heavy and obscure style, they are poorly received, and Humboldt is very sensitive to this failure. From then onward, he will painfully feel the inadequacy of his writing, as is seen from his correspondence in the following years. A subsequent letter (from Rome, 30 April 1803, quoted in Seidel 1962, 2:240) expresses very clearly his situation vis-à-vis writing: he has no pretension to be a writer, but "as far as ideas are concerned we actually possess only what we can set out of ourselves, and to bring our ideas to exposition we need to expose [them]." We perceive here the deep connection between Bildung and writing, but the repetition of *darstellen,* "to expose," which I have kept on purpose, refers as well to "set out of oneself," so that we could translate this as "we only really possess the ideas that we can express under a communicable form."

Moreover, Wilhelm von Humboldt feels he knows himself well, and he has only a moderate opinion of his abilities. He has always considered himself intellectually globally inferior to his brother, Alexander, especially with respect to inventiveness and intuition, and superior to him only in his faculty to "develop, compare, elaborate ideas."[20] In the "Autobiographical Fragment" of 1816, he comes back to his vocation of critic rather than creator; he writes that he is not destined by nature to great actions or important works, but that his own sphere seems to be life itself, "collecting it, observing it, judging it, treating it, forming it" (*GS* 15:454). Since his child-

---

20. Letter to Jacobi, July 1789, in Leitzmann 1936: 151.

hood, he has practiced paying close, incessant attention to the people around him, comparing them with each other and with the most remarkable individuals. He has not had more experience of the world than others, but beyond doubt he combines experience and reflection in an original way (453–54). We see that Humboldt transcribes here his very notion of Bildung: to gather the most diverse humanity in oneself, to distill it to the point that one sees the idea express itself in its most perfect forms, without ever segregating particulars from universals or the subjective from the objective, in such a way that all things are related and that one no longer knows where to start or where to stop (ibid.). How can this enterprise, closed upon the subject, give rise to the "exposition" of ideas? The text cited indicates that much later Humboldt thought for a short while of an autobiography. At the time, though, he envisages turning his observations on individuals into a theory.[21] Here is the germ of the anthropological project. Actually, a more circumscribed project entitled "Characteristics of Greek Poetry" is discussed in the correspondence with Schiller at the end of 1795 (Seidel 1962, 1:213 ff.), but this is only a matter of providing an acceptable contribution to Schiller's review. The project of defining Greek genius will be taken up again later.[22]

We cannot but admire the sincerity with which Humboldt attempts to analyze the difficulties he encounters with writing in his letters to Schiller of 1795–97, which are very somber years for him. Let us take for instance the letter of 16 July 1796[23] or that of May 3: he is ashamed of his idleness, he must concentrate in order to produce a decent book (Seidel 1962, 2:62). On 4 September 1797 he admits the "imperfection of his being" and the "misfortune of his existence." He is suffering from a dual deficiency: in him, imagination is not independent, and intellect is not sovereign either; they interfere with each other (cf. autobiographical fragment, *GS* 15:458). This is not a problem in life, or in dialogue, but it is a problem when one tries to produce something. There is surely a manner that would suit him, but he despairs of ever finding it. People are not wrong who judge him to be vague, obscure, tangled. Even his friends have not been able to discover the truths contained in his articles for *The Hours*. He does not manage to express what is on his mind; he lacks the basic idea (*Grundgedanke,* underlined), and stylistic talent is denied him once and for all. Perhaps is he improving nevertheless? At any rate, he is deeply desirous, and firmly decided, to produce something out of himself, a genuine work, a work for

21. Letter to Wolf dated 26 December 1796, quoted by Leroux 1958:7.
22. On Humboldt and Greece, cf. Quillien 1983.
23. French translation in Caussat, 1974: 12.

others (Seidel 1962, 2:119–20). We see here that Humboldt is aware of having written mostly for himself until then (cf. Sweet 1978–80, 1:108–9), and of the necessity of passing from this solitary ratiocination to a genuine form of communication (cf. the letter to Wolf cited previously and the letter to Körner in which he will later justify his specialization in linguistics).[24]

Let us note that in all of this Humboldt submits to the negative judgment of his friends and seeks on the whole to adapt to his literary milieu. But what does Schiller himself say? In general, he praises the content of Humboldt's writing but is more circumspect on the style. Thus, according to him, Humboldt's ideas on the sexes will become common currency once they are better expounded (5 October 1795). The failure of these two texts should not deter the author, for the subject matter was too dry and too difficult. Approving of the Greek project, Schiller writes that Humboldt should be less sharp and less intellectual, and he suggests ways to lighten and animate the argument (7 December). Schiller expresses himself more fully in a letter to his confidant Körner, who is also a friend of Humboldt's. Speaking a little later of Humboldt's book on Goethe's *Hermann and Dorothea,* he judges the content to be excellent but the style deplorable, and on 7 August 1797 he speaks his whole mind: Humboldt's conversation is precious, and he needs dialogue to "provide a matter for his sharp intellect, since he cannot create [or "form," *bilden*], but only cut and paste." Schiller's final and complete judgment is found in his 20 July 1796 answer to Humboldt, which Pierre Caussat judiciously chooses to translate in his edition of the *Introduction to the Kavi* (Humboldt 1974: 13). I would only like to proceed a little further in the reading of this letter. In brief, Schiller writes that Humboldt is neither a philosopher nor a poet, but a critic devoted to judgment and aesthetic enjoyment. Producing a work cannot be an end for him; but, Schiller adds, he will not be able to realize his gifts fully without the personal effort and the work of writing. He should therefore

---

24. In French, in Caussat 1974: 12. The editor of Humboldt's linguistic works, Heymann Steinthal wrote a detailed study of Humboldt's style (1883:23—34) in which he even listed the syntactic and lexical shortcomings. Here is his evaluation: "I cannot say that he managed to overcome his stylistic shortcomings; they were too deeply rooted, and originated in his intellectual character. We encounter them in his last and great work just as they were in the essays published in Schiller's *Hours*" (27). Although he admires Humboldt's intellectual abilities and considers him a "born philologist in the highest meaning of the word," Steinthal explains very felicitously that when Humboldt writes, he is still too busy struggling with the idea to make it clear to himself. He has not yet mastered the idea and so "cannot expound it objectively" (26). "Humboldt's style was and has remained purely subjective" (27). In this sense, we can say that Humboldt never, or almost never, wrote but for himself. On this level he remained willy-nilly within the scope of his Bildung.

never give up production, even if for him it is only a means, just as criticism is only a means for one who has the vocation of a producer. This is of course the lesson that Humboldt, as a man devoted to his Bildung, was to gather from his familiarity with the two creators of Jena and Weimar.

Let us point out that Schiller leaves unexamined the question whether Humboldt's works will eventually reach a wide audience. Only a fraction of them seem to have done so during his lifetime. Nonetheless, during these years Humboldt gathers his strength to produce a work, and, searching for a worthy undertaking, he decides on an anthropology. He writes to Wolf that he feels confident he will be able to produce something new by exploiting his particular talent, which consists in "detecting relationships between things usually seen as distinct, in assembling various aspects, in discovering unity in a multiplicity of phenomena" (quoted in Kaehler 1927: 439 n. 11; cf. Sweet 1978–80, 1:176). This is actually, for us, the anthropologist's vocation, but it is only one aspect of Humboldt's anthropology. A subsequent letter to Schiller (12 July 1798) contains perhaps the most concise formulation of the immense ambition of the project. One immediately notices that Humboldt has accepted Schiller's advice, and that anthropology is precisely the framework in which he can express himself while remaining at the level of "criticism": "I am more strongly convinced than ever," writes Humboldt, "that if I possess any type of intellectual vocation, it is that of a critic, and if I can pretend to a virtue, it is that of accuracy [*Gerechtigkeit*].[25] . . . Given this disposition, and uninterrupted reflection, a broad inquiry, a zealous investigation of various men, lands and customs, I can entertain the ambitious hope of finally finding the key to the secret of all human greatness and the formula by which one could *judge all originality and prescribe its orientation*" (Seidel 1962, 2:166, my italics; letter quoted in Kaehler 1927: 11). A twentieth-century critic notes the obvious "chimerical intoxication" (*Rauschtraum,* Kaehler 1927: 12). I italicized the last words of this quotation, for they clearly indicate that it is the preoccupation with Bildung that imposes a normative dimension on Humboldt's anthropology and, in his eyes, justifies its descriptive dimension. The global object of study is the human ideal seen through its various

25. I think that we cannot quite challenge Humboldt's assertion of his soundness of judgment. He is studying France at the time of this letter. In this field—except when writing about the Revolution, a topic that strikes a nerve (cf. below)—we see that Humboldt often concludes his enquiry with balanced judgments and fine remarks that ring true, thus transcending the unfavorable prejudice he shares with many Germans. (The contrast is striking with Herder for instance.) Cf. his study on the French tragic theater (*GS* 2:377–400), later published by Goethe, and what is said below (pp. 123–24) about the "rhythm of global activity" characteristic of the French (*GS* 2:64–66).

forms, as he explains in a general ten-page text entitled "*Ueber den Geist der Menschheit*," which should not be translated, as Flitner warns us (Humboldt 1956: 139), as "on the spirit of the human species" (*GS* 2:324–32). In other texts, however, this spirit or ideal character of humanity can be extracted from its history, as a kind of extrapolated integral of the excellencies that creative periods have successively produced.[26]

•

This is the global perspective in which, in 1795–97, Humboldt thinks he has found his personal mode of expression and which he presents in two texts, the "Plan for a Comparative Anthropology" and "The Eighteenth Century" (*GS* 1:377–410, *GS* 2:1–112). These two texts constitute a turning point in the author's intellectual career and are thus particularly relevant to our discussion, but they are, to say the least, "dense and diffuse" (Leroux 1958: 31) and we will use Robert Leroux's excellent summary in French (Leroux 1958). The first text, dated 1795, was quickly abandoned; the second (1797) was originally intended to replace it and supplement the theory with a particular application, but, for reasons which are clear in the text, this application, the analysis of the eighteenth century, was never written. Leroux notes that "we therefore have, in the second study, a new edition, more detailed, and modified on some points . . . of the theoretical ideas developed in the Plan" (1958: 31 n). The two texts, then, are essentially "programmatic," as one would say today; both, for different reasons, are failures, and Humboldt did not publish them. The second one was read by Schiller, and Humboldt wrote down some of his critical remarks (*GS* 2:5, 32 nn.). As important as these works may be for us, we should not forget that they are abandoned essays that only the devotion of posterity has gathered in Wilhelm von Humboldt's monumental complete works, or, more exactly, in his "collection of writings" (*Gesammelte Schriften*). To read these texts is, in a way, to peer indiscreetly over the shoulder of a man who is struggling to write. We are free to use them to comprehend the method, but we should refrain from taking them at face value, as finished works the author would have agreed to be identified with.

The "Plan for a Comparative Anthropology" shows Humboldt's extreme preoccupation with justifying his enterprise to his friends and to the public. Only a third of the text as it appears (secs. 4–7, *GS* 1:388–400) introduces the discipline's objectives, methods, sources, and limits, and the danger of possible abuses. The preliminary, justificatory sections occupy

---

26. Cf. letter to Schiller dated 2 February 1796; Seidel 1962, 2:23.

another third (secs. 1–3, pp. 377–88), while the last section links this text to his previous studies on sexual differences. The whole appears as a kind of prolix prospectus in which the author is attempting to "sell" his invention to his friends and to followers of Bildung in general.

Section 3, entitled, literally, "Immediate Influence of an Individual Knowledge of Men on the Originality of Character," deals with the relation of anthropology to Bildung. We can understand this title to mean "immediate influence of the differentiated knowledge of men on self-education," for Humboldt says that "comparative anthropology studies the character of entire classes of men" (384), and, as is confirmed from the immediate context, "individual knowledge" here means the knowledge of men in their collective and individual diversity, i.e., in sum, "differentiated knowledge." Moreover, originality (*Eigentümlichkeit*) represents the pinnacle of differentiation, that is, in the case of a single individual, the proper goal of Bildung.

In what way will anthropology promote Bildung? The author answers peremptorily: "Undeniably in the fact that the observer and the observed are both men, that man everywhere adapts to internal spiritual forms without always noticing it, and that the multitude of reigning concepts finally subdues in a way often incomprehensible for us, not only man but also inanimate nature" (386). In other words, man is a social being depending on collective representations; the subject matter of Bildung and of anthropology is identical. Anthropology will therefore be able to help Bildung. But under one condition: it has to be, like Bildung itself, normative in orientation. This is clear in the section under consideration, and the point is fundamental; one notes that it is thanks to a normative preoccupation that the subjective (Bildung) and the objective (anthropology) communicate with each other. Humboldt's anthropology thus rests on a normative foundation.

The last section of the "Plan" (*GS* 1:400–10) is rather redundantly entitled "Main Fact on Which the Idea of a Comparative Anthropology Is Selectively [*vorzüglich*] Based." This refers to the difference between the sexes, the topic of the two long articles published earlier in Schiller's review. We should therefore underscore, as emphatically as Humboldt himself does, the importance of the relations between the sexes in the author's life. Since these relations are fundamental on the level of Bildung, his transition to anthropology must for him be based on this theme. Without going into psychology for its own sake, it is indispensable to touch on this point, and it so happens that what we know can be ordered into a perspective relevant to our discussion.

We shall isolate several levels in Humboldt's relations with the feminine sex. On the deepest level, we encounter a fantasy associating pleasure with brutality toward a humiliated partner, which Humboldt reveals frankly in a page of his 1789 travel diary (*GS* 14:79–80; translated by Sweet 1978–80, 1:63–64). This fantasy originated in childhood, and Humboldt locates it at the basis of his personality, stating that it is from there that his love for, interest in, and empathy for women and for others developed, as well as his refined skill in social relationships. It seems that Humboldt's affirmation has not been taken sufficiently seriously, given the great distance between this fantasy and the egalitarian climate that characterizes his social relations, most particularly his relations with women, which were an integral part of what he conceived as the development of his personality.

Although sublimated most of the time, the rather sadistic motif of the 1789 journal is still present as a secondary theme in the sonnets Humboldt composed in the last years of his life (Sweet 1978–80, 2:488), in which he let himself pour out his heart. One also thinks of some escapades of his when he was following the Prussian army in the final campaign against Napoleon in 1813,[27] escapades that his companions did not appreciate. More generally, we cannot ignore the quite notorious use he made of prostitutes, which he occasionally justified (Sweet 1978–80, 1:94). Humboldt explained what is perhaps the essential on this in an 1817 letter to his wife, which Sweet quotes at length (96–97): "This is something which does not become part of the intimate being of the one who derives pleasure from it, but returns to the global image of the world . . . man possesses it, it never possesses man" (as opposed to love).

In sum, these pleasures are anecdotal, as opposed to Humboldt's genuine relationships with women, numerous mainly in his youth, which were essential to his personality.

Leroux is certainly justified to center his biography and the development of Humboldt's thought on his experience of love as a deep affection between persons of the opposite sex. By the process of love, man becomes aware that he is a totality (Leroux 1932, 81; cf. 273 ff.). Among all the friendships through which Humboldt consciously enriched himself, his friendships with women were the deepest. In his youth, he was the confident of some of the most remarkable women of his milieu, Henriette Herz and Therese Forster among others, so much so that he internalized their problems and identified with them. He also thought carefully and at length about his own eventual marriage (Sweet 1978–80, 1:167–69). Then came

27. Gossip, undoubtedly malicious, spread by Metternich (Sweet 1978–80, 2:151).

his relationship with his bride and future wife: we know from their abundant correspondence that Humboldt, in the context of complete freedom and equality between spouses,[28] strove to share with her all the events of his moral and intellectual life. It is from here that the problem of Bildung is generalized from one subject to other subjects. The "Plan" says that "in practice, every man has the obligation . . . to take into consideration the intellectual and moral Bildung of himself and others" (380); reason prescribes that in any community—and especially in marriage (382)—the subjects respect each other's morality and culture, never do harm to them, but purify and elevate them whenever possible (381). Does the Bildung of women differ by nature from that of men, or do woman and man share the same ideal? As was his habit with all aspects of his experience, Humboldt endlessly pondered and ratiocinated on these questions. Over time, he developed a "sexed" metaphysics and aesthetics, as Leroux says in his analysis of the two articles in *The Hours* (Leroux 1945, 1948). Thus it is that sexual difference led to anthropology, as Humboldt himself tells us, and is granted major status within it, so much so that it is considered to be at the root of personal diversity in the "Plan"—which is no longer the case, notes Leroux (1958: 51–52), in "The Eighteenth Century." Conceivably, Humboldt saw the relationship between man and woman as the main source of the enrichment of personality and, in this sense, the main access to diversity. The association between sexual difference and diversity is so pronounced in him that we almost wonder whether he did not have a premonition of what biologists tell us today regarding sexual reproduction as an agent of diversification for the species. (But this is obviously an altogether different subject.)

It would be superfluous to insist on the contrast in Humboldt between the domination aspect of his childhood fantasy and the presupposed equality in his numerous friendships with women, in his marriage, and in his writings on Bildung and the difference between the sexes. We can wonder whether he managed to completely sublimate his initial impulse in the forms that egalitarian individualism imposed on his life and on his speculations. His correspondence provides the beginning of an answer by revealing two particular episodes of his life.

In 1809 Humboldt met a woman in Königsberg who helped hidden feelings resurface. Writing to her in 1813, he describes a love in which the absolutely submissive woman entirely merges with the man she loves and becomes a part of him. Whatever others may think, Humboldt adds, this is

28. The home frequently accommodates a paramour, while Humboldt is also known for his escapades, which for him are simply a matter of sexual hygiene.

a deeper and more genuine (*eigentümliche,* which we usually translate as "original") kind of love than the one he experiences in his marriage—and he would not confess this to anyone else but her (Sweet 1978–80, 2:85–87; Bruford 1959: 30).

Later, after his retirement and then as a widower, Humboldt corresponded with his protégée Charlotte Diede. These letters, published after his death under the title *Letters to a Lady Friend,* had a great success in Germanic countries as a classic of feminine education. In them, Humboldt plays the role of a director of conscience and, remarkably, proselytizes for Bildung while requiring the most complete submission from his pupil. Here, as in the sonnets of his later years, we encounter a resurgence, albeit partial, of the initial fantasy, as if self-control had weakened with age, letting resurface an impulse that until then had been contained.

Thus, it seems that the original fantasy underlay the conscious effort, which Humboldt did not mention but which is surely present in his own Bildung, to alter on this point his initial "unilaterality" into "originality," establishing equality between the sexes in his friendships with women and in his marriage and then developing his reflection on the characteristics of the sexes, so much so that he placed sexual difference at the heart of his anthropological project. Whatever one might think of these developments in themselves, it seems to me that a healthy interpretation requires that we insist on this voluntary continuity. From this vantage point, the genuine development of Humboldt's life and thought offers a lesson in contrast to some contemporary tendencies.

We are distancing ourselves from two attitudes, both of which would divide what is a living unity in Humboldt. We could, like Kaehler, stress the fantasizing representation and see it as proof of the inanity of Humboldt's project, as the imprint of a torn nature, condemned to failure in everything and in politics in particular. Or, conversely, and according to a tendency that seems very common today, we could condemn the original fantasy in the name of ethics—for instance in the name of the egalitarian principle—and demand its eradication pure and simple, without bothering to know whether that would be viable, and at what price.

We shall take neither approach. We cannot deny that there was some degree of contradiction and conflict in Humboldt, but must we believe, like the most naive representative of the Enlightenment, that good can exist without its opposite, that man should be monolithic, like a diagram devoid of depth? Does not man, as Humboldt attempted to do, have to construct himself from what he already is, developing or modifying himself without uprooting himself, controlling or inflecting his impulses without destroying them? What would sentient life be otherwise? On the contrary, let us thank Humboldt for his sincerity, which gives us a complete man and not an automaton or a ghost. The fantasy he describes is not exceptional, as can be seen from the passages from D. H. Lawrence or Henry Miller cited by Kate Millett in her attack on male sexism (Millett 1969). There is nothing exceptional in his case, apart from Humboldt's sincerity, and his ability to recognize the initial form, and the deep origin, of his interest in the female sex and in the difference between the sexes, and hence the need for sublimation.

At the cultural level, it is clear that the transition from the initial fantasy to equality between the sexes is meaningful. The dimension of domination was, as we know, especially pronounced in Germany, and the success of the *Letters to a Lady Friend* is characteristic. On the other hand, equality was in the air, no doubt in connection with the Enlightenment and the French Revolution. This transition can therefore be taken as a form of contemporary German acculturation.

•

The fundamental character of Humboldt's anthropology can be readily deduced from his conception of Bildung. On the one hand, self-education consists in enriching one's personality by the appropriation of a maximum of diversities in order to attain the excellence the subject is capable of. Self-development tends toward an ideal and is fed by particularities while subordinating them to the ideal development of humanity. The researcher must not simply observe or record, he must also judge, he must be "an observer of nature, a historian and a philosopher" (GS 1:397) all at once. The discipline will combine a normative primacy with an inventory of human diversity: it will have to conciliate, in a way, Kant and Herder. In order to better understand the originality of Humboldt's project, it is helpful to situate its elements in terms of the two perspectives that undoubtedly contributed to its elaboration.

Not only is Bildung a moral duty (GS 1:380) prescribed by reason (*Vernunft*), but, when it is a question of the development of man (390), of his ideal requirements of liberty and dignity (391), etc., one inevitably thinks of Kant, and especially of his 1784 "Idea for a Universal History from a Cosmopolitan Point of View." Let us recall Kant's first two propositions:

> 1. All the natural dispositions of a creature are determined to develop one day completely and in conformity with their end.

2. In man (as the only rational creature on earth), those natural dispositions which are directed to the use of his reason are to be completely
developed not in the individual but only in the species. (Kant 1965: 11)

It is clear that Humboldt adheres to a general perspective of this kind.
Like Kant, he speaks of the human species, of the general character of the
species (*GS* 1:377), of an ideal of the species (380), and of a spiritual development of humanity (380), an idea that underlies his entire project. But
here is a passage that, although it exhibits a formal analogy with the text by
Kant we just cited, actually says something quite different:

> *A*
> Humanity can only achieve its highest form socially, especially because a
> greater diversity better illustrates the wealth of its gifts . . . a man, a
> class of men, corresponds only to a form, but the ideal of humanity ex-
> hibits numerous and diverse forms and can only appear *in the totality of
> individuals.*[29] (*GS* 1:379, my italics; cf. quotation in Quillien 1983:
> 121)

Here then, as in Kant, humanity progresses toward its peak and the ideal is
realized in the "totality of individuals." But this totality is not the species
anymore, it is society, or a society, and above all the ideal is now plural—an
impossible event in a Kantian perspective. However, the primacy of the
ideal is not affected:

> *B*
> One must study the character of sexes, ages, temperaments, nations,
> etc., with as much care as the natural sciences study the breeds and vari-
> eties of the animal world. Although it is only properly a matter of
> determining how diverse man may be, one must proceed as if it con-
> sisted in determining how diverse individual man actually is.[30] (*GS*
> 1:390; cf. 391: to retain only the individual diversities that are compati-
> ble with ideal requirements)

Still in relation to Kant, it is remarkable that Humboldt uses the word
Gattung to designate not only, like Kant, the human species but, in a more
circumscribed and vaguer sense, the varieties he thinks he can isolate

29. And not "of societies," as Sweet wrote.
30. Let us praise here, in passing, and independently of its particular application, a precept relevant to anthropology: always investigate a field broader than the one initially intended for analysis; this is the only way to avoid fixing prematurely the boundaries of the
given system.

within the "species."[31] We encounter both meanings in the first page of the "Plan" (377) at a two-paragraph interval: the objective of comparative anthropology is to "present side by side and to judge comparatively the particularities [*Eigentümlichkeiten*] of the moral character of different human types [*Menschengattungen*]," and further on, this project rests on general anthropology and presupposes that the specific character (*Gattungs-Charakter*) of man is known.[32] In sum, the ideal is plural, given this internal multiplicity of the species.

It is clear that the idea of a spiritual development of humanity is always present [A] and that it no longer refers, as in Kant, to the eschatological perspective of an "asymptotical" progress (Kant 1965: 46) of the species toward the ideal term of a perfect political constitution (ibid., 33–40). That idea is indispensable here as the background for the improvement of man in Bildung on the one hand, and for the implementation of the ideal in the project of comparative anthropology [B] on the other.

The notion of improvement is essential (cf. above), and when Humboldt speaks of progress, he tends to do so in the plural form (all this conforms to the most widespread usage; cf. the important article by Koselleck 1972). The idea will be made more precise in "The Eighteenth Century."

The most remarkable point is that, although the ideal has broadened or diversified—we shall have to come back to the problem this creates for us, if not for Humboldt himself—the moral obligation is absolutely not weakened. On the contrary, knowledge of human diversity is important in light of the obligation (*Obliegenheit*) for all to strive for the improvement of humanity. It is not simply the mission of educators, religious teachers, and legislators: everyone must "take into consideration in practice the intellectual and moral education [*Bildung*] of oneself and of others" (GS 1:380); ". . . and of others": here is the key to the transition, through the characteristics of the sexes, from Bildung to anthropology.

One notes here how, through this transition and the alleged diversification of the Kantian ideal, *duty* evolves into a pretension to *power,* the Kantian imperative becomes aggrandizement of the subject. One thus perceives in this particular case a general trait of the post-Kantian generation. But we had encountered something similar in Calvin, in whom the apparent limitation of predestination produces an exaltation of the "inworldly" will

31. The word *varieties* itself is used in the field of biology. In the previous quotation, Humboldt wrote *Rassen und Varietäten*. He also uses the word for cultures, once with a derogatory nuance (*GS* 1:380).

32. See also *GS* 1:390–92 for the second meaning of *Gattung*. More generally, "two kinds [*Gattungen*] of characteristics" (399).

(Dumont 1986: 54–56). The parallelism between the two phenomena is striking.

Humboldt writes that "comparative anthropology studies the character of entire classes of men, especially [or "preferably," *vorzüglich*] that of nations and periods" (384). It is impossible here not to think of a filiation with Herder, since it was he who asserted the diversity of cultures in the face of the universalism of the Enlightenment and of Kant. I think that Humboldt wanted to bring precision and strictness to the kind of consideration that had remained fanciful and approximate in Herder (Sweet 1978–80, 1:143–44). But apart from the fact that in Humboldt diversity is always subjected to normative judgment, it also extends much further than in Herder. Humboldt applies the term *Eigentümlichkeit,* which designates for him significant particularity or originality—in contrast with "unilaterality" (*Einseitigkeit*), which is a particularity devoid of meaning or purely contingent—to persons as well as to cultures, and even to abstract categories of people.

The two citations above illustrate these uses. In [A], "a man, a class of men" indifferently represent a form of humanity. In [B], Humboldt enumerates as varieties of men, on the one hand, nations (i.e., concrete social entities) and, on the other hand, "sexes, ages, temperaments" (i.e., abstract categories with more or less biological connotations). We see that he reserves the right to have comparison bear on one or the other. Insofar as the latter categories are actually transcultural, we see that Herder's contribution is at risk of being neutralized. It would then not be anymore a matter of social or cultural belonging, except as one determining factor among others. There would actually exist only individuals as representatives of one category or another ("a man, a class of men").

The concern for Bildung obviously predominates here, and through it Kantian normativeness threatens to overcome Herder's insight. Humboldt's anthropology is not a cultural anthropology in the spirit of Herder, or the transition is still incomplete, as the rest of the study shall confirm.

We can however praise certain perceptions in passing. Thus, Humboldt says that "philosophical anthropology can only study a whole, an accomplished form [*Gestalt*], and not a mass of isolated traits" (as in the natural sciences). This sheds light on the content of what he calls *eigentümlich* or *individuell-ideal*. Concerning the place of imitation in Bildung, he notes that nations tend, in their relations, to exaggerate or, conversely, to abandon their originality (388). For Germany, this remark announces the argument in "The Eighteenth Century" regarding the exaggeration of the tendency to imitate (cf. below). Hence, an impeccable argument, addressed to the legislator, in favor of comparison: ". . . how can one possibly know completely a nation's character without having also studied other nations with which it is in close relation? It is in contrast with them that this character actually came into being and it is only through this fact that it can be fully comprehended" (378–79). Here is an entirely valid precept—mutatis mutandis—for today. We are but applying it to Germany here (cf. above, chap. 2).[33]

On the personal level, we believe we can descry how Wilhelm von Humboldt came to construct his formula for a comparative anthropology. Having identified from very early on the seed and the idea of self-education, within himself and from his reading of Greek authors, he used Kantian moralism to help him turn it into a moral law for himself, while his attention, which had always been responsive to the diversity of characters that surrounded him, found in Herder the justification for, and a kind of consecration of, the collective idiosyncrasies that appear as so many living personalities. The meticulous concern for self-improvement by the integration of external diversities ran into the idea of the improvement of the species through its cultures and the diversity of its original characters.

On the level of the history of ideas, what strikes one is the reunion in one theory of two very different types of thought which were clearly distinct and even antagonistic in the previous generation. Humboldt naively undertakes the difficult task of reconciling them. In form, this is a movement characteristic of the development of German thought during this period. It is a movement of integration of diversity, as is that of Bildung itself and the movement Humboldt sees as the root of the German tendency to imitate. Formally, it is logically coherent, insofar as it transcribes hierarchically the difference between the two components.

It remains to be seen, at the confluence of diversity and normativeness, how Humboldt thinks they can be united, or more precisely, how he thinks he will judge the diversity of the actual—and preserve some of it—from the point of view of the ideal.

In principle, man must "preserve the character that comes to him from nature and from the situation—since only within it can he move freely and be active and happy"[34] and at the same time answer to "humanity's general

33. Conversely, French nationalism in the Third Republic is largely of German influence (see below, chap. 8, part 2).

34. More precisely, in accordance with what we shall explain later, a choice has to be made here. Thus, in a November 1795 letter to Schiller, Humboldt writes: "Everyone must study one's originality and purify it, and distance oneself from the contingent. . . ." (cited in Bruford 1959: 31–32).

demands, and set no barrier to its spiritual development" (380). There is here a contradiction, to be resolved in practice by the study of the relations between the various particularities and the ideal of the species. As "ideal demands," Humboldt mentions the "dignity of man" (391) and the "liberty of individuals" (393). Man will have to judge, for each particularity, whether it is in conformity with these demands or not. On the very level of description, Humboldt hesitates between a monistic view (interaction of material circumstances and spiritual characters) and a dualistic one opposing chance and necessity, or rather the contingent (*zufällig*) and the essential. The latter distinction plays a major role here and an even greater one in the text on the eighteenth century. It will turn out to be very cumbersome, not so much for its arbitrariness, which strikes us more than it did Humboldt, but for its instability. We shall here only register a few judgments. There are blamable varieties, "indeed not every difference deserves to be preserved" (380), and it seems that this is especially the case with national characters, which too often result from chance alone (380–84). Yet, Humboldt cites the example of Switzerland as a case where no one could see particularities disappear without deep compassion (380), apparently because of the alloy of civilization and simplicity the country embodies.

We learn in fact that a population needs a certain cultural development to attain a truly individual character, since particularities are first external and contingent, and therefore insignificant. In Europe itself, the author distinguishes three levels. Russians and Turks, found at the third level, have obviously no "individual-ideal" character (393). We see here that the normative point of view results in excluding from anthropology everything that is not civilized in the most restrictive sense of the term. At this stage of Humboldt's thought, the field of his comparison is after all very limited. In modern times, he thinks of only a few European nations.

All in all, the same will be true of the later text on the eighteenth century. We see, therefore, that the field of Humboldt's "anthropology" is restricted in practice to classical antiquity on the one hand, and to modern civilization on the other. In this limited framework, one understands better the introduction of categories such as sex, and even the supremacy of a normative approach. In the end, Humboldt's enterprise at this stage boils down to an attempt to introduce scholars, within their familiar world, to a systematic and progress-oriented consideration of human diversity.

Humboldt will implement this view a little later during his long stay in Paris, and it is open to some expansion, since he will study Spain during a first trip and subsequently return to the Basque country. In the present text,

Spain was only at the intermediate level, between genuine individualities and others.

We do not exactly know what failed to satisfy Humboldt in this first text and led to its abandonment. Only developments in the text that replaces it can shed light on this question.

•

More than a year after the "Plan," Humboldt again took up his project for a comparative anthropology, this time with the intention of limiting himself to the study of the most recent historical period, hence the title "The Eighteenth Century." But in spite of the increased length of the text—112 large pages in volume 2 of the *Gesammelte Schriften*—it still remains an introduction. Moreover, Humboldt concluded, once the project was rationally formulated, that its execution was almost impossible, so much so that he never pursued it. We shall not linger on the first half of the text (*GS* 2:1–51), which more or less repeats the "Plan" on the justifications and the general a priori characteristics of the study and adds a justification for the choice of the period. Schiller was impatient at the moralizing pedantry of these justifications, and posited that it is simply necessary for the modern individual to adapt to totality, a necessity for moderns that did not exist for the Greeks (*GS* 2:5, n).[35]

The eighteenth century opened a period of movement, and the choice of the period is justified by, among other things, the importance of the intervening changes, that is to say, as a function of progress. For Humboldt, who is close to Kant here, progress is above all a task of reason busy reducing the place of the contingent in nature and humanity, and especially in transforming man into a citizen of the world, although he adds that man must also cultivate his originality. We find here, again, the difficulty we had encountered earlier in the dual concern for normativeness and "character."

For our author, progress resides mostly in the more or less imperceptible changes in mentalities, but one is struck nevertheless by the care with

35. Further on (*GS* 2:32 n), Schiller adds another criticism to which we can only subscribe. He complains that the general line of development escapes the reader, and that the frequent restrictions found even in the general propositions lead him astray (on "side ways," *Seitenwege*). It is true that this text, like others by Humboldt, becomes a labyrinth when one attempts to follow the development step by step. Humboldt disorients and confuses his reader—at least this reader—with his twists and turns, his asides, his undefined digressions, his liberties with vocabulary and syntax. As a result, it is especially difficult to follow the general rule we have set for ourselves of translating literally even when we do not use quotation marks. We have resigned ourselves to introducing approximations here and there in order to avoid obscuring the text beyond measure.

which this text (*GS* 2:21) minimizes the impact of the French Revolution. It is not mentioned by name but only alluded to, as an "extraordinary and remarkable fact, whose future consequences are unknown," and then as "the greatest external phenomenon, the richest in consequences, the strongest commotion that can be," but, all things considered, it remains less important than the increase in liberty of thought against traditional constraints. The Revolution is undoubtedly part of this increased liberty, but it adds to it, along with violence and chance, "the impulsiveness of a quick wisdom"—which we shall see a little later is, for Humboldt, characteristic of the French rhythm of activity.

Fortunately, we have at our disposal a slightly later text, written from a very similar vantage point—i.e., the ideal character of humanity—to put somewhat in perspective this interested underestimation of the French Revolution. It offers a more sincere and exact view of the "external phenomenon" in question:

> . . . when everything vacillates around us there is no safer refuge than ourselves, and since a genuine upheaval of all conditions has occurred in one of the most significant and cultured places on earth, it is more than ever doubtful whether anything [how much] will remain from these conditions elsewhere, especially since this upheaval appears, in a philosophical era, as something absolutely and morally necessary. ("Ueber den Geist der Menschheit," *GS* 2:324)

Concerning the difference in content, we notice that this text was probably more confidential than the previous one, since it was not destined to be communicated immediately. According to the editor, it dates from the beginning of Humboldt's stay in Paris (*GS* 2:405), after the Humboldts were prevented from going to Italy by the war there. It seems to me that the idea of a "refuge" within oneself sheds light on the intention that led to the attenuation of the event in the first text: rather formally addressing his German peers, did not Humboldt propose, in line with his study of mentalities, the internal refuge that was to transform Bildung into a national institution (cf. above)?

We see from this example that "The Eighteenth Century," unlike the "Plan," leaves room for the concrete realities of the time. One also thinks of what is said about the immoderate tendency of Germans to imitate others at the cost of their own particularity. Humboldt writes that this tendency originates from a laudable propensity toward diversity and that its exaggeration is only contingent (Leroux 1958: 41 n. 2). Schiller's reaction to his assertion was recorded by Humboldt:

> The tendency to imitate is a phenomenon that is too permanent in the
> German character to be resolved entirely in an ideal effort toward diver-
> sity, and as a defect, to be due simply to chance. The reason for it could
> well lie mainly in the political constitution (*GS* 2:32 n).

For the reader who would want a commentary on this point, let us say that
(1) it is vital to see these authors insisting on the importance of this trait; (2)
in order to understand it, we shall consider it together with the tacit acceptance of subordination in society, on the one hand, and—in parallel, on the
external level—with a feeling of inferiority toward Western cosmopolitan
culture, and French culture in particular, on the other hand. The political
divisiveness on which many others insisted after Schiller was probably perceived as a symptom of cultural inferiority (cf. chap. 7 below).

Two concrete developments concern France. Humboldt shows, using
the example of French character, how one can go beyond the consideration
of isolated traits, in this case lively imagination and a preponderance of understanding, by focusing on the relation between faculties and the rhythm
of global activity, i.e., "a relatively short-lived vehemence, which is prompt
to act and which, together with a cold and thoughtful assurance, inclines to
get externalized in actions rather than internalized" (Leroux 1958: 46).
This allows one to characterize more precisely understanding and imagination (*GS* 2:64–66). Further on, concerning the difficult distinction between
the contingent and the essential, Humboldt retraces and judges positively
the long cultural predominance of France at the time (*GS* 2:107–9).[36]

As to the century itself, Humboldt delineated its principal traits along
the way with enough precision for Leroux to attempt an outline of it in a
few pages, while Humboldt himself, his hands tied by the methodological
requirements he had accumulated, stopped before a task he now deemed
insurmountable. The matter of uniting "triumphant rationalism" and the
sudden appearance of an "irrational tendency illustrated by the birth of the
historicist spirit and a strong affirmation of sentimental tendencies"
(Leroux 1958: 46) is in the end condensed to a Franco-German dialectic in
which the synthesis, and with it the future, is electively located in Germany.

We cannot discuss at more length these concrete aspects and judgments,
which are scattered throughout Humboldt's unfinished essay and distinguish it from the "Plan." Yet we should say something about the program-

36. It is unfortunate that Muhlack, in his large work on contemporary France and Humboldt's politics, systematically ignores Humboldt's positive or balanced opinions of French
culture. These are of minor importance in the overall framework of Muhlack's demonstration
(cf. above), but their omission impoverishes the thesis, especially on the plane of chronology,
and furthermore distorts the global picture for the uninformed reader.

matic equipment Humboldt perfected, to the point that it blocked the passage to actual realization. He himself refers to the difficulty inherent in applying a model centered on the human individual to an entire period in all its diversity. Let us note, as a reminder, two other aspects already encountered in the "Plan," namely, the combination of the normative and the descriptive, or comparative, points of view and, consequently, the necessity of distinguishing between contingent and essential traits, which occupies the author in the last section of the text (86–112). We know that in principle Humboldt subordinates diversity to the ideal. For a particularity to be recognized as "originality," and not rejected as "unilaterality," it must fulfill certain conditions. Most often, he says that it must constitute itself as a "harmonious plenitude." He is sometimes more precise, for instance when he writes that the development of particularity must not alter the soundness of judgment, be it a judgment on facts, values, or tastes. Here is, at a minor but operational level, an articulation between normativeness and diversity which seems to impose rather narrow limits upon the latter. The point is perhaps decisive concerning the question of the relative places of the universalism of the Enlightenment and the German claim for diversity. The latter is located *within* the former, as we pointed out for Herder (Dumont 1986: 118–19), and this is not contradicted by the global picture of the century (cf. above) but contributes to clarifying it. Germany proposes a diversified, deepened universalism and not, or not yet, a historical relativism.

Today's anthropologists may consider Wilhelm von Humboldt's anthropological enterprise to be rather limited and timid. But, on the one hand, it is interesting to see the emerging point of view lean so squarely against the universalism of the Enlightenment; on the other hand, it is clear that although Humboldt underestimates the gap between the ideal and diversity, we ourselves are still not free from all relation to a universal norm. The relation has simply shifted levels: if not found within the "pure" discipline itself, it is indeed present at the juncture where it inserts itself into social life, as we are reminded in France today [1988] by the New Caledonia problem or a trial concerning the ritual excision of girls.[37]

37. In both cases, it is a problem of a conflict between modern values and other values, that is to say, between the universalistic individualism of French law and the acknowledgment of a particular nonmodern culture. In the case of New Caledonia, the referendum of 6 November 1988 delayed the examination of the fundamental question, namely, is it possible to legitimate, in the framework of the Constitution of the French Republic, the maintenance of Kanak cultural identity? On ritual clitoridectomy being challenged as a mutilation inflicted upon a human being, see Lefeuvre 1988 (on recent trials, pp. 65–66; I had mentioned the problem in Dumont 1986: 208–9 n. 5).

As Leroux is careful to point out (1958: 53), in "The Eighteenth Century" Humboldt adds a draconian requirement for his anthropology to the
ones he had already compiled in the "Plan." In his search for a global characterization that would go beyond the mere gathering of empirical traits, he
comes back to the "internal form," the essential plastic force that governs
the person's unity. He no longer connects it to sexed characteristics, as in
the "Plan," but sees it as the "the primitive force, the original self, the personality given with life itself" on which man's liberty rests (*GS* 2:90), and
he requests a direct intuition of it. It is a rather arduous task, since in the
ordinary course of life this essence is hidden under a multiplicity of more or
less contingent traits resulting from the subject's era, nation, social standing, or profession (106). Thus to seize this essence one must evoke either
the rare moments when the subject feels in full possession of himself or,
objectively, the exceptional circumstances, the great actions that unveil his
deep character. In such a consideration, the domain of the contingent, i.e.,
what is foreign to the essence of the person, broadens, and Humboldt undertakes to distinguish three degrees of contingency. . . . This is how the task he
had undertaken finally appears to him to be more or less insurmountable.

Let us attempt in our turn to characterize what is occurring here. First,
we are indeed in the eighteenth century insofar as the psychology of the
human individual provides the perspective from which all social life is apprehended. Let us note in passing that psychology is here monistic and dynamic: we are in Germany, very close to Herder in particular, and not far
from the Leibnizian entelechy. But the most remarkable point for us is that
the stress on the individual human being with its endless refining is ruining
the promise of a cultural anthropology that we had found in Humboldt in
Herder's wake. We pointed out previously the widespread use of the word
Gattung to designate, other than the human species, various categories of
men or varieties of the species, be they cultural (nations), social (profes-
sions), or biological (sex, temperament, age), varieties that were all, up to
"the period" (*das Zeitalter*), taken more or less as individualities of a
higher order. Here Humboldt attempts to show that the distinction between the essential and the contingent, and even the degrees of contingency
derived from individual psychology, can apply to a period, in this case the
eighteenth century (*GS* 2:107–9). We see that the *Gattungen* an individual
belongs to are responsible for the more or less contingent traits he exhibits
and that he is truly himself only in his essence,[38] i.e., a differentiated mani-

38. The contradiction between *Gattung* as real and as contingent is obvious when, for
instance, one encounters "particularities," resulting from social status, national origin, or a
specific time, listed as (durable) "contingencies" (*GS* 2:106, 1.11–15).

festation of the human species. We had already found something like this in the "Plan," where supposed lower nations, as opposed to higher nations, exhibited only contingent particularities. But now the hierarchy extends everywhere and reveals its origin—the normative individualism that forms the foundation on which Bildung is erected. There are no longer any cultures in the anthropological sense of the term. It is therefore not surprising that the author had to renounce writing an anthropology of the eighteenth century.

•

We have now completed our study of Humboldt's comparative anthropology, but we have presented only the first stage of the transition that will eventually lead him to devote the last years of his life to the study of languages. But before turning from anthropology to linguistics, we shall mention the founding of the University of Berlin, which we are now able to consider from the point of view of Humboldt himself.

CREATION OF THE UNIVERSITY OF BERLIN

In 1809–10, in only eighteen months, Wilhelm von Humboldt reorganizes public education in Prussia and founds the University of Berlin, which will later be considered the prototype of the modern university. Our main concern is to see the connection between what is usually thought to be Humboldt's institutional and political success and his ideas, as we have come to know them, that is to say, of course primarily—but not exclusively—his theory of Bildung as self-education. In order to do so, let us begin by removing an adventitious obstacle out of our way. The word *Bildung* having come to designate education in general and public education in its institutional form, we would risk confusion if we ourselves used it in this sense, while we know perfectly how to designate in our language public education and its successive levels. We shall therefore restrict as much as possible the use of the term Bildung to self-education, as we have been using it, without neglecting the connection that naturally occurs between institutional education and the one the subject exercises on himself.

Concerned with the establishment of an institution or a set of institutions, Humboldt could only partially apply his ideas on man's self-improvement. He would also have to turn to what we called the "objective projection" of these ideas, that is, his comparative anthropology. Moreover, he obviously had to take the environment into account and adapt his views somewhat vis-à-vis the state and the enlightened public, especially the philosophers.

People are sometimes surprised to see someone who earlier, in the name of Bildung, had pronounced himself in favor of restricting the activities of the State to a minimum assume a role in a state project precisely in the field of public education. In fact, there is no contradiction on Humboldt's part, although there is undoubtedly a change. In order to appreciate this change and to understand Humboldt's role and the future of his reform, we must consider the historical circumstances and the place Humboldt occupied in the Prussia of the time.[39]

After the defeat of Jena, Prussia was in a very precarious position: its territory had been reduced, and it was occupied by Napoleon's troops and subjected to heavy tribute that it did not manage to pay. The king thought it safer to seek refuge in Königsberg. At the same time, the scope of the disaster caused a national renewal and brought to power, with an eye toward recovery, advocates of profound reforms toward democratization. Since Fichte's *Addresses to the German Nation,* enlightened minds closely associated the Prussian state and the "German nation," that is to say, German culture, and saw in education for all, i.e., in public instruction, the key to a rebirth. The senior civil servants themselves were in the process of becoming adepts of Bildung in the full sense of the term, and the day was not far off when what is called the class or rather the estate (*Stand*) of educated or cultured people (*gebildete*), whether noblemen or not, would replace the nobility in its governing functions.[40]

It is quite important to precisely situate Humboldt within this conjuncture. Until the moment he assumes his new position, he remains moderately patriotic. He fears the consequences of French domination over German culture, although he is as removed from the nationalist extremists who are calling for an uprising as he is from the cosmopolitan minds such as Goethe, who, from outside Prussia, agree to this foreign domination. Humboldt arrives from Rome, to which he would prefer to return. He even temporarily contemplates renouncing his Prussian citizenship in order to save threatened property he owns in Poland. His attitude contrasts with that of his brother, Alexander, who during the subsequent upheaval will not leave Paris, where, thanks to his fame, he enjoys favorable working conditions and publication opportunities, and where he will even be able to use his connections to save the two brothers' property in Poland. Alex-

39. I shall make use here of the very thorough biography by Sweet (1978–80, 2:1–71), without specifically citing it.

40. Thus, in Hegel's *Philosophy of Right* (1821), the class of civil servants will assume, as the "universal class," the position previously occupied by the landed nobility in the Jena writings.

ander is Francophile and his brother is not, but this is not the essential difference between them, which stems from the fact that Wilhelm serves the
Prussian State and accomplishes his duty while simultaneously remaining
faithful to his ethics of detachment. Later, the contrast between the two
brothers will be at its highest when, during the peace negotiations, Wilhelm
will attempt to impose the harshest possible conditions on France, in Prussia's name. Let us add that Alexander always benefited from the favor of the
king of Prussia. Perhaps the Humboldt brothers embody an example of
people for whom national belonging was less important than it is today.

For now, Wilhelm has had to accept a minor appointment. He is the
head of the section on cults and education in the Prussian Ministry of the
Interior. He tried in vain to avoid the nomination: the recommendation of
some of his peers, their pressure most likely, and finally the inflexible order of the king forced him to accept. But he entertains no illusion about
the fate of his efforts, although we do not know whether he thinks mainly
of the external level, where Prussia will finally prevail, or of the internal
level, where his fears were all too justified. He may have foreseen that if
Prussia were victorious it would no longer have any need for the liberalism he had implemented thanks to the crisis—which is what in fact occurred. Yet, if Humboldt went, the university stood.

One will probably agree that this situation differs widely from the implicit presuppositions of the *Essay on the Limits of State Action*. Let us
recall that, unlike other early texts in which Humboldt showed the necessity of acknowledging the actual and its foreseeable reaction to change in
political action ("Remarks on Constitutions"), the *Essay* was as abstract,
as removed from context, as the French revolutionary creed; it was a kind
of utopian counterpoint to utopia: given man's inalienable right to the
free intellectual and spiritual development of his personality, which activities can be tolerated on the part of the State? This implicitly supposes
that everyone possesses the means to develop oneself, including, among
other things, a minimum of education. Now the humiliated Prussian State
discovered precisely that it needed to spread education among its subjects. Which adept of Bildung could refuse to serve this goal? Let us note
in passing that in his reform activity and his memorandums or instruc-
tions Humboldt never questions the primacy of Bildung over the State. He
even occasionally asserts it, in derived forms, for instance as the primacy
of the point of view of knowledge (*Wissenschaft*) or of the university over
that of the State. A convenient area to study Humboldt's attitude, since it
was also under his authority, is censorship. Characteristically, Humboldt
bows to circumstances without ever relinquishing principles. It would be

best to have no censorship at all, but in the meantime, he strives to limit it and to graduate it (between the publications destined for educated people and those accessible to all).

Yet it is obvious that, in the reform of education at all levels, Humboldt did in fact increase the role of the State, as others had begun to do before him. This was probably unavoidable, in Prussia as elsewhere, in the modern era. On the level of ideas, the only remnant from the early *Essay* is the principle of the subordination of the State to Bildung in a very wide sense, as for example in the expression *Bildungsstaat,* "education state."

Not only did Humboldt create the University of Berlin; he also reformed elementary or primary education and secondary education as well, although he played a less personal role in those instances. In elementary education, reform was already underway under the influence of Pestalozzi, and Humboldt had only to generalize and systematize the movement. This accomplishment represented a step toward the requirement of Bildung, for Pestalozzi himself had insisted on the need to awaken and mobilize the child's attention.

Circumstances were also favorable in secondary education, since the idealistic reaction against utilitarianism had grown among educators in favor of a broad humanist teaching emphasizing what we in France call *culture générale*. Humboldt therefore could, in agreement with the teachers, set forth the principles for the application of the Bildung ideal in secondary education. The *Gymnasium* was to be devoted to general education, leading to the university and to higher professional training. (There were other secondary schools as well.) The teaching, which included mathematics, history, and languages, could be individually modulated in response to the needs of the students. This plan was not put into practice in the long run, nor were the means of control designed at the beginning. Yet, as far as we know, the *Gymnasium* remained in large part an establishment devoted to humanist education.

Remarkably, the university, according to Humboldt, represents a discontinuity, a true break with secondary education concerned with general education. There are no longer any students per se; the goal of the establishment is of a different nature: in the university, teachers and students are in equal measure at the service of *Wissenschaft,* literally, "science," or rather "knowledge." This knowledge is never complete but is rather a process, or, as a first approximation, what we call *research*. Education is replaced here by *Wissenschaft,* which according to Humboldt provides the necessary materials for Bildung and imposes itself as a higher end in relation to the State as well as to practical ends and to the subsequent careers of the students (this differs from the utilitarian inspiration of the French Ecole Polytechnique, prestigious at that time, where scientific teaching was designed to train the high State officials).

From the point of view of the continuity of Humboldt's ideas, the connection thus established between Bildung (self-education) and *Wissenschaft* inevitably evokes the passage from the subjective to the objective reference in a comparative anthropology, or even linguistics, that would not be exclusive of history.

What should detain us here is above all the idea of *science,* of the unity of Knowledge. No doubt it is understood in Humboldt from the unity of Bildung, but the idea of the deep unity of all knowledge is general in Germany, albeit under different conceptions. We should at least state here the confluence of this idea with the contemporary philosophical perspective in which it is more strongly stressed than in Humboldt himself, as we shall see. We know in particular that Fichte and Schleiermacher had both written memoirs on the creation of a University in Berlin to replace that of Halle, which had been lost during the war, and that Humboldt confronted the two authors, siding with Schleiermacher's liberal formula against Fichte's authoritarian one (Ferry, Pesron, and Renaut 1979: 10).[41] For Humboldt, as for Schleiermacher, the unity of knowledge is to be found on the level of an "aspiration of the spirit" (ibid., 323), rather than on the level of a supposedly complete and enclosed philosophical system, as in Schelling and Hegel, or of a system conceived as an "organic entity," incompletely realized as of yet, as in Fichte (ibid., 189). It is right to say that Humboldt conceives of the unity of knowledge in a Kantian perspective, as a regulative idea (ibid., 21–23).

The intervention of the theory of Bildung, or, if we may say so, its intersection with the German philosophical tradition, can be detected in the distinction Humboldt makes between disciplines (though in an adventitious document). Humboldt limits to four the number of disciplines that will be represented on an advisory committee designed to uphold the humanistic inspiration of secondary education against the eventual hostility of the State bureaucracy. These four higher disciplines are philosophy, mathematics, philology, and history. We see that in Humboldt's mind the natural sciences are relegated to a subordinate level, the reason being that

41. This work, *Philosophies de l'université,* includes, among others, the translation of Fichte's and Schleiermacher's memoirs, and of Humboldt's best known text: "On the Organization Internal and External of the Superior Scientific Establishments of Berlin" [9 pp].

contrary to the higher disciplines, they do not possess the capacity to transform the acquisitions of a given field into "genuine intellectual Bildung"
(Sweet 1978–80, 2:50–51).[42]

In order to better discern the intervention of the theory of Bildung here,
we can compare Humboldt's classification with the views Fichte and Schleiermacher expressed in their memoirs. Both authors are especially concerned with replacing the old but still dominant trilogy of theology, law,
and medicine with the supremacy of philosophy. Fichte enumerates five
great divisions: Humboldt's four disciplines plus natural science. For
Schleiermacher, *Wissenschaft* is philosophy, and while he acknowledges
the existence of distinct disciplines, he insists that subdisciplines should not
be rigidly compartmentalized in university education. It seems that Humboldt diverges mostly in making philosophy share its prominent role with
the three other major disciplines. If we compare the four major disciplines
acknowledged by Humboldt with those that dominate his own practice—
i.e., anthropology, history, and philology (or linguistics)—we see that, in
order to adapt to the needs of the State or of the society, he consented to
replace anthropology with philosophy and, like Fichte, to accept mathematics. We are therefore justified in saying that, on this point, the orientation of Humboldt's university issues from the intersection of his Bildung
ideal with contemporary philosophical views. Moreover, the fact that
Humboldt excludes the natural sciences, or lowers their status, indicates
that in the end he does not adhere to the contemporary German idealist
philosophical viewpoint, which does not by any means exclude the possibility of a philosophical recovery of these partial viewpoints. The essential
point is that, for Fichte and Schleiermacher, philosophy ensures, and even
constitutes, the unity of *Wissenschaft,* whereas in Humboldt the principle
of unity is found in the relation to Bildung, which helps acknowledge several higher disciplines on an equal basis.

As a result, although in passing we translated as "research" Humboldt's
Wissenschaft, which is in progress, never complete, it still differs from what
we today call scientific research, even in the "human sciences," which
would in part correspond to Humboldt's cardinal disciplines. Humboldt's

42. Humboldt's thought on this matter is clarified and qualified in a letter to Wolf (14
July 1809, *GS* 16:174) in which he attempts to persuade him to join the planned committee:
"There shall only be" a philologist (Wolf), a theologian (it will eventually be Schleiermacher),
a mathematician, a pedagogue-philosopher, and a historian, in the broader meaning of the
word; one could also separate physics and the natural sciences from mathematics, or choose a
linguist (nonclassical languages), etc. Let us note in passing that Humboldt applies the word
"terrible" (*schrecklich*) to chemistry, botany, and other disciplines, which could only be represented in extraordinary cases.

university cannot, without misunderstanding or an unexpected shift in meaning, be seen as a prototype for the modern university, as has sometimes been done in the Anglo-American world. It is only its precursor in its emphasis on research in the broader meaning of the term and in its introduction, by virtue of its close connection to Bildung, of individualistic demands, such as the ones we later encounter in student movements, as in France in 1968.

The only law in Humboldt's university is freedom. It aims at "an uninterrupted common activity, which lives and ceaselessly renews itself, without any constraints or determined finality" (Ferry, Pesron, and Renaut 1979: 321), but given that each member "faces the pure idea of science," isolation and freedom (*Einsamkeit und Freiheit*) are basic principles (*GS* 10:250).[43] Another text adds that freedom is necessary (*notwendig*) and isolation useful (*hülfereich*) (Humboldt 1956: 79; Vierhaus 1972: 530). Humboldt does not insist on courses, on teaching proper: those who find it useful to the advancement of their research read papers; others give few lectures or none at all. Here Humboldt innovates—even when compared to the liberal Schleiermacher, who planned, among other things, a kind of philosophical propaedeutic for all students.

The relation Humboldt establishes between the university and the State is clear in principle and, from his own admission, problematic in practice. The State must support the university, while simultaneously acknowledging the superiority of university values over its own, and consequently refrain from intervening in university life and in everything relating to those values. *Wissenschaft* is not at the service of the State; it simply provides the materials from which the individual constructs his Bildung.

Humboldt initially thought the university would achieve financial independence by obtaining a sufficient land grant from the king. But he fought in vain to obtain it and had to content himself with regular budgetary credits (Sweet 1978–80, 2:58, 63). In providing these means, it is clear that to the Prussian State the decisive factors were its own self-interest and the prestige Prussia thought it would gain from the institution in the eyes of all Germany. We perceive this when we see Humboldt hide the truth for once and assert, inaccurately, that all the scholars who were approached accepted to join the University of Berlin.

The teachers will be chosen by the State, for co-optation is not desirable here—contrary to what is true for the academy. Humboldt moreover privileges the university over the academy as far as the advancement of knowl-

43. Translated as "independence and freedom" in Ferry, Pesron, and Renaut 1979:321.

edge is concerned. He uses the argument of recent history, and he also fears the compartmentalization of disciplines. But in order to avoid stagnation he counts above all on the vitality and passion of youth, once it comes into contact with the most distinguished minds. The proximity of the ideal of Bildung is tangible here.

Humboldt is fully aware that in spite of precautions, the intervention of the State can be harmful. He even tends to make the State feel guilty for its positive interventions: the State has "the duty to provide structures and means," but by doing so "it plunges what is spiritual and elevated into a material and inferior reality." The State must therefore "set its sight on the internal essence" to remedy what it has destroyed and prevented, "even if it has done so unwittingly."

We see that Humboldt, even in a position of power—a short-lived one—never ceased to express his mistrust of the State. To be sure, a kind of utopia still prevailed at the time, and later, either after he left the ministry or on a larger scale during the antiliberal turn that will bring about his retirement in 1819, the University of Berlin moved away from the model he had prescribed. It still remained exemplary for its combination of teaching and research. If we may extrapolate here and venture a hypothesis concerning the relations between the State and the university and educational institutions in general, it seems, on one point at least, that the distance marked somewhat caricaturally by Humboldt did survive. That, at any rate, is what the comparison with France in regard to the teaching of politics suggests: in Germany, the political domain seems to have escaped teaching altogether, in accordance with the tradition of Bildung,[44] in France the République managed to impose itself only thanks to Jules Ferry and through compulsory secular schooling and "civic education."

THE CONVERSION (CONTINUED): LINGUISTICS

We know that from his retirement in 1819 until his death in 1834 Humboldt devoted himself mainly to linguistic studies. However, among his other writings from this period, we must comment on a 1821 communication to the Academy of Berlin entitled "The Historian's Task." Taking advantage of the existence of a good French translation and of a detailed commentary by Jean Quillien (Humboldt 1985), we shall only indicate the place of this text in relation to what concerns us here. Given the once again "programmatic" aspect of the title, one could believe that it is simply a de-

---

44. See above, the chapters on Thomas Mann and especially on Troeltsch (chaps. 4 and 3).

velopment, an application to history, of the anthropological views we studied in the "Plan" and "The Eighteenth Century." But that is not the case, for, as the title indicates, the accent has shifted from the object of the research to its author or subject, in this instance the historian, which allows for a decisively greater depth of perspective. Moreover, we have here surely one of Humboldt's happiest texts, for once clear and skillful in the presentation of its main idea.

The felicity is perhaps due to the fact that both the concern with objectivity and the subjective activity are here present and united, in opposition to earlier works. The central thesis is that the historian extracts from himself what has to be added to the given so that it may be understood as history. Seeing Humboldt thus explicitly drawing together the historian and the literary creator (*Dichter*), we immediately think of Schiller, who, by the way, had also written history. And Humboldt in fact wrote in a letter to Goethe that the idea originated in a remark by Schiller that "the historian must proceed exactly as the poet. Once he has assimilated the material, he must re-create it in an entirely new fashion from within himself." Humboldt added that at first he did not understand what Schiller meant (the letter is quoted by Quillien in Humboldt 1985: 94). This confession is precious for us, for it illustrates well the difference between the 1790s texts and this one. While it was previously a matter of grasping characteristics or "originalities," or an "internal form," which were supposedly present within the object, the historical given now resembles a lifeless chronological and causal chain to which the historian must add something in order to reanimate it. What he must add is of the order of thought; this explains why thought is needed for this re-creation, by an operation which is both a *bringing in* and a *taking out,* since there is "a preexisting and original agreement between subject and object. Comprehension is never simply a development stemming from the former, nor simply an extraction from the latter, but is both simultaneously" (Humboldt 1985: 78).

This sentence says everything, explicitly and implicitly. Explicitly, naive positivism, according to which the past is immediately meaningful without recourse to interpretation, is abandoned. A subject, in this case the historian, is needed to make the past meaningful. This incontestable view, transcendentalist in essence, is in fact linked to the Kantian distinction between determinism and liberty—since only liberty is meaningful. But the meaning the historian confers upon the past is not indifferent or gratuitous: it was to some extent contained in the past, and it is unique—this is the implicit aspect of the quoted sentence. There is *one* historical truth, which the historian may grasp depending on his ability and success. Humboldt stops short of relativism, for the historian himself is in history and his comprehension could well vary as a result.

If it does not, it means that history in its global unfolding has an orientation, a purpose, so that one must postulate a "governing of the world" in the sense of this teleology. Thus, we encounter again, underlying the "historian's task," what we previously called normativeness. It is because history is oriented toward the good that it is progress, when taken globally, and that the historian conscious of this orientation is assured of attaining the truth. We are here at the extreme end of the eighteenth century. Kant *genuit* Schiller, Schiller *genuit* Humboldt. Is the same true of Hegel? He does not invent anything; he discovers what is there already, history has one meaning and one only. But as a result of this—major innovation—history ends.

One may wonder why Humboldt did not, earlier and on his own, bring into relief this aspect of the study instead of borrowing it from Schiller. It is perhaps due to his development of anthropology as a counterpart to Bildung, to what we called the projection of the subjective into the objective: the subject was at work, unbeknownst to himself.

It remains to be seen whether "The Historian's Task" is as isolated from Humboldt's subsequent linguistic works as it is from his earlier anthropological writings. As far as I can tell, I would venture to say yes: languages are a hard given for Humboldt, as categories (*Gattungen*) of men were earlier. He will not be aware of the need to complement them with his intuitions, so much so that he will assert his ability to weigh objectively the relative spiritual merits of different types of languages. In sum, Schiller's clear insight allowed Humboldt to write, for once, a "programmatic" text, a text of principle, that is clear and incontestable in its central idea.

•

Let us come back to our main purpose. We set out to reduce the apparent discontinuity in Humboldt's preoccupations between self-education, which was the exclusive concern of the first part of his life, and the construction of a comparative linguistics, which occupies most of his later years. In order to do so, we have studied in detail a first transition, which, in 1795–97, led him to set forth a program for a comparative study of individual and collective characters, thus of cultures in particular, within civilized mankind. This first stage in the overall transition is essential for us: it stresses Humboldt's intention to project out of himself in an objective form, in a written work, various human contents—representations, values, sentiments—that in their original state were essentially experienced, linked to the subject.

But there is more to it. Even if one grants that the passage from the subject's inwardness to an *objective comparison* is essential, we would still have to show how a comparison between cultures could evolve twenty years later into comparative linguistics. Moreover, the original comparison involved only a few supposedly higher cultures, whereas linguistic comparison will be in principle more open, or even universal.

We notice first that the problem is not exactly posed in these terms. We speak of cultures for simplicity's sake, though Humboldt spoke of isolating the characteristics of some categories of people, including nations and periods. Moreover, "characteristics" have to be understood here both as distinctive traits and as psychological aspects, as "characters" in the sense that one speaks of a person's character. The examples we cited illustrate this—the "rhythm" of the faculties among the French, for instance. This results from the fact that for Humboldt, at the stage of the "Plan" and "The Eighteenth Century," the basic model is still the individual. But we have seen his comparative requirement culminate in the search for the "internal form," for the plastic force, the principle of unity, of order and growth at work in the living man. It is precisely this principle, more or less impossible to grasp at the level of the eighteenth century, that Humboldt will find in language. In the end, when compared to language, civilization and culture appear as secondary, superadded developments and even, except for the conscious recapture of culture in the activity of Bildung, as more or less inert products, as for example in the *Introduction to the Kavi*.[45]

The decisive turn occurs in relation to Humboldt's journey to Spain, and especially his discovery of the Basque people (Sweet 1978–80, 1:231).[46] We know that in 1799–1800 Humboldt traveled through Spain with his family for seven months, and that he went back alone to the Basque country for two months of additional investigation in 1801. He was immediately seduced by the originality of the Basque character, although the language—so obviously linked to the collective identity of this people—remained impenetrable to him (ibid., 234, 241). He will return to study these people, who, in contrast to his usual research subjects, occasionally appear to him as barbarous (ibid., 278). Still, thirty years later, in a

45. French translation, secs. 6 and 7, Humboldt 1974, esp. 159–66.
46. We shall retain from Aarsleff (1982: 348) the idea that this "turn" may have been prepared, and Humboldt's attention drawn to the Basque language, during his contacts with the Idéologues in Paris.

general work, Humboldt will stress the importance of this experience in a beautiful text that we are fortunate to find translated by Pierre Caussat in his preface to the *Kavi* (Caussat 1974: 16–17). Caussat also includes a partial translation of a letter to Schiller dated September 1800 (17–19), which we shall consider at length, for two reasons: first, it includes a peremptory statement that introduces a notable discontinuity with what we have learned of Humboldt so far; and second, this declaration makes sense only in connection with what precedes it, a context that itself needs to be ordered along a few dominant ideas.

In order to remain brief, we shall depart from our usual rules. Forbearing to give a literal translation and instead directing the reader to P. Caussat's translation, which is skillful and generally correct, we will propose a reconstruction of Humboldt's text, along with commentaries aimed at grasping the new from the known. The reader shall be the judge of the exactitude of the summary, in particular on the few points where it diverges from the published translation (German text, Seidel 1962, 2:206–9).

The text is an excerpt from a very long letter, a kind of essay on Schiller's *Wallenstein,* which Humboldt had just spent two weeks studying. The reference to Schiller, which was explicit a little earlier in the text, is implicit in the last paragraph of the excerpt, in which Humboldt deduces the eminent role of the writer's art (*Dichtkunst*). A previous letter, from June 1800, alluded to the recent journey in Spain, which is not mentioned here.

Humboldt categorically proclaims the superiority of the present over the past and the future. He justifies this by saying that man as "a thinking and acting being can find his greatest satisfaction only in his own act and in an undivided instant, in the present. The future evokes need and the memory of the past is painful or cold." (We have encountered no precedent of this kind of view in his earlier writings).

We should add that the present in not conceived as absolutely distinct from the past and the future, but that in a way it encompasses them. This is true above all for the past, whose genuine existence stems from the fact that it underlies the present moment. Thus, in music, the note that resonates now is pregnant with previous and subsequent notes. It is the same for language: the instantaneous, individual linguistic utterance is pregnant with the long collective creation of which the language is the fruit. In spiritual activity, similarly, the force that is active at the present moment issues from the subject's entire past activity.

Where does this stress on the present—so new for us—come from? We perceive that the essence of language is placed in the act of speech, but it is man's finitude that imposes the preeminence of language, for, as a finite creature, man aspires to the ideal and inaccessible infinite. Humboldt seeks in the finite a kind of small-scale model of the infinite. The infinite, that is eternity, and the present as he conceives it strongly bears the image of eternity, even if he does not say this. Now, "our finitude comes from the fact that we can only know ourselves in another." Therefore, linguistic communication, implicitly conceived as instantaneous, is here installed at the summit of our being. One only has to make this privileged present as perfect as possible.

In sum, what is new in this development is the exaltation of language in its most important aspect, according to Humboldt, for spiritual activity. At the same time, one encounters echoes of earlier concerns, but they are in some way transformed, and we obtain a view of human duty slightly different from the one we knew. Concerning the infinite and the finite, we recall what Leroux called Humboldt's sexed metaphysics: it is through the relation between the sexes, conceived as the model for all relations, that man can overcome the unilaterality his finitude binds him to, and combine activity and passivity, intensity and perseverance, initiative and conservation. In a somewhat different manner now, the complementarity between human beings appears in the form of the linguistic act. The linguistic act is not indifferent; it is, as was Bildung, oriented toward perfection in virtue of its increasing intensity and richness. When it is said that the essential does not lie in the content or in the final objective itself but in the intensity of the force used in the pursuit of this objective at any given time, we are still seemingly within the dynamism of Bildung, taken more as a process than as a final result. In the conclusion, we encounter on the contrary a break in this solemn proposition that we would do well to ponder:

> It seems necessary to me to thus set forth man's destination [we know the weight of these words] and to seek it neither in an activity [*Wirkung*], nor in mankind as a whole, nor in the duration of an entire lifetime. (Seidel 1962)

Bildung, too, precluded a specialized activity, but it was not indifferent, as we have seen, to the development of "mankind as a whole," and above all it did require "an entire lifetime," at least as a framework for its progress. The idea of totality itself, to which Bildung remained faithful, at both the collective and the individual levels, is here expressly challenged. It is replaced, if one looks closely, by the *present* as a hierarchical totality that encompasses the past and possibly the future. Let us add that the past is present inasmuch as language issues from the collective spiritual effort of men: the instantaneous, individual act of speech contains in itself in some manner the past of the linguistic community. This clearly underscores a shift, a pivoting, from the individualism of Bildung to the holism implicit in the global consideration of a language.

Does this mean that Humboldt's cherished themes, the duty of Bildung and of human progress, are solemnly relegated to the background, and that man's purpose is simply linguistic communication, the most common human activity? Did a ray of common sense actually pierce the arrogant cloud of ideology? And is this not setting man's dignity in its proper place? But let us not be mistaken. A halo of perfectionism still surrounds the practice and the cultivation of language, for it needs to be lifted to an ever higher instant of communication. We can even detect an atomistic aspect, an element of intensification toward romanticism, in the substitution of the present moment for "an entire lifetime."

If we set this surprising development back into the context of the whole essay, we see that the exaltation of language serves immediately for the analysis and illustration of Schiller's art. And as we see that the concern with, or the duty of, improvement persists from Bildung to the succession of instants of linguistic communication, we are led to a hypothesis: the concern to raise language above everything else will have determined the supremacy of the present, by pushing back Humboldt's habitual ideas.

Yet we have before us more than just an occasional writing. On the personal level, Humboldt justifies in advance as it were the long years he will devote almost exclusively to the study of languages at the end of his life. We can even go a little further. We discern that a change occurred in Humboldt's lifestyle in subsequent years. It seems that the duty of Bildung is progressively overshadowed by a career as a scholar and researcher, as was the case during the studious, albeit official, stay in Rome (1802–8), or during the retirement in Tegel from 1819 onward, and even during the intermediate years, filled as they were with political and diplomatic functions and contacts. The personal relationships, the discovery of others, have lost the urgency they possessed during his youth and the stay in Paris, their relative importance diminished, progressively perhaps, in relation to study and cabinet work.

The primacy of linguistics in Humboldt's studies established itself slowly. The idea of an encyclopedia of languages probably came to him as early as 1802, but the stay in Rome reestablished the primacy of the classics and of higher civilizations while the study on the Basque language will only be published in 1816–21 (Sweet 1978–80, 1:277–78). The linguistic work proper is beyond our purview, except for remarking on the permanence of the normative viewpoint (for instance, the respective merits of the different types of languages, etc.), in continuity with the anthropological views. Contrary to the German view—according to which Humboldt's linguistic theories are in continuity with Herder, Goethe, and the German tradition in general—Aarsleff has maintained that they originate mostly in Condillac and in Humboldt's contacts with the Idéologues in Paris (Aarsleff 1982). Whatever the case may be, and in spite of the laudable effort to reestablish the role of international contacts, which Germans often tended to minimize, the fact remains that Humboldt's Paris journal, so uniformly critical of the philosophy of his French interlocutors, does not mention linguistic ideas much. This in turn does not mean that there were no borrowings or influence, but they cannot be surmised.

We still have to elucidate the transition from anthropology to linguistics. At first, we encountered an anthropology that included physical characteristics (physiognomy among others) as well as psychology and what we call culture, and dealt primarily with the spiritual originality, the "character," of men taken individually and by category. From there, we move to an exclusively linguistic anthropology, which apprehends the originality of linguistic communities through their languages. It is clear that the second undertaking is easier to pursue in the study than the first one, especially at that time. (Humboldt, however, still writes to Schiller in 1802, at the time he is settling down in Rome, that the comparative study of languages would necessitate periods of travel.) The point is banal but not negligible, as far as the future is concerned. But the underlying reason for the shift from anthropology to linguistics cannot be found here. In his "Eighteenth Century," we have seen Humboldt capitulate in the end before the impossibility of globally characterizing a period from a model based on the human individual. We can add that the problem would not have been very different for an actual society. Later, we saw how Humboldt, in the Basque country, was enthusiastic about the discovery of a well-characterized population whose collective identity was inseparable from an original language. Language here allowed—or seemed to allow—unmediated access to the collective character; the individual character of each Basque receded to the background to the point of being neglected. I believe that this is the essential point: language emancipated the researcher from his compulsory reference to the human individual and embodied the promise of an unmediated grasp of the society itself. It substituted a holistic perspective for the individualistic perspective imposed until then by the contemporary civilization, and deeply internalized in Bildung. Hence the pivoting we have noted in the text we examined.

In order to shed light on the situation, we can use a contemporary example, that of anthropology as it is conceived in the United States. Americans are deeply individualistic. For them *society* cannot be grasped directly and globally, as Durkheim had attempted to do in France. Society is definitely an aggregate of individuals. Since the anthropologist needs to grasp things globally, American anthropology resorts to another concept, "culture." *Culture,* which is here a German legacy—since the first American anthropologists were of German intellectual parentage—allows the anthropologist to consider society as a whole, in a holistic mode (cf. Singer 1968, esp. 532, col. *b*). Language played the same role for Humboldt, who, in continuity with his own Bildung, could until then speak only of the originality (*Eigentümlichkeit*) or the "character" of a community or individual.

•

We intended to show that there is a continuity between three successive stages in Humboldt's thought and preoccupation. In the first stage he is essentially concerned with his personal formation, while in the second stage he seeks the conditions for a comparative anthropology, and finally, in the third stage, he devotes himself to the comparative study of languages. The continuity resides in the permanence of what could loosely be called the human content and, in consequence, in the permanence of the normative preoccupation, which is very pronounced at first and which extends to the other two periods in a manner that has become foreign to us. We explained the transition from phase 1 to phase 2 by the introduction of a dual constraint, consisting of an inscription in the literary field and an objectification of the content which at first related to the subject. This phase quickly leads to the impossibility of an adequate understanding of human communities as unified totalities, and phase 3 opens with the revelation that language allows direct access to the spiritual originality of these communities.

This realization requires that we go further in the exploitation of continuity and interpret each of these phases in light of one another and of the set they constitute. It will especially be a matter of refining our idea of Bildung in the light of what followed.

We noted previously, concerning the instantaneous linguistic act, a "pivoting" from an individualistic to a holistic view, which is, I believe, characteristic not only of Humboldt but of his cultural milieu. It is quite easy to detect a similar "pivoting" in Humboldt's very conception of Bildung. The concept that governs the whole matter is obviously the originality (*Eigentümlichkeit*) the subject must strive to reach and cultivate, from his own positive particularities. Humboldt does not insist on the uniqueness of each

individual and does not—not yet?—conceive of individuality as irreplaceable, as German tradition will do from Goethe onward (cf. Weintraub
1978). But he at least attempted to know himself and define his own
originality.

We should keep in mind that a value judgment is present here: the particularities that are compatible with universality are the only ones to be
retained, others are rejected. We have seen that this normative aspect imposes itself throughout in Humboldt, though the value judgments themselves may seem in detail rather weak. It is essential to realize that this
judgment of universality sanctions the introduction of particularity into a
mode of thought that, in principle, excludes it. For, in what we elsewhere
opposed to holism as individualism *stricto sensu,* the individual is directly
universal, and consequently devoid of any particularity. Here, German
thought distends universalitic individualism and introduces a measure of
particularity, which Humboldt calls "originality."

But "originality" also possesses another aspect. The Bildung subject
must, according to Humboldt, draw from his environment the largest
number of diversities compatible with what is positive in his own particularity, that is to say, with his "originality," in order to enrich it and constitute it as a whole. One may wonder about this demand, which is heavily
accentuated in Humboldt: why would originality not stay simple? We notice that it enriches itself, or becomes more complex, by the multiplication
of relationships with other subjects and the constitution of a network of
relationships, a kind of small-scale society. Now, Humboldt is a nobleman,
whose affinities with the social totality we have noted: let us say that he
aspires most of all to establish within himself, as a function of his own originality, something analogous to a society. Beginning with a simple, "unilateral" being, he aspires to turn it into a totality. (We encounter the same
movement in Hegel's dialectic, from thesis, or simple entity, to synthesis, or
totality.)

The ideal of Bildung can be seen as a conjugation of particularity and
totality; the individual of Bildung renders himself homologous with a society, which explains why the transition to the idea of an anthropology is so
painless. Even the idea of comparison is implicit in Bildung. Finally, Bildung, as Humboldt perceives it, appears to conciliate universalistic individualism, initially distended in virtual "originality," on the one hand, and
the demand for social totality, a kind of implicit holism, on the other.

In sum, throughout the three phases we distinguished in Humboldt, we
never left the notion of social totality—either implicit in the ideal of Bildung, or difficult to grasp in the eighteenth century, or present as a given in

the totality of a language. We also never left the individual as original, that is, as a particular being seen through the screen of the universal, either as the human creature itself or, by extension, as categories of men, human communities, or languages. In all of this, we have always encountered a mix of individualism and holism in the strict sense we gave these terms. More exactly, these two elements, which we distinguish more or less arbitrarily, are constantly present, under various combined forms. This is how we perceive Humboldt's representations and researches taken in their continuity; how we perceive Bildung, still in a nascent state in him; and, to anticipate, how we perceive German ideology analyzed in the terms we have chosen, in a way following Humboldt, to compare cultures.

7

Bildung **Represented:** *The Years of Apprenticeship of Wilhelm Meister*

Our hero of the preceding chapter can well introduce us to the hero of this one. For it so happens that the literary work most representative of Bildung is composed by Goethe at the same time that Humboldt is living close to Schiller in Jena. There has just been a rapprochement between Goethe and Schiller, and Humboldt is made to share in some manner the intellectual life of the two German geniuses at the beginning of their friendship. There is here something more than a coincidence—we can almost discern Humboldt's silhouette in the novel—and yet we shall see that the distance between Humboldt's Bildung and Meister's apprenticeship is great.

Wilhelm Meisters Lehrjahre (*The Years of Apprenticeship of Wilhelm Meister*) appeared in 1796. It seemed to call for a sequel, which Goethe would much later decide to provide under the title *Wilhelm Meister's Journeyman Years* (1829). This later book was actually a very different work from the *Apprenticeship,* and posterity gave its interest to it only secondarily. We shall do the same, limiting ourselves to searching in it occasionally for the development of some fundamental themes of the earlier book, which will retain our attention as it has held the interest of posterity.

DIFFICULTIES AND PRECAUTIONS OF ACCESS

To tell the truth, as much as the *Apprenticeship* recommends itself for our study by virtue of the resounding echo it aroused, so much does the task of interpretation appear hazardous. The ideal of Bildung is known to reign in educated Germany during the nineteenth century and beyond. Also, Bildung is more than an ideal, it is an institution that has its literature in the form of the *Bildungsroman,* the "novel of Bildung." That the *term* was coined only in 1870 by Dilthey is not important, since the *thing* itself can be followed throughout the century (see *The German Tradition of Self-Cultivation,* Bruford 1975). Now, the *Apprenticeship* has remained the prototype and the model of the *Bildungsroman,* so that one has the feeling of touching here the heart of culture as it is understood by the Germans. Unfortunately, the novel in itself is found rather insipid today and does not hold our interest much. True, that does not matter greatly, since our aim is

Translated by Christophe Robert and revised by the author.

first of all to reach an understanding of the place of the work in German culture. This is no easy task. As far as possible we shall make use of the existing commentaries on the novel. A special mention must be made of Max Wundt's solid and copious monograph, first published in 1913, whose title refers to the "development of the modern ideal of life" (Wundt 1932). We shall see that the commentaries that have accumulated, generally full of praise, enlighten us especially through their disagreement on problematic aspects of the work. Let us give an extreme example. A recent critic, Kurt May, could maintain with some plausibility that the education of the hero is not accomplished when the novel ends and that, moreover, Goethe did not intend to write the novel of such an education. The critic is of course puzzled that posterity more or less unanimously took the novel to be something that it was not (May 1957).

Is the criticism justified, or is it simply a sign of the times, the mark of a radical discontinuity that the nineteenth century, supplemented by the brief but debasing Nazi episode, would have hollowed out in German culture? What are our hopes, as a latecomer from another culture, of being able to penetrate these delicate questions? To go further: what Kurt May's critique, intent on demystification, ends up showing us is that the kind of popularity or exemplariness of *Wilhelm Meister* does not rest on explicit signs but rather touches upon a deep and sensitive area of the mentality, which requires of us, if not total anesthesis, at least precautions and some subtlety.

To tackle the novel with a solid common sense of the Voltairean or French petit bourgeois variety would be fatal. Even a distinguished Germanist like Robert Minder, in a comparison of French and German literature (Minder 1952), failed to acknowledge the novel of Bildung (*Bildungsroman*) as a German counterpart of the French social novel (*roman de société*). And we shall see here itself how the Goethean penetration of Luckács finally succumbs to his desire to establish himself as a champion of the Enlightenment, which leads him to subordinate German culture to a materialistic universalism.

Against such errors, we have a few assets, such as being able, thanks to Troeltsch, to recognize *Gemeinschaft* next to *Gesellschaft* without being stopped by the individualism of Bildung as a contradiction. In general, our distance from the work would expose us to gross mistakes of interpretation were it not for two safeguards: on the one hand, the comparative views we have already acquired (chap. 2), and on the other, the abundant literature surrounding the work, which should teach us to read it as it was read. But we are lucky, to begin with, to be able to listen to the very intentions of the author and the reactions of his first reader.

The correspondence between Goethe and Schiller is of exceptional interest for our purpose: it begins at the same time as the decisive phase in the composition of *Meister,* and the two friends will assiduously discuss the novel during the following two years. Let us add that Schiller appears almost as an intermediary between Goethe and us, anticipating our reactions while he is intervening in the writing itself and obtains changes from the author.

Moreover, this friendship, as we know it from their writings, is surely remarkable, but it is not unique in the German intellectual milieu of the period. One thinks of the three boarders of the *Stift* in Tübingen—Hölderlin, Hegel, and Schelling—who seem to have looked at themselves as conspirators for liberty; or, in Berlin, of the close friendship, described by Dilthey, between Schleiermacher and Friedrich Schlegel, at the source of the romanticism that will animate the whole Berlin group. One may wonder whether the history of ideas has fully exploited those communications and communions between friends. Individualism permeates our culture and leads us to focus our attention on each of the great creators taken individually; and in spite of the insistence of the romantics on "philosophizing together" (*sum-philosophieren*), these great friendships have probably not revealed all their secrets, even though, as counterparts to the current "quarrels" (*Streite*)—for instance, during this period, the "quarrel of pantheism" triggered by Jacobi concerning Lessing and Spinoza, or the "quarrel of atheism" menacing Fichte in Jena—they perhaps characterize best the German milieu. At any rate, the sociologist must certainly make the most of these forms of restricted and intense socialization.

The case that concerns us, however, is very particular. The friendship between Goethe and Schiller is in a way the living basis of German classicism. Without slighting the emotional importance of their friendship, we think we can safely say that it was eminently functional at the professional level. We shall see this more clearly later, but it must be said here already, to make one feel how insufficient the usual biographical approach is. One can naturally speak of the rapprochement between the two poets, of the mutual sustenance they gave each other in a difficult phase of their artistic life, of the stimulation and support that Goethe for his part found in Schiller at Jena, where he came to refresh himself now and then, especially in the long conversations to which both say they are much attached. But this is probably not enough to do justice to the relationship—"unique," according to Goethe—between the two men. We shall see them exchange in writing a promise, one could say a commitment, to *community* of work. The collaboration is not limited to the review published by Schiller. To speak of a literary crusade would be only slightly excessive; let us say at least that the two writers were engaged in a common enterprise that included all they wrote, each on his side and in his own way. Thus of *Wilhelm Meister*. Moreover, they will both confess that their friendship gave them back a lost or compromised fecundity, as if it had re-created a propitious environment for creation, perhaps its natural environment. In sum, friendship modified something in their personalities, in their respective powers of manifestation. Without suppressing differences, their friendship united them in depth. We shall find proof of this when we see a conflict—related precisely to *Meister*—remain momentary and encompassed in the lasting solidarity of the two men. We must see Goethe and Schiller as deeply united.

How can we relate this solidarity to the study of the *Apprenticeship*? We know from Goethe himself that he managed to complete the novel, with great effort, only with Schiller's help, and that without him he would not have written the novel as we know it. If Goethe is the undisputed author, we have to leave some room for Schiller as a coauthor, much beyond the minor changes he obtained from Goethe at the last hour. In sum, there is a secondary author, a kind of subauthor, namely, the pair of friends, an idea that should help us to understand the work better. Thus, in order to be able to ask the more important questions concerning the nature and the ambition of the novel, we shall begin by retracing the living and vital relationship between the two authors, which represents a sort of microsocial foundation for the literary work.

THE RAPPROCHEMENT BETWEEN GOETHE AND SCHILLER

At first, the two men were quite distant from one another. They had never met, though they both contributed to the literature of *Sturm und Drang*. We know Schiller's feeling toward his great elder, so different from himself, from his letters to his friend and confidant Körner. He admires the genius at a distance; he does not like the man. Schiller goes so far as to candidly admit his jealousy. While he must struggle hard in the pursuit of his ideal—consumed as he is by disease—and manages to produce something only in the utmost tension, nature, to him a cruel stepmother, seems to have given perfection by the armful to that figure who dominates him with all his serenity. "This man is in the way and constantly reminds me of the harshness of my destiny" (Schiller 1973: 109; trans. Herr 1923; 1:ix). Schiller is in Weimar when Goethe returns from Italy; he finds him distant, stiff-mannered, and secretive, and finally turns away.

Goethe later revealed the reason for this calculated coldness (*Erste Be-*

kanntschaft mit Schiller, 1817, in *Briefwechsel,* Staiger 1966: 11–14). Returning to Germany, he found a literary climate quite contrary to his definitive, "classical" orientation as it had crystallized in Italy. Thus, for instance, he detests Schiller's *Robbers,* in which "a powerful talent lacking in maturity had poured on the land in a powerful torrent the ethical and theatrical paradoxes from which I had precisely attempted to purify myself" (ibid., 11). He contemplates giving up everything: how could one ever get the better of these productions of genial value and wild form, when one is trying to nurture and communicate the purest intuitions?[1] There is even here a danger of artistic ruin for his friends Meyer and Moritz. Goethe avoids Schiller, who is his neighbor, and after the presentation of *Don Carlos* (1787) opposes all efforts to bring them together. Then appears Schiller's essay entitled "Grace and Dignity." According to Goethe, Schiller has happily embraced Kantism, which lifts the subject so high while seeming to limit it, and the proud sentiment of liberty and self-determination has rendered him ungrateful toward the great mother, who has certainly not treated him cruelly. Moreover, Goethe could also have perceived that some of the rather harsh judgments in the essay applied to him.

Goethe, on the contrary, tries to cultivate himself (*ausbilden*) in all the arts, as a practitioner in literature and as an amateur in the plastic arts; he strives to see nature as an independent, living order of production (*gesetzlich hervorbringend*) from the lowest to the highest. In sum, the two men are at the antipodes of each other . . . and yet, all these misunderstandings would dissipate and be replaced by a friendship that, according to Goethe, would go beyond all his wishes and hopes.

Here is how it happened, still according to Goethe. Schiller has gone to live in Jena, which is very close to Weimar. A natural science society has been founded there, which Goethe frequents, and once he meets Schiller there. By coincidence, they leave together.[2] The conversation can be summarized as follows.

1. We will use Goethe's expressions as much as possible. One will note the notion of an assumed superiority and the repetition of the idea of purity or purification; there is also an emphasis on the self-education of the artist.

2. In fact, it is likely that Schiller had just written a very ceremonious letter to Goethe to ask for his collaboration on the review he was preparing, *The Hours* (*Die Horen*). If that is the case, since the letter was dated 13 June 1794 and Goethe replied on 24 June, the meeting would have taken place between these two dates, and it is conceivable that it was not a coincidence that the two men left the meeting together: Schiller wanted to break through Goethe's reserve.

SCHILLER, *speaking of the session they are leaving.* —Such a fragmentary
way to see nature cannot hold the attention of the profane for very long.

GOETHE. —It can remain strange even for the initiate. There is another
way to view nature, however, this time as living and acting, by going
from the whole to the parts.

SCHILLER. —Really? And you maintain that this mode of consideration
necessarily results from experience?

They arrive at Schiller's house. Carried along by the conversation,
Goethe follows Schiller inside; he becomes animated and expounds his
Metamorphosis of Plants, with the help of a few strokes of the pen to depict
for Schiller a symbolic plant, the Original Plant (*Urpflanze*). Schiller listens
and watches intensely.

"But when I had finished," writes Goethe,

> he shook his head and said: "This is not an experience, it is an idea." I
> was disconcerted, somewhat vexed, for the point that separated us had
> been rigorously designated. The affirmation of *Grace and Dignity* came
> back to my mind, and with it something of the old resentment, but I con-
> tained myself and replied: "I can very well accommodate myself [*das
> kann mir sehr lieb sein*] with having ideas without knowing it, and even
> seeing them with my own eyes." Schiller, who had much more practical
> sense and manners than I, and who cared more about attracting than re-
> jecting me because of *The Hours* he was about to publish, replied as a
> consummate [*gebildete*] Kantian, and since my intransigent realism gave
> rise to many a pronounced disagreement, we struggled a lot and finally
> reached a truce. Propositions such as the following chagrined me com-
> pletely: How can there be an experience corresponding to an idea, since
> the characteristic of an idea is precisely that it could never be congruent
> to an experience? If he saw as an idea what I called experience, there
> must exist between them a mediation, a relation! However, the first step
> had been taken. Schiller had a great force of attraction, he would hold
> all those who approached him. I associated myself to his intentions and
> promised to give to *The Hours* many things that lay dormant with me
> and thus, through the radical and perhaps never appeasable rivalry
> [*Wettkampf*] between object and subject, we sealed an alliance that was
> never interrupted and produced a lot of good, for us and for others. For
> me in particular it was a new spring in which all things germinated hap-
> pily together, where seeds and boughs began to grow.

Thus begins the unique friendship testified to by the correspondence exchanged between June 1794 and Schiller's death in 1805, a correspondence

that Goethe was to release for posterity under the patronage of the king of
Bavaria in 1829.[3]

Goethe and Schiller will now progressively strengthen their union.
Goethe is in Jena from 20 to 23 July, and the two men have long meetings in
which, according to Schiller, they discuss "all aspects of art and aesthetics"
and share "the main ideas" they have "reached by different paths." These
ideas show an "unforeseen agreement," which opens the possibility of an
exchange fruitful for both of them (letter of Schiller to Körner, 1 September
1794). On 23 August, Schiller writes a long, still rather solemn letter to
Goethe in which he draws his intellectual portrait as a genius. Goethe is a
Greek mind born under Germanic skies, and Schiller analyzes the exceptional relation between the concrete and the abstract resulting from this
union. The letter is designed to completely disarm Goethe, and on the
whole it succeeds: Goethe answers on 27 August, flattered, probably a
little amused, but won over by the obvious sincerity of the letter, where, he
writes, "you draw the balance sheet of my existence with a friendly hand,
and where you show a sympathy which heartens me" (letter 5, Herr 1923,
1:9). He sees their recent conversations as inaugurating a new epoch in his
life. He congratulates himself on henceforth pursuing his way together
with Schiller, assures him of his high esteem, and presses him "to reveal the
movement of his mind, particularly in the last years." (We are no longer
dealing with the author of *The Robbers*!) Let them better each other's
knowledge, to work more easily in community (*gemeinschaftlich*). On 31
August, Schiller picks up the expression in a parallel letter in which he sa-
lutes the meeting of their two existences and describes himself in contrast
to Goethe; he is prone to speculation as well as to poetic creation, and now
that he finally knows how to discipline those two forces, he sees the disease
threatening to ruin his physical resources. He knows that his days are
counted: "It is rather unlikely that I will have the time to perfect in myself
the great and total revolution of my mind." The two poets exchange confidential texts. Trust has been established, the "work in community" has
begun.

The union was unexpected on both sides—for Goethe, who was not
aware of Schiller's evolution, and for Schiller, who desired a rapprochement
but did not believe Goethe capable of it. It is to the advantage of both men,

3. We will quote the correspondence in Lucien Herr's translation as much as possible
(Herr 1923) and the German text in the Insel edition (Staiger 1966). It is convenient to refer to
individual letters by their number, which is the same in both editions. Thus the complete reference will be of the form: letter 368, Herr 1923, 2:11; Staiger 1966: 302.

since each was encountering a difficult period, more or less sterile even for Goethe. In contrast with the isolation in which both had worked until then, the confident exchange and mutual support they experience in their friendship must actually represent for them a natural state of things: one has only to see with what eagerness Goethe, and then Schiller, evoke a community of work. They esteem one another and are conscious of dominating their times. They have the same enemies—the philistine, mediocre, and dilettante—and the review they will jointly animate will show a pronounced polemical aspect.

The correspondence between Goethe and Schiller echoes and extends their conversations. Goethe often visits Schiller for a few days at a time in Jena, which is only twelve miles from Weimar, during which time the two friends have long tête-à-têtes in which they freely exchange their views.

On a practical level, the first two or three years of the correspondence are filled with the preoccupations relating to their literary activity in the monthly review published by Schiller, which they prepare in common, *The Hours,* to which will soon be added an annual collection, *The Almanac of the Muses.* They also discuss extensively Goethe's main work at the time, *The Years of Apprenticeship of Wilhelm Meister.* Schiller would have liked to publish it in the review, but Goethe already had an arrangement with a publisher, and he sends the manuscript to the printer book by book. Schiller receives and comments on the successive books one by one. Goethe thanks him warmly for his comments and occasional criticisms, and encourages him to express himself fully. He said in the end that without Schiller he would not have been able to complete the work as he did (letter 185, Herr 1923, 1:249). On 9 December 1794, Schiller receives the first book already composed. He is enthusiastic, as is Humboldt, who is visiting him (letter 32). On 26 June 1796, Goethe sends, with pride and relief, the eighth and last book: the "great work" is now completed! Schiller can then consider the work as a whole. His correspondence swells up, long letters follow each other in quick succession between 28 June and 9 July, still with Goethe's encouragement (letters 177 to 189)—except for the last one, in which Schiller, imprudently encouraged by Goethe, suddenly goes so far as to demand a place for philosophy in the novel, claiming as it were for Wilhelm the benefit of a Kantian education. This is more than Goethe can bear.[4] He breaks contact, adopts dodging maneuvers, and finally sends the book to press on 16 August before settling in Jena to start a new work. Two months later, upon seeing the printed book—and the modifications made

4. Let us note that a year later, solicited by Goethe, Schiller will demand some philosophy in *Faust* (letter 329, 23 June 1797).

by Goethe following his advice—Schiller has nothing but praise for the novel (letter 230). The friendship is intact; the exchange between the two poets, which is vital for both of them, will go on until Schiller's death in 1805. Goethe has only fenced off what he felt was a trespass by Schiller on his personal ground. He will confess to Eckermann in 1829 he had "always needed an infinite strength of resistance to hold his own" (Herr 1923, 1:297, note by Herr).

Allow us to complete this general presentation by citing two letters from the beginning of 1798 in which the two poets confess to each other what their friendship has done for them (letters 398 and 399, Herr 1923, 3:6–8). Schiller, who is still working on *Wallenstein,* writes:

> It is obvious that I surpassed myself, and I owe it to my knowing you, for only the prolonged and frequent contact with a mind so different from mine and which I can consider at a distance to be an objective reality, and then the intense movement which draws me to it and the dual effort which I apply to contemplate it and simultaneously assimilate it in thought—only this fortunate circumstance could render me able to move back so far and in all directions the boundaries of my own nature.

And Goethe answers him:

> If I rendered you the service of being for you the representative expression of a good number of objective realities, in return you have brought me back from a too rigorously objective observation of the external world and its laws to withdrawal into myself. You have taught me to look with more attention at the complexity of the inner man, you have procured me a second youth and made of me once again the poet I had practically ceased to be.

BRIEF SUMMARY: WILHELM'S BECOMING

In order to be able to follow the exchange of views between the two friends, we shall first summarize the *Apprenticeship* very briefly, and only from the viewpoint of Wilhelm's becoming. We shall distinguish three very different parts.

The first five books have something of a picaresque novel. The young hero Wilhelm, son of bourgeois shopkeepers, has affinities for the theater. A deep aversion for bourgeois life and a serious sentimental crisis provoked by the unfaithfulness of his friend the actress Mariane have led him to join a small troupe of actors. There he leads a bohemian life in the midst of very lively contrasting characters, from Philine, an animated actress who enjoys life fully, a to a little girl named Mignon and the old harper, who are nostalgia and poetry incarnate and whom Wilhelm gathers into his troupe.

The troupe sojourns in a castle for a while and is later attacked by robbers. Wilhelm, who feels increasingly responsible for his friends, manages to get them hired in the city by a permanent theater, where, having reflected on Shakespeare, he directs *Hamlet* and plays the leading role. Is he successful? Quite the contrary, the whole thing appears as a misunderstanding. Wilhelm has already from time to time encountered mysterious strangers who seem to take a lot of interest in him and who wish to influence his development, and now they call upon him to leave the theater straightaway. The theater experience is bankrupt, this is symbolized by the death of Aurelie, a quixotic actress and a very close friend of Wilhelm's.

Book 6, entitled "Confessions of a Beautiful Soul," is apparently an aside skillfully connected to what precedes and follows. It is a long presentation of the inner life of a pietist lady, a counterpoint to the picturesque movement of theater life, and it actually brings up an indispensable element of reference for the subsequent equilibrium of the hero.

With the last two books, 7 and 8, the novel assumes a markedly didactic turn. We are now among provincial nobles, in the family of the "Beautiful Soul" of the preceding book, and Wilhelm discovers the Society of the Tower,[5] a small group of men responsible for the mysterious interventions of the first part, and who now avow themselves responsible for his education and grant him a certificate of apprenticeship and, with it, integration into their group. Wilhelm is now responsible for Felix, a healthy baby he has taken in who is actually his son, while, their sinister history exorcised, Mignon and the harper disappear, and with them their nostalgic poetry. Wilhelm errs once again by choosing Therese for his wife, a person with an exclusively practical mind—thus causing Mignon's death. He must indeed, according to the Tower, become an active man, a useful man, but it is Natalie who is destined for him. He had earlier caught a glimpse of her, as an ideal figure, an amazon; the niece of the Beautiful Soul of book 6, she is goodness incarnate, thus the Beautiful Soul par excellence. In the meantime, he is going to leave with his son, Felix, on a long journey to perfect his education.

That journey will be the subject of *Wilhelm Meister's Journeyman Years,* which Goethe wrote many years later (1829). In fact, in the *Journeyman Years* the description of a communitarian and pedagogical utopia and

---

5. The "Society of the Tower" evokes the vogue of Masonic lodges, or even secret societies, before the French Revolution. One notices that Goethe suggests, very deftly, that the society, while still active, belongs to the past. Although they exhibit great respect for their leader, the Abbé, the members of the next generation keep their distance vis-à-vis his ideas.

a number of disparate narratives gathered together by the author's fantasy relegate the story of Wilhelm and Felix to the background.[6]

THE NOVEL IN THE CORRESPONDENCE BETWEEN SCHILLER AND GOETHE

Let us turn in detail to the correspondence between Schiller and Goethe, which should help us familiarize ourselves with the novel and read it as it should be read. We have already said that some of the criticisms proposed by Schiller are similar to objections we could formulate today. More broadly, the correspondence will reveal the origin of some general traits in the novel that are different from what our contemporary sensibility would expect, such as its didacticism and the passive character of the hero.

Schiller comments on the novel as a whole between 28 June and 9 July 1796 (letters 177 to 188). We shall not mention his general praises and the studied progression of his criticisms, and we will systematize his remarks somewhat. In his penultimate letter in this series, on 8 July, he chooses two important points. First, the "machinery." He begins by justifying it:

> The novel, as it appears here, resembles an epic on more than one ac-
> count. Among other similarities, it uses a machinery which, in a certain
> sense, assumes the role of the gods and of fate as sovereign. The topic re-
> quired it. (letter 186, Herr 1923, 1:252)

The topic, says Schiller, is apprenticeship, which itself refers to mastery. But the hero cannot be aware of the idea of mastery: "it therefore must neces- sarily stay behind him to guide him"; there is a need for "a higher intel- ligence" to vigilantly accompany Meister, namely, "the powers of the Tower."

Goethe could have written all this himself. In general, the two friends are very anxious to properly define the literary genres in order to conform their works to them. Thus, it is important to characterize the novel, a new or modern genre, in relation to the classic genres of the epic and the drama. Goethe introduces in *Meister* itself a brief comparison between the novel and the drama. He is talking about *Hamlet,* in the seventh chapter of book 5:

> In the novel it is predominantly sentiments and events that are to be pre-
> sented, in drama, characters and deeds. The novel must move slowly and
> the sentiments of the main personage must, in some way or another,
> hold up the progression of the whole toward the conclusion. Drama

6. For an attempt at a global symbolic interpretation, see Charbonnel 1987.

must move quickly and the character of the hero must press toward the denouement and only be held up by the obstacles. The hero of a novel must be passive, or at least not active to a high degree; from the hero of a play we demand effective action and deeds. Grandison, Clarissa, Pamela, the Vicar of Wakefield, even Tom Jones are, if not passive, yet "retarding" [*retardierende*] personages, and all circumstances are to a certain extent fashioned after their dispositions of mind. (Pléiade: 652–53; cf. Goethe 1989*a*: 185–86).[7]

Similarly, Wilhelm appears to be a "passive" hero. In fact, we recognize here the interaction between subject and milieu characteristic of Bildung. Roy Pascal put it very well: "he meets a vast number of incidents and his character gives them a meaningful shape." "He develops in time . . . almost unconsciously he absorbs what an occurrence offers, and the result takes shape slowly or quickly, according to the tempo of his inward growth" (1956: 24–25). Moreover, the somewhat dull character of Wilhelm facilitates the reader's comprehension. Schiller emphasized this aspect:

> Wilhelm gathers in, so to speak, the spirit, the meaning, the substance of all that goes on around him, transforms every obscure feeling into an idea and a thought, expresses each individual thing in a more general formula, he brings home to us the meaning of all and, thereby fulfilling his own character, most perfectly fulfills the purpose of the whole. (letter 182, July 5, 1796, Herr 1923; 1:242; Pascal 1956: 25)

To sum up, as far as the character of the hero is concerned, the novel resembles an epic, as Schiller indicated in the beginning. By virtue of being closer to the epic than to the drama, the novel is a hybrid genre, or as Goethe will say, an "impure form" (letter 370). We shall see later that this

7. "Pléiade" refers to the French translation of *Meister* in the Bibliothèque de la Pléiade volume of Goethe's novels (Goethe 1954). Page numbers for an English-language version are also provided.

In a recent and very rich article ironically entitled "The Theatrical Mission of the *Lehrjahre*," Jane Brown points out the many common points between *Meister* and English novels, and shows as well that the mid-eighteenth-century English novel developed in continuity with Shakespeare's theater and particularly with *Hamlet*, to which novelists frequently, one would almost say normally, make reference. She insists on the fact that this development is fueled by a critique of neoclassical aesthetics, and she sees in *Meister* an attack against such an aesthetics. Thus, as far as the requirement for verisimilitude in the theater is concerned, Fielding mocked it by ridiculing a spectator taking the ghost in Hamlet seriously, and Goethe went further by having Wilhelm, playing the role of Hamlet, believe for a moment that the ghost's voice is that of his own father (Pléiade: 667; Goethe 1989*a*: 195; Brown 1983: 78–80).

Perhaps can one note here that afterward Goethe, in *Poetry and Truth*, made a comparison, on the whole similar, between *Hamlet* and later English literature, with which he was very familiar. But there it is mainly a matter of poetry and its sinister aspects, in relation to the *mal de vivre* of the young contemporaries of Werther.

idea surfaces often in the correspondence. Moreover, the exchange of views on the drama and the epic is not limited to *Meister;* it is most lively in 1797 (letters 300 and following), about Goethe's *Hermann and Dorothea* and Schiller's great drama *Wallenstein,* and concludes at the end of the year (letters 391–95). Goethe encloses in a letter a short study signed with both their names in which he generalizes from the preceding discussion, and that Schiller discusses. Goethe distinguishes now five kinds of motifs, three of which are common to both genres.[8] The old "retarding" motif has been decomposed and only the "regressive" motif remains foreign to drama. Schiller insists on the mixture of traits, on the proportion between them and on the general effect. Jane Brown justifiably concludes (1983: 69–70, after Blackall 1976) that the difference between the genres posited in *Meister* is later relativized by Goethe, and even finally erased.

Naturally, if the two friends discussed literary genres with such seriousness, it was because of a practical interest. It was for the benefit of the work that they thought it advantageous to observe the rules that preside over the elaboration of these genres. We find a passage in his letter of 7 July (letter 185, Herr 1923, 1:249) in which Goethe, thanking his friend for his help, reveals something of how their conversations affected his work.

> . . . it is beyond doubt that, without our friendly relations, I should not have been able to bring the work to conclusion, at least in the manner I did it. A hundred times, while I was conversing with you of theoretical problems and concrete examples, I had present in my mind some of the dramatic situations that are now under your eyes, and I was judging them silently in the light of the principles on which we were busy coming to agreement.

We can imagine the scene: the two poets are discussing, perhaps, problems of the novelistic genre from the vantage point of the difference between drama and epic. Goethe applies the insights to a situation in *Meister* that he has in mind but is careful not to mention. We could have guessed from the correspondence at the kind of prudent reserve maintained by Goethe, even in his relationship with Schiller. It is now revealed: beyond the effusions, the artist jealously guards the secret of the work in gestation.[9]

What does the correspondence say on the relation of *Meister* with

8. The study is enclosed with letter 391. It is found only in the German edition (Staiger 1966: 521–24).

9. One sees that Schiller was attempting to pierce this reserve in a passage where he writes: "You can well see that the confidences you told me concerning your *Hermann* while you were working on it, have absolutely not compromised its unity and purity" (letter 369, Herr 1923, 2:281; Staiger 1966: 492).

drama, and with theater in general? More than a year later, having read
again both *Hermann* and *Meister,* Schiller sharpens his critique, in contrast
to his unqualified praise of *Hermann and Dorothea,* to the point of declaring peremptorily:

> There is, without the shadow of a doubt, too many tragic artifices in
> your *Meister,* I am speaking here of the vague forebodings, of the incom-
> prehensible, of the innerly wonderful, all things which . . . [are not]
> compatible with the excellent clarity which fills your novel. (letter 367,
> Herr 1923, 2:278)

We are dealing here with traits that are common to the drama and the epic
(cf. Goethe, in Staiger 1966: 520, 523) but foreign to the pure understanding to which the novel belongs, according to Schiller. Already in the first
letter we mentioned, that of 8 July 1796 (letter 186, Herr 1923, 1:254), he
criticized the pursuance of "a more theatrical end and by more theatrical
means than is necessary and allowed in a novel." Perhaps Schiller touches
here, inadvertently as it were, on the deep relation that there actually is between *Meister* and the theater, and that will become clear to us little by
little. But this is one aspect of a more general criticism. Let us return to the
letter from 8 July. Schiller began by justifying the "machinery"; he continues by criticizing the fact that it remains external, foreign to the novel.
He wishes that Goethe had "made clearer to the reader . . . the necessary
connection with the deep spirit of the work." It is not enough to provide, in
the eighth and last book of the novel, the *historical* key to all the events, one
also needs the *aesthetic* key "to the poetic necessity of all the parts of the
edifice," and "I myself," adds Schiller, "needed a second and a third reading to fully penetrate it." A few days earlier, upon communicating his first
general impression, he had written that he perceived the continuity but not
yet the unity of the work (letter 180, Herr 1923, 1:229). On this point he
shall more or less prevail, for, Goethe having answered that he could easily
have given the second part of the certificate of apprenticeship (letter 187),
Schiller insists that he do so (letter 189, Herr 1923, 1:265), and the final
version of the novel summarizes and excerpts this certificate in chapter 5 of
the eighth book (Pléiade: 880; cf. Goethe 1989a: 335–39).

Having thus criticized the absence of aesthetic unity resulting from the
treatment of the "machinery," Schiller gets to the second point of his critique. He has already given his first impression in these terms:

> Globally, what in my eyes is most striking is that gravity and pain slide
> by and vanish as a play of shadows, while a spiritual and light fantasy
> definitively and completely takes over. (letter 177, Herr 1923, 1:225)

On 8 July, Schiller goes a little further. He reproaches Goethe with having pushed the "free grace of play" of the imagination, or even of the theater, farther than is proper in a novel, thereby playing into the hands of the "weaker portion of the public." At the same time, Goethe insufficiently defined the apprenticeship and the mastery, remaining short of what is concretely presented in the novel, so that, if the fable is true and the moral also, the relationship between them is not evident. All this touches on Goethe's aesthetics. On the first point, Goethe admitted elsewhere his aversion for the purely tragic. The idea of writing a "true tragedy" terrifies him and he declares that he is "almost convinced that it could destroy me to even attempt it" (letter 384).[10] As to the criticism that he was not explicit enough, his answer contains a precious confession:

> The fault which you notice comes from my innermost nature, from a certain "realistic tic" that makes it seem pleasant to me to withdraw my existence, actions, and writings from men's eyes. (letter 187, Herr 1923, 1:259)

He adds that it is Schiller's urging alone that prevented him from giving in completely to this propensity as regards the novel, which, "considering the immense trouble I have taken over it . . . would have been unpardonable."

What Goethe calls his "realistic tic" is actually a tendency to use litotes, or more generally, understatements, which leads him to remain beneath what could be more categorically cleared up or more precisely expressed. It is an inclination altogether more aesthetic than philosophical.

We have just seen Goethe mention the difficulty of the task. He returns to it more than once. On 22 June (letter 172), as the work is nearing completion, he calls it "an almost impossible thing," and he adds on the 24th: "The demands this book places upon me are limitless, and cannot by the very nature of the topic obtain full satisfaction, and yet it is indispensable that everything be given its solution, at least up to a point" (letter 174, Herr 1923, 1:221). But when Schiller evokes fantasy triumphing over gravity and pain, Goethe declares that it is a testimony that "all things considered,

---

10. In response, Schiller, finding in his friend's works all the required tragic power and depth, and in "*Meister* itself, as far as sentiment is concerned, more than a tragedy," suggests that "what your nature loathes is simply the rigorous rectilinear line which the tragic poet must follow" (letter 385, Herr 1923, 2:309). On this theme, see the remarkable essay by Erich Heller, "Goethe and the Avoidance of Tragedy", in Heller 1961: 33–55. In book 10 of *Poetry and Truth*, concerning Herder's reading the *Vicar of Wakefield*, Goethe declares his "agreement with this ironic disposition which is lifted above things, above happiness and misfortune, good and evil, death and life, and which thereby attains the possession of a genuinely poetic world." This description applies to Goethe himself and to the consciousness he has of himself.

I have managed in this production to adapt what is in conformity with my own nature to what the nature of the work demands" (letter 178, Herr 1923, 1:227).

We see here another aspect of the complexity or of the hybrid character of *Meister*. Goethe feels that he had to conciliate opposite demands, those of his own aesthetics and those resulting from the nature of the work. Other passages can be read similarly. Thus, in December 1794, while thanking Schiller for his favorable judgment of the first book, Goethe writes: "After the strange vicissitudes this production has encountered from without and from within, it would not be surprising if I had completely tangled the threads" (letter 33, trans. M. Arnault, Goethe 1924: 12). And he adds: "I have finally remained as close as possible to my idea, and I would be pleased if you helped me out of this labyrinth" (letter 33, Herr 1923, 1:50; cf. letter 163, May 1796). We shall encounter the external vicissitudes later. The inner ones are likely to be related to what has just been recalled. Then, much later, Goethe will confide to Eckermann: "This work ranks among the most incalculable productions. I myself have almost lost the key to it. One arduously searches for a center without ever succeeding" (quoted in Goethe 1924: 10). (Let us add, in order not to exaggerate the impact of this last judgment, that Goethe consoles himself by observing that everything in it is in the last analysis symbolic.)

According to Goethe himself, he overcame the difficulties thanks to Schiller's friendship and assistance. He says it more than once (cf. above, letter 185). We should not forget what a great role Schiller played in the gestation of the work. While expressing his agreement with Goethe, he delicately pointed out in what sense, according to him, the evolution of the hero was truly an education. Wilhelm finally finds "his place in a beautiful median human region equidistant from unregulated fantasy and philistinism" (letter 181, Herr 1923, 1:240). In a fine page of which we can only give an incomplete idea here, Schiller identifies "the ultimate goal that Wilhelm attains after a long series of errors." "From an empty and confused ideal, he progresses toward an active and precise life, without losing in this passage the power which creates the ideal." "The two opposite paths which tend to deviate from this state of satisfaction [i.e., an ungrounded inwardness and an activity devoid of ambition] are described in the novel" (letter 186, Herr 1923, 1:256). In the end, Wilhelm, now anchored in reality thanks to his son, Felix, "but without relinquishing his admirable mobility," appears "engaged on a path which will lead him to limitless perfection" (257). We see that for Schiller the hero has indeed been educated in some measure.

In the end, it is clear that the two friends agreed on certain aesthetic conceptions as well as on a didactic intention. We possess another testimony of this aesthetic and didactical convergence, in the complete approval down to the practical level that Goethe expressed concerning Schiller's first *Letters on the Aesthetic Education of Man* (letters 20 and 22). It is clear that the teaching of the *Letters* and that of *Meister* are not identical, they may even seem to be at odds, but one should take into account the different levels on which the works bear: their orientation is similar concerning their articulation to social life.

The didacticism that pervades *Meister*, and that makes the second part of the work rather strange to us, reflects the aesthetic attitude of the two poets, who are at the time busy affirming what has been called their "classicism"[11] against the ambient mediocrity, against utilitarianism, and especially against the risk of an unregulated inwardness, of an abandon to the *Schwärmerei*, the famous German reverie, about which Grillparzer will note later (in 1828), thinking of Novalis:

> That the Germans attribute so high a value to this unsteady dreaming, this capacity for boding without clear image or idea, is the very misfortune of this nation. . . . They think it is something proper to their nation, but other peoples know this state of mind too, only with them boys in the end grow into men. I do not speak as one to whom this dreamy daze is strange, for it is my state. But at least I recognize that one must work one's way up out of it if anything is to be achieved. Monks and hermits may intone "Hymns to the Night," but active men need the light. (Grillparzer 1916: 327; translated in Pascal 1956: 19)

It is ironic to notice that in this same page of his notes, Grillparzer sees Novalis as a "Wilhelm Meister without terminal leave, forever entangled in his years of apprenticeship."

Goethe and Schiller were united, after all, against what they perceived more or less as the threat of a romanticism. This is why Schiller naturally adopted Goethe's idea that the novel, instead of portraying an artist, should depict a common man who believes he is an artist, and then open his eyes and show him the reasonable way to self-accomplishment. Hence, the down-to-earth pedagogical aspect that brought Goethe so much trouble. Schiller began by praising the alliance of fantasy and realism, but ended by writing, on 8 July 1796 (letter 186, Herr 1923, 1:254): "It seems

11. Let us borrow from the study by Jane Brown quoted above a suggestion concerning a definition of German classicism as "a sort of compromise between Neoclassicism and Romanticism" (Brown 1983: 83).

to me that you have pushed the free grace of this game a little farther than poetic gravity requires."

Eventually, the two friends will suddenly split on this very issue of didacticism. Until then, Goethe not only agrees with his friend's criticisms but also praises their relationship as "unique in the world" (7 July, letter 185, Herr 1923, 1:249). Finally, on 9 July, 1796, he enumerates seven modifications that he proposes to introduce and apologizes for his "realistic tic" with unexpected exaggeration:

> And if it came to happen—since men's shortcomings are unfortunately insurmountable—that with the best will in the world I should be unable to proffer the last indispensable words, I request that, to put an end to it, you add with a few bold strokes of your brush what the bizarre fate which holds me in bondage will have prevented me from saying. Do continue to send me this week again your criticisms and your suggestions. (letter 187, Herr 1923, 1:261)

These were very unwise words. Thus prodded, Schiller loses all restraint. The same day, he decides to go to the end of his thought. His 9 July letter sounds bombastic and sententious (less, however, than it appears in Lucien Herr's strange "translation," in which these traits are heavily exaggerated —probably as a result of the translator's strong antipathy toward Schiller, which surfaces in the foreword). Schiller writes:

> I would therefore strongly advise you not only to leave aside this half of the Certificate of apprenticeship, but also to introduce in it, more or less explicitly, the philosophical content of the work. (Staiger 1966: 246; my translation)

The word has been let out: for Schiller, the novel, being a product of understanding, must deliver its own key in rational terms. He insists:

> . . . I have to confess that it is rather cavalier, in our times of metaphysical speculation, to write a novel of such content and broad extent, in which the "only thing which is necessary" is so silently expedited. . . . (ibid., 247; Herr 1923, 1:265, modified translation)

Schiller moreover develops a coherent argument, which can be summarized as follows: everyone needs the help of philosophy, except Goethe, for whom aesthetics suffices (by a kind of divine gift, which is not mentioned here). But the exception cannot be extended from Goethe to Wilhelm, who therefore needs philosophy. The reasoning is formally correct, since, in the novel, it is precisely a matter of making Wilhelm realize that he had no artistic vocation.

This is too much for Goethe, who breaks contact: he uses the "strength of resistance," which he will later tell Eckermann that he had needed "infinite" amounts of, "not to give in" (Herr 1923, 1:297 n). At first, he pretends to believe that Schiller is requesting a sequel, and he says that they shall discuss it (letter 191). He then visits Jena from 16 to 19 July, but the novel is almost not mentioned; it is "taking a nap" (Goethe, 30 July). Eventually, on 10 August (letter 208, Herr 1923, 1:295–97), Goethe indicates, with a little irony, that he has tried to take Schiller's observations into account, but he adds:

> I would almost be tempted to send the work to press without your looking at it anymore. The difference between our natures is such that it will never be able to satisfy entirely your demands. . . . (Staiger 1966: 271–72, my translation; cf. Herr 1923, 1:296)

The planned departure for Jena is postponed. Six days later, Goethe finally sends the last book to press and announces his departure for Jena. He will stay there for a month and a half. To Schiller's amazement, during that time he will write the first four chants—that is, almost half—of *Hermann and Dorothea,* which represents that miracle: a bourgeois epic.

It is clear that this is Goethe's spontaneous reaction to the constraints he had imposed upon himself to complete *Meister.* The correspondence of the following year confirms it. Upon receiving a printed copy of *Hermann,* Schiller praises its "achieved perfection in its genre." By contrast, he stresses once more the hybrid character of *Meister,* which lacks a certain "amount of poetic boldness" because it is a novel and, since the author is a poet, "a certain settled sobriety (which we may yet rightfully demand, to a point)" (letter 367). Goethe answers concerning *Meister:*

> . . . all this is true and even more. It is precisely its imperfection which gave me the most trouble. A pure form helps and supports, while an impure form constricts and pulls about everywhere. But let it remain as it is. I shall no longer be so easily mistaken about topic and form, and we shall see what our good genie will grant us at the end of our life. (Herr 1923, 2:283; modified translation)

This disavowal of the novel is exceptional and probably only momentary in Goethe. It is clearly connected to the revenge he enjoyed with his epic. We may also discern a bit of temper, as if he had understood that he had been

led to that situation by his didacticism, or more precisely by the didacticism
of his friend, which had reinforced his own.

FROM THE THEATRICAL MISSION TO *MEISTER'S*
APPRENTICESHIP

An unpublished text by Goethe, discovered at the beginning of this century,
helps shed light on the genesis of the *Apprenticeship* and allows us a better
grasp of the author's intention. It is part of a work entitled *Wilhelm Meister's Theatrical Mission,* which represents a primitive form of the novel,
written during the first part of Goethe's stay in Weimar. He will use it years
later, after his Italian journey, and turn it into the first four books of the
Apprenticeship. To begin with, this text represents an intermediary stage in
Goethe's work between *Werther* and the *Apprenticeship,* a transition that
reduces for us the discontinuity between them. Also, the comparison between the two versions of *Meister* should allow us to ground somewhat our
interpretation of the later one, "incalculable" as it is according to Goethe
himself.

The hero of the *Theatrical Mission* is in many regards similar to the author: when he was a child, a family puppet theater aroused in him a passion
for the theater and the vocation of a dramatic poet—which is what also
happened to Goethe himself, according to his autobiography. But the family is less refined than Goethe's; the father especially has narrowly mercan-
tile concerns, and the young bourgeois Wilhelm feels spiritually alienated
in his milieu. A tragic love affair and a series of events lead him to join a
troupe of traveling actors. He is thus thrown into the beginnings of an acting career, and he eventually joins a professional troupe. The half of the
work that has survived allows us to surmise that the hero is promised a high
destiny. His name even evokes William Shakespeare, who was both an author and an actor, and the "master" (*Meister*) of the English theater; Wilhelm takes Shakespeare as a model as soon as he discovers him. In short, it
seems that Meister's mission is to give Germany a national theater.

Beyond the parallel with Goethe, who at the time in Weimar expects a
lot from the theater, Wilhelm is here, in the perspective inherited from the
Sturm und Drang, a representative of Genius. Yet, he is no longer a sensitive or passive Genius who clashes against the outer world and is destroyed
by it, like Werther, but rather a creative personality, an active Genius who
faces the world, naively perhaps, but courageously and, in the end, effectively. As in the life of Goethe himself, there is in Wilhelm, in the *Theatrical
Mission,* an adaptation or the beginning of an adaptation of the genial personality to the world; the relationship between the subjectivity and its envi-

ronment is now constructive instead of destructive. It is art that allows this relationship, and, very symbolically, it is the art of the stage, it is theater as the representation of life, as the mediation between the creative spirit and everyday life. It is on the level of the theater that the Genius gets reconciled with the world in order to leave his imprint on it.

Now, it is precisely on this point that the *Apprenticeship* introduces a break, a radical discontinuity, with the *Theatrical Mission*—and by the same token with *Werther*. We should not be deceived by the fact that the name of the hero remains the same: he is no longer the same man. Wilhelm is no longer genial; he is now a common man. It is true that he still goes through the experience of the theater, but it is no longer in order to develop himself but finally to escape from it, as from a dead end into which he has strayed. This indicates a radical change in the author's intention, on which we shall have to insist.

However, we would first like to single out a point that went unnoticed, except by Hegel,[12] and that remains common to the *Mission* and to the *Apprenticeship* beyond the differences between the two Wilhelms. Whether the young man is a genius or not and whether his vocation is genuine or not, we see that he first distances himself from the social milieu he grew up in, in order later to adapt to social life under a new form. It is true that Goethe does not insist on the social aspect of this break, or defection, but rather concentrates on the depiction of the relation of the subject to others from the vantage point of the development of his personality. Yet, in order to situate the novel within modern culture, we have to bring into relief the underlying theme of the rebellion of adolescence and subsequent reconciliation, since, through it, *Meister* participates in a phenomenon of great magnitude, which is encountered and in a way acknowledged throughout mankind, and to which our own culture is deeply indebted.

We could perhaps find the principle of all this in the customary distance between father and son and contiguous generations in general. In tribal societies, very generally, kinship terminologies distance children from their parents, and conversely draw grandparents and grandchildren closer together or even identify them with each other; it seems that among Australian aborigines, in particular, the alternation of generations should be held as a structural principle of the first order (Dumont 1983: 200–201). In

12. In a page of the *Aesthetics* that Lukács quotes at length, Hegel vigorously stresses and develops this theme of adolescent rebellion—which he links to chivalry—and of the return to reality through the education (*Erziehung*) of the "years of apprenticeship." As Lukács points out, Hegel cannot but have been thinking of *Meister*, even though he speaks of a general social phenomenon (Hegel 1979, 2:347–48; Lukács 1947:40).

these systems, the continuity between generations is obtained only after making allowance for their alternation. Now, we encounter everywhere, down to the moderns, enough parallel behavioral traits to assume that an underlying universal disposition is present here. (It is pleasant to remark that Goethe introduces a clear opposition between generations in Wilhelm's family: the father straightaway sells off the art collection the grandfather has assembled.)

But in our modern individualistic societies the major phenomenon corresponding to the alternation of generations occurs on the level of individual development. An identity crisis is under way during adolescence when the subject must either define himself within the boundaries of the societal role he is assigned, or else find another role altogether, thereby rejecting his relatives' expectations, his father's especially. In the latter case a transitional period opens, characterized by maladjustment, irresponsibility, and even rebellion, which can be lengthy and will close only upon the readaptation of the subject to society in a role he accepts. This is what Hegel called the "years of apprenticeship," and the sarcastic tone he uses to mention it seems to indicate an allusion to personal experience (Hegel 1979, 2:347–48).

This crisis of adolescence is not without its effect on the culture. In an important book, Erik Erikson showed how the Reformation stemmed from it, how Luther first used the monastery against his father and finally, after a long "moratorium," destroyed the monastery itself in the name of the immediate relation of the Christian individual to his God (Erikson 1958). In an unpublished lecture, Jerrold Seigel, an emulator of Erikson, applied a similar analysis to two other "radical thinkers," Saint Augustine and Karl Marx.[13] From the example of these three geniuses, we realize what promises of innovation are contained in the adolescent crisis of identity.

We can expect to see this phenomenon proliferate in our societies, which contradictorily combine excessive specialization and a secondary education that still promotes individualistic universalism and the ideal of the *honnête homme*. The rebellion of the student and of the young intellectual would seem to be the natural outcome of this situation, and such rebellion can become a mass phenomenon, as in Paris in May 1968.

All this perhaps allows us to speak of a general background against which Goethe develops his own themes in the *Apprenticeship*, and, as far as

13. I must here warmly thank Professor Carl Schorske, who very kindly supplemented my failing memory and thereby contributed to a better orientation of this development.

we know, in the *Theatrical Mission* as well. But let us now return to the relation between the two works.

While the theater was to allow a younger brother of Werther's to develop his innate skills and thereby reconcile himself with the world, now, another young man with the same name, who is honest and full of goodwill, open and sensitive, but devoid of particular aptitudes, undergoes the apprenticeship of life, which poses the problem of Bildung in all its extent and generality. How can we understand Goethe's decision to alter his novel so deeply? But we are still stating the problem in the wrong terms: the new work is radically different from the previous one, in terms of both content and intention; it simply uses the earlier work as available material upon which to erect something new. The *Apprenticeship* proceeds from Goethe's decision to deliver a message relating to the common man rather than to present the story of the adaptation of a young genius to the world. We should understand this capital decision. In order to attempt to do so, we need a series of remarks.

First of all, it is clear that this decision is linked to the change in Goethe's ideas resulting from his Italian journey. Goethe now perceives himself as a child of Nature, he has emancipated himself from the absolute distinction between subject and object, and he has learned, in the perspective of his self-development, to conjoin the pursuit of his craft and an objective and devout study of nature (cf. *The Metamorphosis of Plants*). On the literary level, it can be seen in *Torquato Tasso* that he has abandoned the notion of the Genius withdrawn into himself. Henceforth, what the exegetes will call "the ideal of Humanity" prescribes that each individuality grow and reveal its universal value by opening up to the action of the environment, by enriching itself through contact with all forms of ambient life (Wundt 1932: 169).

At the same time, the first consequence of this transition from the Genius to the common man is the increased distance separating the author from his hero. Goethe obviously no longer identifies with the Wilhelm of the *Apprenticeship* as he did with the hero of the *Theatrical Mission*. Wilhelm is no longer an irresistible and sparkling personality, the "dear dramatic portrayal" of the author (Goethe 1924: 21 n). Upon rereading the novel much later, Goethe will call the hero "a poor dog" and add, "[B]ut it is only in such a being that one can clearly show the successive phases of life and its numerous and diverse duties—rather than in 'beings who are already formed and firm'" (*Conversations with the Chancellor F. von Müller*" [1821], Goethe 1930: 72). In the same conversation, Goethe explains how painful his "constant effort toward the most universal" has been. This is because he could never completely cease to identify with his hero. We notice that Wilhelm has not ceased to be liked by women; and in a letter to Schiller, speaking of his modesty—what he calls his "realistic tic"— Goethe naively writes that he almost could not bring himself to mention favorably, even in passing, Wilhelm's physical appearance (letter 187, Herr 1923, 1:260). The fact remains that Goethe no longer tells about himself, even under a broadened or abstract form. Dealing with the common man, Genius prescribes or legislates, inevitably and, as he is careful to add, *up to a point*. As author, he affirms himself through the liberties he takes in composition, in step with the literature of his time. Thus, he interrupts the course of the story to insert the autobiography of a pietist lady, the "Confessions of a Beautiful Soul," which occupies the whole of book 6. Much later, he will develop the device to the extreme with the *composition à tiroirs* of the *Journeyman Years*. We shall have to remember this marked presence of the author beside his hero when we review the attitude of posterity vis-à-vis the work.

Given the deeply innovative character of the *Apprenticeship,* it is surprising to see how much of the *Mission* Goethe actually preserves in it. He strips Wilhelm of his theatrical mission and yet leaves him his theater adventures. Though in a greatly modified form, they fill most of the work, five out of eight books. The reader will not complain about this, given the liveliness and the animation of the first part—which recalls the *Theatrical Mission* from which it originated—in contrast with the subsequent chapters, where rather shady but quite lively characters are replaced by abstract and vague figures, in the name of the ideal (Butler 1935: 123). We can surmise that Goethe also had a weakness for this motley group of characters, this small traveling theater troupe whose "objective" presentation as a social microcosm was also in line, in his mind, with the "epic" perspective the novel as a genre demanded.

We certainly also need to state a biographical element. It so happens that the false theatrical vocation he was now attributing to Wilhelm Goethe had in fact encountered in the person of Karl Philipp Moritz, whom he had met in Rome in 1786–88 and whom he liked to treat as a younger brother. Let us recall here the originality of the aesthetics of Moritz, to which we devoted chapter 5. Moritz had by this time published three of the four books of *Anton Reiser,* a rather miserabilist autobiography, the story of an endlessly humiliated and starving youth who finds solace in poetry and theater. This turns out to be, for lack of real skills, a false vocation, as Moritz will explicitly state in the introduction to the fourth book, published in

1790 (French trans. Moritz 1986: 319). It is easy to imagine that Goethe helped him distinguish or strengthen this insight, but the influence was probably reciprocal (Bruford 1933: 36). Whatever the distance between Moritz and Meister, it is clear that the meeting with Moritz has, to say the least, catalyzed in Goethe the transformation bearing on the place of the theater and the personality of the hero.

In a more limited way, another encounter probably influenced some aspects of the *Apprenticeship,* namely, that with Wilhelm von Humboldt. This paragon of Bildung was staying in Jena precisely at the time of Goethe's writing, and while it is true that the relationship with Schiller was more intimate, Humboldt was also for Goethe a valued interlocutor. Impossible for us, who have made his acquaintance, not to see some traits of Humboldt in the nobleman Goethe depicts in book 5 in Wilhelm's important letter to Werner, which we shall encounter later on.

But let us not be mistaken: the meetings with Humboldt and even with Moritz are only anecdotal elements that have come so to speak to strengthen Goethe's decision to choose a universally significant hero or topic—in the German context of course. This decision, moreover, although it is based on the Italian experience, is essentially located on the *literary level.* Remarkably, the first important work arising out of the genial subject's reconciliation with nature, i.e., out of Goethe's own Bildung (Gundolf 1922: 337), is a novel that depicts the apprenticeship to life of an ordinary man. In such a situation, we should probably admit in principle that the author has here satisfied a deep need, which we have still to discover. It is certain at least that this need corresponded to his literary objective, we would say today to his literary strategy, at the time. Goethe began to rewrite the novel shortly before his meeting with Schiller, in the same state of mind he was in when the two friends inaugurated their militant association. Goethe was determined, since his stay in Italy, to unite subjectivity and objectivity in his life and in his work. He also had the premonition of an eventual drift of unbridled subjectivity in line with the *Sturm und Drang,* from which he had distanced himself, and he intended to fight against it and against that propensity to divagate (*Schwärmerei*) that Grillparzer would later avow as the true misfortune of the German nation (see above). The novel even seems to suggest that Goethe perceived a social danger in this German bent toward an unbalanced inwardness. The genre of the novel was well suited to the treatment of this theme, notably because, according to the conventions of the time, it allowed some didacticism, but also because it required a down-to-earth realism. We have seen the two friends, as good classicists, anxious to define this literary genre, closer to the epos than to the drama, in order to give firmness to their writing. Among other things, the epic hero is passive, and we previously cited Goethe's after-the-fact justification of Wilhelm's passivity and insignificance in terms of didactic necessity (Goethe 1930: 272).

But while we think we perceive what he attempted—something akin to sending the dreamers back to gainful occupation—we still have to ask what internal necessity this work, which was so arduous to write, satisfied for Goethe himself. To understand this, we should perhaps transfer the problem inside the author and ask whether Goethe was struggling against something entirely foreign to himself. Obviously not: he had had to tear himself free from pure subjectivity; he had found within himself enough strength to overcome it by means of an unremitting effort—to which his whole life testifies—toward Bildung, that is, toward self-development in the intimacy of nature, in the interaction of subject and object. Just as he would devote as much time and effort to works he believed to be scientific as he would to literary works, similarly, at the turn of the 1790s, he wanted to use a prosaic, realist, "objective" form of literature not only to deliver a social message but also to distance himself personally from a disorderly inwardness.[14] In an indirect form, the author remains present in *Meister*, there is still something of him in the figure of Wilhelm. Without this abstract but deep identification, without this commitment, it would be hard to understand the subsequent immense resounding of the work.

There is one point that requires specification: we have supposed that Goethe had perceived a social danger in the eventual generalization of an unbridled subjectivity. He seemingly perceived the danger menacing educated young Germans of a complete dissociation from social reality, and he wanted to contribute to bringing them back to it and to anchoring them in it. This social aim will be more readily apparent in the *Journeyman Years,* the novel's later sequel, although it is already present to some degree here in a very general way. The Society of the Tower is in the process of becoming an instrument for social reform and the development of resources. The novel ends with several marriages, which, as Schiller approvingly points out, are misalliances from the viewpoint of the ancien régime. The model hero of the last two books, Lothario, fights for American independence, contemplates granting land rights to the peasants who reside on his estates,

14. Only three years after writing *Werther,* Goethe wrote a comedy, *The Triumph of Sensitivity,* to ridicule the sentimentality à la Werther that was then in fashion. The play was given in Weimar in January 1778 (cf. Goethe 1988: 1606 ff.).

and engages in agricultural improvement schemes. These are traits that very subtly recall the proximity of the French Revolution.[15]

Two external facts support this view. As soon as he was relieved from the burden of his novel, Goethe began to write *Hermann and Dorothea*, in which, he says, he "strove to show how the great movements and changes which were taking place on the great stage of the world were reflected in a small mirror" (letter cited in the French ed., Goethe 1947: xxxiv). In chant 6, he exalts the ideals of the French Revolution before depicting its evils and condemning in the very last verses of the poem the idealism of Dorothea's first fiancé, who, having left for Paris, was jailed and died there: "Germans ought not to propagate this terrible movement . . . We must hold firm and last." We see that in this epic the poet takes position completely, a position in essence similar to that of Kant's or Schiller's.

On this point also the agreement between Goethe and Schiller needs to be emphasized. While Goethe works on the *Apprenticeship*, Schiller publishes the *Letters on the Aesthetic Education of Man*, in which, starting from the failure of the Revolution, and with the goal of enabling its ideals to be put effectively into practice in the future, he proposes a moral transformation of mankind through aesthetic education. We know that Goethe explicitly approved of the *Letters* in their first part. While granting that the *Letters* and *Meister* are not working on the same level and do not give the same place to Beauty, we must obviously admit that they are parallel and must be considered compatible, on the plane of the German reaction to the great contemporary upheaval or, to be more precise, on the plane where German culture integrates the German experience of the French Revolution into its own constitution.

In other words, it is impossible not to search in *Meister* for a message relating to the French Revolution. It may be found in two aspects. On the one hand, as Lukács noted, the Society of the Tower constitutes a kind of utopian island in which Goethe sets, within the German world, a minuscule equivalent of the French social reform—although this particular aspect will be developed only in the *Journeyman Years*. (We see clearly, against Lukács, that it is a matter altogether different from the rise of the bour-

---

15. Before the *Apprenticeship* Goethe had written three plays about the French Revolution. It matters little to us that they have been forgotten, and probably justifiably so. We see here the sign of his preoccupation with the Revolution, which he himself confesses, writing after the lack of success of the first of these plays: "What preoccupied me internally kept appearing to me in a dramatic form" (Goethe 1988: 1665; cf. the complete commentary, ibid., 1660–84).

geoisie.) On the other hand, and above all, we think of the hero and his becoming. It seems that Goethe had perceived and feared a potential link between the literary tendencies he combated and the revolutionary idealism he condemned in Dorothea's fiancé—in other words, a possible transition from the individualism and the *Schwärmere* inherited from the *Sturm und Drang,* which would blossom in romanticism, to a political commitment such as that of Georg Forster, who, after having taken an active part in the revolution in Mainz, died heartbroken in Paris in 1794. It is perhaps by surmising in Goethe the association of literary and aesthetic objectives on the one hand, and a national, and indirectly political, preoccupation on the other, that we can best understand the great care he took in portraying his hero, now a common man who must absolutely be brought to accept his place in the community.

We can even go a little further, at the risk of anticipating what we shall discuss later. We probably have to grant critics that the development of Wilhelm's personality is still incomplete at the end of the novel, since Goethe does consider writing a sequel. However, a decisive point has been gained. Wilhelm, who was running away from society into the theater, now reintegrates society proper. Not quite, you will say, since the society he now enters differs from the one he left. The distinction between social ranks or orders is symbolically abolished—let us recall the four "misalliances"— and values are different. This point was noticed by Roy Pascal: the transformation of the hero is accompanied by a transformation of society.[16] There is here a complementarity that supposes an equivalence of function, an underlying equivalence between Bildung and the French Revolution, on which we shall have to ponder.

In sum, the French Revolution must be taken into account in order to understand the genesis of *The Years of Apprenticeship of Wilhelm Meister* out of the previous *Theatrical Mission.*

A FEW LESSONS

Thanks to the *Theatrical Mission* and to the correspondence with Schiller, we are now somewhat more familiar with the *Apprenticeship* and Goethe's intent. That this intent was in great part didactical is clear. We can therefore continue our inquiry by attempting to grasp the lesson that should emanate from the work. Since, according to common opinion, this is a matter of Bildung, in what exactly does this Bildung consist? There is no unani-

16. Roy Pascal rightly shows that Wilhelm can agree to the unilaterality that results from the division of labor only because he joins a society founded in a completely new spirit, in which the best of the nobility and of the bourgeoisie are united (1956: 10–11).

mous agreement on this today, and the traditional viewpoint has been radically questioned in Kurt May's long and carefully argued article (May 1957). We have already alluded to it, in particular to acknowledge that Wilhelm's personal development is not completed but only underway at the end of the novel. May's central thesis is that when the book ends, Wilhelm does not exhibit a harmoniously developed personality (in the sense of the Bildung of Winckelmann, Herder, Schiller, and Humboldt). May concludes that there is no Bildung here; that, moreover, Goethe did not attempt to put any here; and that posterity, by assuming he did, was purely and simply mistaken. To this, we could already oppose that Bildung cannot be reduced to an end result, that it is also, and first of all, a *process*—as in Humboldt, for instance. Where May is right in his assertion is that it is impossible to apply the established concept of Bildung to Goethe's novel: we ourselves also noted that Bildung was contradicted in the novel: Meister is not Humboldt. May's argument is quite formal: he demands, for instance, a harmonious alliance between the religious, aesthetic, and ethical aspects of Bildung, to which we shall come back later. Hence the idea of proceeding here in an opposite fashion in order to identify the teaching of the *Apprenticeship:* we shall try to isolate a few concrete lessons that, once gathered, could give us a more precise idea of Wilhelm's development than Schiller's remarks, while avoiding preconceived formulations.

If we seek to find out what Wilhelm's development between the beginning and the end of the novel consists of, we can perhaps isolate three main changes. As we have seen with the *Theatrical Mission,* it is essential that Wilhelm decides not to place himself under the banner of art, in other words, that he renounces the theater for life itself. But Wilhelm had found that the theater represented for him the means to develop into a complete human being, to constitute himself into a self-sufficient totality. The activity on the stage was for him a kind of Bildung. It is therefore essential to see what is going to replace it. We find that Wilhelm joins a group, becomes a member in a collective totality. This presupposes a profound transformation in the relation, quite essential for the novelist, of the subject to the world, of the self to others, which is exhibited in Wilhelm's relationships with a series of characters, each of whom—especially the women—embodies a major psychological orientation. Let us not forget, moreover, that this entire development is guided or controlled by the Society of the Tower.

Goethe is clearly concerned with having the reader understand that Wilhelm is not an artist. The Society of the Tower is convinced of this from the start, but it will let the theater episode run its course, in conformity with the Abbé's doctrine according to which the subject really learns only

by exhausting his errors. In the first two books of the novel, Wilhelm successively encounters two strangers who harshly criticize his outmoded and
complacent beliefs about fate and genius and attempt to awaken in him a
responsible attitude toward himself. These men are obviously messengers
of Bildung, emissaries of the Society of the Tower, and they attempt to stir
doubts in Wilhelm's mind concerning his artistic calling.

The first stranger had known and highly appreciated the art collection
assembled by Wilhelm's grandfather. He deplores that Wilhelm remembers
only a mediocre painting for its sentimental anecdote—a sick prince consumed by passion for his father's bride[17]—thereby exhibiting an inability
to get out of himself, in sum, a lack of aesthetic sense (Pléiade: 426ff.;
Goethe 1989a: 37 ff). The second stranger, who meets the itinerant troupe
on one of its excursions, provocatively declares that familiarity with a puppet theater and traveling with a company of mediocre actors are a poor
start for a stage career (Pléiade: 475–76; Goethe 1989a: 68).

Toward the end of the narrative, Wilhelm, now ready to leave the stage
for good, is shocked to hear Jarno, the person closest to him among the
members of the Tower, deny that he has any kind of theatrical talent
(Pléiade: 806; Goethe 1989a: 287). A little later, at a time when Wilhelm is
deeply unhappy, Jarno, who is in charge of explaining the attitude of the
Society of the Tower toward him, finally justifies the judgment: "A man
who knows to play only himself is not an actor" (Pléiade: 883; Goethe
1989a: 337): Wilhelm played quite well roles that corresponded to his
character, and the reader could have been mistaken by that, especially as
regards *Hamlet,* which in a sense was both the beginning and the end of
Wilhelm's theatrical career. The matter is so important that Goethe was
careful to give it a complete symbolic development. Wilhelm's imperfection is present in an extreme form, as a caricature, in the person of his pas-
sionate friend Aurelie, who feeds her acting with her personal torment. In
fact, Aurelie's death puts an end to Wilhelm's career; her tragic fate sym-
bolizes his failure.

If Wilhelm is not an artist, what path is open to him? A distich of
Goethe's (Goethe 1951–82, 2:428, quoted in Korff 1957: 333) answers
this very question. It is imperative:

> Always aspire to the whole: if you yourself cannot become a whole, fas-
> ten yourself to one, as a limb to its service.

17. This painting reappears insistently at the end of the novel (Pléiade: 829, 847, 851,
934), so much so that we are surprised that N. Charbonnel, who is usually keen on this type of
theme, did not exploit the trait (Charbonnel 1987).

Indeed, we see the hero of the *Apprenticeship* first attempt to build himself into a totality and then, having failed, let others persuade him to join a collective whole.

Rather late in the novel, after having learned of the death of his father and having received a sordid, utilitarian letter from his brother-in-law Werner, Wilhelm answers him with a categorical declaration and joins the theater of Serlo. "To develop myself, as I am by my nature," writes Wilhelm, "that is, obscurely, since my youth, my desire and my intention" (bk. 5, chap. 3, Pléiade: 636; Goethe 1989*a*: 174). He goes on, stating that the harmonious development of his nature is refused him by his birth as a bourgeois. In Germany at the time, only the nobleman has license simply to be himself, while the bourgeois lives under the motto of property and specialization, which forbids any harmony. Only the theater will allow Wilhelm to be as free as a nobleman:

> On the stage, a cultured man can put forward his full radiance just as in the upper classes of society. There, mind and body keep step in all one does, and there I will be able both to be and to appear as well as anywhere else.

Here it is obviously a matter of developing oneself into a harmonious totality. It is true that the word *totality* is not used, but the contrast between nobleman and bourgeois is clearly the same as the one between totality and fragment. The nobleman is self-sufficient: "If he knows how to remain always equal to himself . . . there is nothing to be added in him and no one would wish him otherwise." An expression used by Goethe is very remarkable: he says that the nobleman is a "public person," and similarly, Wilhelm wants to become a "public person." The expression emphasizes a homology between the person of the king, and by extension of the nobleman, and the social totality (cf. Gundolf 1922: 359–60). We insisted on this in regard to Humboldt (chap. 6): the "public person" is reminiscent of Hegel's "universal class," i.e., a person or a social category is in charge, not of a particular function, but of society as a whole.

When Wilhelm writes this letter he is about to devote himself entirely to the theater with Serlo, but in fact he will not stay there for long, and he will soon, only implicitly at first, admit his failure. Had he been an artist, he would have found his personal development in his devotion to his calling, but we see that he wanted, on the contrary, to put art at his service. Hence his failure.

He must therefore devote himself to the second branch of the alternative presented by Goethe, namely, to give up art and serve a whole greater than himself. This implies a shift from aesthetics to ethics as the major category of Bildung, and presupposes that Wilhelm has now accepted the specialization or division of labor that he initially felt was an unbearable limitation. It is clear also that we are turning our back on Humboldt's ideal here, and we shall have to keep this in mind. However, here is, strictly speaking, the message of the book, the teaching of the Society of the Tower.

Actually it is the sequel to the *Apprenticeship,* written much later, *Wilhelm Meister's Journeyman Years,* that is perfectly explicit concerning the division of labor and communal participation:

> . . . our age is one of specialization. . . . Become an organ and wait to see what place humanity will assign you for the best in the general life. . . . The best is to limit oneself to one single craft . . . and the most gifted, by doing one thing will do them all . . . , in this one thing which he does very well, he will see the image of all that is done well. (bk. 1, chap. 4, Pléiade: 970, modified translation)

But this is in 1829. In 1796 Goethe is much vaguer; he simply indicates the path in general terms. Jarno cautiously prepares the conversion when announcing to Wilhelm that he will be initiated on the following day:

> When man first enters into the world, it is good that he begins by counting a lot upon himself, that he dwells on acquiring many advantages, that he exercises all his faculties, but when his education has reached a certain degree of development, there is profit for him in knowing to lose himself in a larger mass, in learning to live for others and in forgetting himself in an activity accomplished as a duty. (bk. 7, chap. 9, Pléiade: 828)

Wilhelm's certificate of apprenticeship states that "only all men taken together make up mankind and all forces together make up the world. [A long enumeration follows.] All this, and much else besides, lies in man and must be developed, not just in one man but in many" (Pléiade: 884). Jarno adds the subjective version of this for his ward's use, namely, that "no one is ever happy until his unlimited yearnings have set themselves limits" (885).

These formulas barely indicate to Wilhelm the direction in which he should develop. Similarly, the projects of the Society of the Tower still seem very vague. The economic and social project will later become more consistent. For the moment, one hears of agricultural developments, and Lothario is concerned with his peasants. Jarno at one point discusses strange ideas: property is not safe in these revolutionary times, and it would therefore be in the society's best interest to spread its estates: in Germany under

Lotharioʼs direction, in Russia with the Abbé, and in America with himself, whom Wilhelm could join.

We can also discern in Wilhelmʼs apprenticeship the search for, and the establishment of, a satisfactory relation of the subject to the world. We have previously seen Bildung defined as the development of the subject according to his own dispositions, thanks to the resources of the milieu. In Goethe himself we find this view fully articulated in his autobiography *Poetry and Truth*. Bildung, or at least its principle, is therefore the establishment of a satisfactory relation, a true relation, between the subject and the world. The *Apprenticeship* lends itself to this viewpoint, for we often see that Wilhelm is conscious of having a false relation to his milieu and is searching for a genuine one.

We realize from many details that Wilhelm suffers from his mistakes in his relations to others, which cause his errors about himself. His false theatrical vocation is his major error, and the two strangers of the first books, who try to inspire some doubt in him in that regard, criticize his resort to the ideas of genius and, especially, of fate as a substitute for a more active attitude toward the outer world. At least at one point in the novel, Wilhelm shows that he does not know what he should ask of himself and of others, respectively (Pléiade: 631). He generally laments each of his errors after the fact. It is true that some of them are truly spectacular. For instance, he hesitates for a long time to begin a career in the theater, and he finally makes his decision when his calling is fading and failure is imminent. Toward the end of the novel, he chooses the wrong spouse: elated by the discovery of his son, he is obsessed with providing him with the best mother possible in the person of Therese, an eminent housekeeper and organizer, only to be forced to reverse his decision when his heartʼs desire, Natalie, manifests herself.

This question of the relation between the subject and the world is central for Wilhelmʼs development. We can see this from the fact that some characters seem to be introduced in the novel in order to offer the hero a gallery of possible attitudes. This is the case with four women who seemingly face each other two by two on either side of a line separating introversion from extroversion, as if to caution Wilhelm against extremes: neither this nor that, neither Philine the plain girl nor Aurelie the egocentric actress, neither Therese the majordomo nor the Beautiful Soul lost within herself. No doubt, we can more precisely distinguish religious, ethical, and aesthetic orientations or propensities—which is what commentators have done most of the time—but I believe it is essential to distinguish, behind these known rubrics, the simple dichotomy that any equilibrium between the self and the world must put to work. In this sense, although we cannot say that at the end of the novel Wilhelm harmoniously combines in himself these diverse values, we can probably state that something has been accomplished on the level of Bildung, since Wilhelm appears to have replaced a false relation to the world with a genuine one, that is to say, a relation underlying a positive interaction, in which the milieu enriches the personality and the personality acts upon the milieu. Schiller is thinking of something akin to this when he praises Wilhelm's moral progress between universality and individuality:

> That he should, under the beautiful and joyful conduct of nature, that is of Felix, move from the ideal to the real, from vague velleity to action and to consciousness of reality, yet without sacrificing anything of what his original state of tension and effort implied of positive content . . . it seems to me that all the inventive dispositions of the work converge perfectly toward that goal. (letter 186, Herr 1923, 1:257)

Ernst Ludwig Stahl stresses this essential aspect of the structure of the *Apprenticeship*. He quotes at length from an analysis of the novel contained in a letter from his friend Körner published by Schiller in the twelfth issue of *The Hours*. Körner writes:

> I find the interweaving of destinies and characters very skillful. Both act reciprocally on each other. Character does not simply result from a series of circumstances, as the sum of an addition, and fate is not simply the action of a given character either. Personality develops from an independent and unexplained core, and this development is only promoted by external circumstances. . . . The whole thus approaches nature itself, in which man, not devoid of his own vital force, is never simply determined by the world which surrounds him, and yet does not develop everything from within himself either. . . . As for myself, I see the unity of the whole as the presentation of a beautiful human nature developing gradually by the reciprocal action of its own dispositions and external relations. The goal of this development is an accomplished equilibrium—harmony and liberty. (Stahl 1934: 160 n. 15; Schiller and Körner 1973: 251–52)

As Stahl surmises, this is obviously the passage to which Goethe was "especially sensitive" when in a letter to Schiller (19 November, 1796, Herr 1923, 2:49) he writes, praising Körner's analysis, that "he touches precisely on a point to which I never ceased to pay the most constant attention, and which, according to me, is the main thread which secretly holds the whole assembled together. . . ." Here is an admission we shall keep in mind: Goethe acknowledges that he based his writing on the principle of the combination of *Ausbildung* and *Anbildung,* on which Stahl rightly insists (except more precisely, that Stahl refers to the same subject what Körner saw as the "reciprocal action" between two entities). We notice that Goethe, in the twelfth book of *Poetry and Truth,* mentions a similar disposition concerning the composition of *Werther.*[18]

Yet we still have to introduce an important point. There is no symmetry or equality between the "inner dispositions" and the "external relationships," any more than there was between the figures of introversion and extroversion mentioned above. In Goethe's very idea, the individual principle of subjectivity (and therefore of *Ausbildung*) ranks above its indispensable complement found in the milieu (and *Anbildung*).[19] This is underscored by the fact that the entire book 6 of *Meister* is devoted to the biography of a pietist soul.

•

By depicting precisely and tactfully the successive stages of the internal life of a pietist lady, Goethe certainly attempted first of all to contrast them with the more or less vain agitation of the stage, as a warning addressed to Wilhelm by the intermediary of his friend Aurelie not to lose himself in grandiloquent gesticulation. This does not mean that the Beautiful Soul is given as an example: Goethe will tell Schiller that the "whole rests on the most noble illusions and on the most delicate confusion of the subjective and the objective" (letter 56, 18 March, 1795). But if this is so, why did Goethe devote so much space and care to this biography of a soul? It is precisely because for him everything originates in pure inwardness, here pietist inwardness, which constitutes the basis for the entire development of the individual.

In fact, Goethe had himself experienced this developmental stage in his own life, so that the "Confessions of a Beautiful Soul" is also a stela dedicated to the memory of a very dear friend of his youth. We know from his autobiography that a friend of his mother's, Suzanne von Klettenberg, who was pietist, had a great influence over his adolescence, sharing with him her esoteric readings and, to a lesser degree, her mysticism. Thus, book 8 of *Poetry and Truth* ends with a more or less gnostic profession of faith. Further on, Goethe explains that he was for a time close to the Moravian Brethren,

18. "That resolution to let my inner nature follow its own course and to let outer nature influence me in its own capacity brought me to the strange climate in which *Werther* was conceived and written" (Goethe 1974, 9:540–41).

19. The point is vigorously emphasized by Simmel in his study on Goethe's individualism, which is difficult to find in German and has recently been translated into French (Simmel 1990: 74–75).

until his unrepenting pelagianism—his refusal to accept that man, after the Fall, is absolutely incapable of any good on his own—led him to forsake their company. His friend, on the contrary, represented a rather benign pietism, since the Beautiful Soul is essentially someone whose natural bent is to do good and love God, someone who can say: "I hardly know of any command, nothing appears to me in the form of a law, it is an impulse that draws me and guides me always well; I follow freely my feelings and know no restriction nor repentance" (quoted by Wundt 1932: 220). We are easily persuaded that Suzanne von Klettenberg was, by virtue of the affection that united these rather similar natures, the great educator of Goethe's adolescence. We thus understand not only how Goethe was able to write this chapter of mystical literature but also why he enjoyed doing so, even if, as some have surmised, he may have used notes of the Beautiful Soul herself, which would have been in his possession, to help him. This is also probably why he could not conceive of Wilhelm's education without the chapter on the Beautiful Soul. Here is a trait that links in depth the hero and the author. Let us insist on this. As much as we saw Goethe distance Wilhelm from himself, as a common man or a "poor dog," it is clear that they both belong to the pietist heritage of inwardness, insofar as they are both incomparable or irreplaceable individuals. Here lies the very foundation of personal development, that is, of Bildung.

•

This development presupposes that in Goethe's mind, the subject, as opposed to the Beautiful Soul, should turn his inner energy toward the outside. On this level, we have found that Wilhelm learns during the novel to relinquish any artistic pretension and to find totality outside himself, in a community that he will serve, and that he progresses by a process of successive corrections toward a set of balanced relationships between self and milieu. In order to grasp more precisely the level of development Wilhelm reaches at the end of the novel, we shall have to carefully scrutinize the last two books, which are rather eventful.

Other than three adventitious stories, we find three major themes intermingling in these two books.

With his arrival at Lothario's castle at the beginning of book 7, Wilhelm fortuitously has access to the place from which his fate has been directed all along, namely, the Tower and its Society, into which he will be solemnly initiated and from which he will receive his certificate of apprenticeship. This is the end of one cycle and the beginning of another. We note that even as a full-fledged member of the Society, beside the Abbé, Lothario, and

Jarno, Wilhelm remains unsure of himself for a long time. He is melancholy and saddened by a rapid series of events, but he does not rebel against the total obedience required by the Abbé until the very end, thus agreeing to serve a "larger whole," the Society.

Sentimentally, Wilhelm finds again the amazon of his dreams, Natalie, and marries her, or at least intends to, but the last two books are taken up with a broad detour through another woman, Therese, who is herself a very remarkable person, but whose choice by Wilhelm is another monumental error. Natalie does not appear until Chapter 2 of the last book, and it is only at the very end that Therese leaves her her place. Natalie is Lothario's sister, and by marrying her Wilhelm enters into a noble family. We recall that Schiller emphasized the union, in three of the weddings, between nobles and commoners.

More important than the formal conclusion of Wilhelm's apprenticeship and his admission into a distinguished circle, and related to them, is the transformation that has taken place in him, which is marked mainly by the recognition and the adoption of his son, Felix. Naturally, marriage, paternity, and initiation all go together; they complement each other and combine to bring about the change in Wilhelm's status. This is specially obvious in the care Natalie takes of Felix and in the unfolding of the initiation, which in a way seals the acknowledgment of paternity. It is clear that anyone who becomes a father gets out of himself and becomes "part of a larger whole," but the change is emphasized in the novel in an even more dramatic fashion. The access to or the identification with Felix is counterbalanced by the loss, the death of Mignon. Thus the strange and genial girl who had become attached to Wilhelm, the sublime and disturbing romantic figure whose nostalgic poetry permeated the first part of the book, is replaced by a boy who is quite simply life. At the same time the curse to which Mignon owed her extraordinary fate is exorcised by the narration of her incestuous birth.

To sum up, the conclusion of the novel marks at the same time an end and a beginning: the end of apprenticeship and the inauguration of a new life, which is still very indefinite. In 1796 Goethe seems to have been anxious mainly to give the novel a denouement, a little in the manner of a comedy, by bringing to their conclusion the developments under way and providing a solution to the immediate problems.

ART AND LIFE

When Goethe confesses the difficulties he encountered in attempting to reconcile the demands of the subject with his own, we can see it as a conflict between the didacticism with which he consciously filled the novel and the aesthetic sense he cannot abandon. There is here an uncomfortable relationship between the novel as a work of art and the message it must convey, which tends to turn it into what will later be termed an *ouvrage à thèse*. Concurrently, the teaching of *Meister,* according to May, has no place for art or beauty. We shall therefore pay special attention to the aesthetic dimension.

Considering the novel first, the fundamental heterogeneity between the didactic intent and the work of art is manifested in the reception of the work by posterity, beginning with Friedrich Schlegel and Novalis.

In 1798 Friedrich Schlegel published a review, or rather a long study, of the *Apprenticeship* in which he celebrates the genius of the work in chosen and careful words (Schlegel 1970). He scarcely questions its unity or the point Wilhelm finally reaches in his development. He notes that the author sometimes indulges his facility, but the arbitrariness of Genius is justified by the high poetic value that is achieved. It is remarkable that Schlegel carefully studies the work of art and completely neglects the didactic dimension, to the point of considering Mignon to be the "central element" of the novel. We also note that he accepts straightforwardly the kind of "regency" exercised by the Society of the Tower—which was perhaps not absolutely to be expected of a beginner romantic—and judges its members as favorably as did Goethe himself. It is clear that Schlegel the artist is guided by his admiration for Goethe and does not bother about Wilhelm.

Novalis at first expressed a similar admiration, but in 1800 he records a categorical opposition in his notebook of fragments:

> In the end, it is a harmful and inane book, full of pretension and preciosity, prosaic to the supreme degree in its spirit, as poetic as its form may be. It is . . . a *Candide* aimed against poetry. . . . It only concerns itself with human things of everyday life, nature and mysticism are entirely absent. . . . Poetic atheism, that is the spirit of that work. (Novalis, n.d., 10)

Leaving aside the personal engagement that led him to write *Heinrich von Ofterdingen* precisely to oppose it to *Meister,* it is clear that Novalis perceived Goethe's didactic purpose, and with it the dual nature of the *Apprenticeship,* which seems to have eluded Schlegel, fascinated as he was by the author and his genius.

The contradiction between the poetic form and the prosaic intention extended to posterity. In the novel Mignon is finally buried without too much ceremony in order to make room for Wilhelm's son, much as noctur-

nal melancholy yields to the dash of dawn. Goethe's poetry got her her revenge, however, in France at least, and it is the nostalgic Mignon who has
held the favor of the public, first in the paintings of Ary Scheffer and later in
the *opéra-comique* of Ambroise Thomas (1866).

To come now to the didactic element, Kurt May in a way echoes Novalis
when he asserts that the aesthetic dimension is absent from the ideal proposed in *Meister,* which, for this reason among others, cannot be accepted
as a *Bildungsroman.* According to May, although the aesthetic dimension
is indeed found in the novel, it is eventually overridden: we encounter, successively, the religious aspect with the Beautiful Soul, the aesthetic aspect
with the uncle, and the ethical aspect with Natalie. The uncle's aesthetics
supersedes the religion of the Beautiful Soul, only to be supplanted in its
turn by ethics, unambiguously symbolized by the marriage to Natalie, an
ideal ethical personality devoid of religious as well as aesthetic sense. According to May, the harmonious combination of the three dimensions,
which alone would allow one to speak of an accomplished Bildung, is still
missing. Instead, ethics imposes itself in the end at the expense of the other
two aspects, in line with the categorical formula of the certificate of
apprenticeship.

The critic thus excludes the possibility that a genuine value could mi-
grate from one rubric to another. Beauty is the major concern of aesthetics,
but not its monopoly. As Pascal points out, Wilhelm learns from the uncle
that, in contrast with the pure inwardness of the Beautiful Soul, one should
be "active in such a way that a harmony is established within oneself, and
between oneself and a community" (Pascal 1956: 21). And Schiller saw in
Natalie the Beautiful Soul incarnate, an aesthetic personality in the sense
that she embodies absolutely disinterested pure love, free of any preference
and selfishness. In truth, each dimension does not obliterate the previous
one here, as May supposed it does. Between ethics and aesthetics, it is a
matter of hierarchy: ethics does not destroy aesthetics but *encompasses* it,
thereby introducing beauty into everyday life. In order to fully appreciate
the place of aesthetics in *Meister* we have to consider the transformation
that occurs in Wilhelm between the beginning and the end of the book. Is
there not an aspect of beauty in substituting a true relationship between
oneself and others for a false one, in knowing how to judiciously limit one's
striving, or in becoming a full-fledged member of a community of persons
united in their common convictions and highly valuing each other? Does
this not represent something of an aesthetic as well as ethical relation to
reality? I am here following Korff, who well perceived the aesthetic aspect
in the conversion to the community (1957, 2:325–40). According to him,

the romantics did not grasp that beauty would thus become part of life, that the ideal of the novel was a transformed, "transfigured" (*verklärtes*) practical life (ibid.: 338).

Yet, Korff adds, here a qualification may be added. Goethe's aesthetic success is not complete: the second part of the novel does not carry the reader's conviction, it is aesthetically inferior to the first part; furthermore, poetry is encountered in abnormal, morally illegal figures, whereas legality should triumph in all things by incorporating beauty under a satisfactory form. *We feel that Mignon calls Natalie's validity into question.* Legality is missing a final depth, which it will attain only in *Faust*. There is thus some validity in Kurt May's critique and in the attitude of posterity rejecting moralism and exalting Mignon.

Let us also point out that a hierarchical relation inverse to that of the teaching of *Meister* (beauty encompassed in life) is encountered in the work itself: for Goethe, the aesthetic aspect encompassed the didactic one. This hierarchical inversion may provide the law of transformation from Goethe to Wilhelm and from Wilhelm to Goethe, or the passage from the level of the message to that of the literary work. After a remark suggested, if not explicitly formulated by Jane Brown, we would say that there is an osmosis between the theater and life: if life—that is, Wilhelm's development—is not in the theater, the theater is in life. In other words, the real life Wilhelm enters is itself theater; in sum, he leaves one kind of theater for another. One has only to think of the Tower, and a scene such as the granting of the certificate of apprenticeship. The end of the novel resembles the denouement of a comedy of that period, with its weddings—including Therese's change of identity, which makes her wedding to Lothario possible. Let us just ponder this: it is rather as a series of tableaux that the novel can still come alive for us.

Thus, if Wilhelm gives up the theater, Goethe does not. By becoming, in contrast to the Wilhelm of the *Theatrical Mission,* a common man, a "poor dog," the hero abandoned the dignity of playwright to his creator. The educated reader who cannot identify with him any longer may turn back to Goethe. We shall take up this essential aspect again in our conclusion.

INDIVIDUALISM OR HOLISM?

If we attempt to grasp *Wilhelm Meister* with the help of the single distinction between individualism and holism, we are likely to find that the Germans and the French view the novel differently, locating it on either side of the opposition. The Frenchman, on the one hand, is aware of the strength of the holistic component in German culture. Taking the *Apprenticeship* and the *Journeyman Years* together, he will undoubtedly be struck by the stress the novels set on the insertion of the person into the social group. It is true that the theme is elaborated—profusely—only in the 1829 book, but it was already indicated or presupposed in 1796. Although less explicit in the earlier work, the orientation is the same: at the heart of the *Apprenticeship*, as opposed to the *Theatrical Mission*, one encounters the curvature that brings the fugitive Wilhelm back to society, that leads him, in default of constituting himself as a totality, to aggregate into a larger totality.

The German reader, on the other hand, essentially sees in *Meister* a problematic of the realization and development of individuality. For him, the social aspect is a commonplace matter, a sort of obligatory accompaniment, which he will be surprised to see others insist on.

But this is too simplistic and we should look into the matter more closely. We can begin by following Georg Lukács, who offers the advantage of introducing a historical perspective and, for the *Apprenticeship*, of taking into account the great contemporary event. Lukács was concerned with reacting against a tradition that, according to him, limited and distorted Goethe's message; he wanted to restore his eighteenth-century aspect, his close connection to the Enlightenment. Lukács went very far in this direction. He explains himself most fully at the beginning of his book *Goethe and His Age*, originally published in 1936, in the chapter on *Werther*, which precedes the one on *Wilhelm Meister* (Lukács 1947: 35ff.). He reproaches the "bourgeois historians of literature," including the great Goethe specialists such as Gundolf, Korff, and others, with having radically separated the *Sturm und Drang*, including especially *Werther*, from the Enlightenment, thus cutting off German classicism from the eighteenth century in favor of the subsequent "reactionary" developments of romanticism.

For Lukács, on the contrary, there is a perfect continuity between the eighteenth century, the French eighteenth century in particular, and the *Sturm und Drang*. Not only is *Werther* a natural continuation of *La Nouvelle Héloïse*, but "the popular-humanistic revolt in Werther is one of the most important revolutionary expressions of bourgeois ideology in the preparatory period of the French Revolution" (Lukács 1947: 25), and along with the other works of the young Goethe, it represents "a revolutionary peak of the European Enlightenment, the ideological preparation for the great French Revolution" (21). The novel is not only "the proclamation of the ideals of revolutionary humanism, but also the perfect formulation of the tragic contradiction of these ideals" (26), a "perfect expression of the inner contradiction of bourgeois marriage" (28).

It is not our intention here to discuss *Werther* and Lukács's interpretation of it, but only to underscore that Lukács goes very far in his desire to react against a tendency to close German culture in upon itself to the benefit of romanticism—so far in fact that he replaces interaction by identification and loses track of all German specificity. We have thus passed from one extreme to the other: from an all-German culture, we have arrived at one that is anything but German.

We encounter similar problems in the chapter of the same book on *The Years of Apprenticeship of Wilhelm Meister*. Lukács is undoubtedly justified in speaking of the "deep ideological influence of the French Revolution on Goethe, as well as on all the great German figures" of the time (41). We only find that he conceives of this "influence" in a somewhat mechanistic fashion. He sees the novel as a positive expression, in literary form, of the human goals of the French Revolution: it focuses on "man, and the realization and development of his personality," expressed this time in an especially clear and suggestive fashion (36) in bright and somewhat utopian colors, resulting precisely from the fact that it is a particular reflection on the experience of the French Revolution (49).

All this is correct up to a point, the point where the difference between national cultures is neglected. We would prefer to speak of refraction rather than reflection: the trait is inflected, inwardly modified, upon passing from one environment to the other. Here individualism receives a curvature, which sends it back to the community: Wilhelm joins a collective whole. Lukács is silent on this aspect. The holism Goethe thus reintroduces, distinctly as early as 1795–96 and more profusely later, is purely and simply disregarded by Lukács as a result of his overarching concern, which is to identify a universal chronology for the rise of the bourgeoisie and the development of capitalism: for him, individualism may be in difficulty in 1830 but not as early as the revolutionary period. As a result, Goethe's true preoccupation in the *Apprenticeship,* as opposed to the *Theatrical Mission*— the essential change that consists in passing from the genial individual to the "poor dog," the common man who can exist only in the community— is completely ignored, and the message Goethe enshrined in the novel is distorted. For instance, Lukács sees it as a veiled polemic against the categorical imperative, while in fact the theory of the Abbé on laissez-faire in education is rejected in the next generation by Natalie, who corrects it in the name of irrevocable moral commandments. There is no reason to doubt that it is Goethe who speaks through Natalie, for in his next novel, *The Elective Affinities,* he will insist on the sacrosanct character of marriage. (Even though many readers, such as Herzen [cf. Malia 1961: 45], detected the opposite message in the *Affinities,* in a distant parallel with Lukács.)

Another consequence of Lukács's exclusively individualistic reading is that although Goethe's antiromantic preoccupation is recognized, it remains a literary matter only, thus autonomous and superficial, while, as we indicated, it is actually intimately linked to the social preoccupation.

I would like to note a point of detail in what precedes. With Lukács, we admitted in passing, in general terms, that the "human goals" of the French Revolution were "the realization and development of [man's] personality." Yet we should make a distinction here from a narrower point of view. Although this may have been the long-term intent of the French revolutionaries, their immediate objectives were much more circumscribed and precise: they were largely absorbed in political transformation. What Lukács's formula of "the development of personality" exactly describes is none other than . . . Bildung, so much so that this passage of the text actually contains a translation, on the cultural level, of the French word *révolution* by the German *Bildung*.

However, Lukács remains essentially on the plane of Western Enlightenment and of the rationalist individualism of the French Revolution. The contrast with Georg Simmel's entirely different perception of the novel will be readily apparent:

> Here for the first time a world is depicted which rests on the individual specificity of its protagonists: it is organized and develops only through them, without any adverse effect resulting from the fact that the characters are conceived as types. As often as these figures may be repeated in reality, the internal meaning of each one in particular remains, so that each one differs in its ultimate foundation from the others toward which fate pushes it, and the imprint of life and of development does not bear on what is similar[20] but on what is absolutely their own. (1989: 300–301)

An individualism of specificity, of the qualitative uniqueness and the incomparability or the irreplaceability of each human creature, surfaces here, in contrast with the individualism of equality and identity of the French, and truly transfers us into Goethe's universe. I am using here Simmel's expressions, albeit from other texts. We find here, facing the individualism of the Rights of Man, a very strong feeling of the unique and irreplaceable individuality of each human being, which is what a German immediately thinks of when one speaks of individualism to him.

Allow us to mention here a characteristic linguistic detail, the dual meaning of the word *gleich*, which means both "equal" and "identical" (or

20. The German *gleich* means "equal," as well as "identical" or "similar." The French translator used *égal*, but I prefer "similar," given the context.

"similar"). Naturally the German speaker can here, as elsewhere, borrow from Romance languages and say *egal,* but the German term proper is ambiguous: it contains and renders unconscious or automatic the passage from equality to identity, which is probably as imperative in French, although there it needs to be thought.

Simmel clearly perceived the distance between the individualism of equality and the quasi cult of the incomparable individuality of the subject. About the latter, he says that "it seems inadmissible to construe equality from the fact that each individual is as special and as incomparable as every other" (1971: 286).

The individualism of difference results in inequality, whereas the individualism of equality implies identity. Here, Simmel is close to Thomas Aquinas, but in reverse fashion: it is difference, *disparitas,* that refers to an order, an entity of a higher order (cf. Dumont 1986: 248 n. 22). We thus encounter the "curvature" we saw at work in *Meister,* which brings the individual involved in his own development back into the community by the intermediary of the division of labor. Moreover, this is not a particular trait, but a characteristic of the "irreplaceable individuality" that one usually encounters in Germany. We see that, contrary to Lukács, Simmel perceived the true purpose, the spirit, of *Meister.* He saw that holism is implicit in the *Apprenticeship,* so much so that Wilhelm's opening to holism truly represents the Bildung that he has acquired when the work ends.

Simmel came back to individualism, or rather to the two forms of individualism, in several places, and these texts shed light on our present inquiry. He clearly emphasizes the distance between the two kinds of individualism. We could even wonder whether these are not in fact two different phenomena that need to be distinguished in vocabulary: if we keep "individualism" for the first form, we could call the second one "singularism." If Simmel does not do this, it is probably because he insists on maintaining the historical, genetic link between the two. He sees the second form as originating from the first by a continuous development, an intensification. Having conquered his autonomy, the individual wants to establish himself further as incomparable, the only one of his species. It is a progress in the modern tendency toward differentiation. Simmel's view is perhaps too simple here: more than a formal continuity, the two forms represent a change in the field, or the level, of application. The intensification seems to us rather to mark the internalization that accompanies the shift from Western to German culture.[21] The fact remains that individual differ-

21. Moreover, as Vincent Descombes notes in a personal communication, this singularism was, to say the least, prepared by Leibniz with his principle of the indiscernible, and before him by the Thomistic theory of angels.

ence points to the division of labor and tends toward the establishment of a higher whole, an overall organism (Simmel 1981: 159). Once again, we encounter the "curvature" that brings Meister back to the community, as well as the hymns of praise to specialization of the *Journeyman Years*. Here is Goethe's real message for the common man, which has nothing to do with 1789, and which Lukács lost sight of. For Lukács, the individual could only subordinate himself to the law, as Simmel quite rightly recalls in contrast, and as Rousseau and the French Revolution itself reminded us. Without pretending here to exhaust Simmel's view on individualism, let us at least add that he clearly perceived and expressed in a striking manner how Germans, or more precisely Kant and Goethe, mix up the two forms of individualism (Simmel 1989: 286 ff.), as if the "Germanic" form was untenable on its own—although he only calls it dangerous (289–91)—and had to be attenuated by a recourse to the Latin or Romance form.[22]

To conclude our discussion of Lukács and Simmel, let us insist on some connections that Lukács missed but that should be obvious. Bildung presupposes an individualism rooted in difference, and conversely, the conception of individuality as unique and incommensurable includes the duty to nurture and develop it. While the individualism of equality is a formal principle, externally applicable to take exception to any holism in political and social life, the individualism of difference corresponds, on the contrary, to the inner feeling of the pietist subject, or subject of Bildung. And *Meister* teaches us that this feeling leads the subject, if he is a common man, to aggregate with a whole, a group, and become an organ of it.

Thus, following Simmel, if not Lukács, we can now preserve both the proximity and the difference between French and German culture. By the same token, we can see Goethe both as close to the Enlightenment and, at the same time, as busy weaving together the legacy of the Beautiful Soul and that of the *Encyclopédie*.

A work entitled *The Value of the Individual*, dealing in large part with Goethe—in fact arising out of him and centered upon him—can help us complement somewhat the views we have expressed so far. In this book, Karl Weintraub, an author of German background, wants to show that the

---

22. Given the amplitude and the interest of Simmel's views cited above, and their frequent convergence with ours, the reader could wonder why we did not mention them earlier in our research. The reason is simply that we were not aware of their existence. The first encounter took place in 1986–87, thanks paradoxically to a critic who tried to use Simmel against us (Béteille 1986; reply Dumont 1987). Other relevant texts became accessible later through recent translations. An overall view will have to wait until we have taken a more comprehensive view of Simmel's work on culture, which is made difficult by its richness, diversity, and dispersion.

autobiographical genre culminated in Goethe, in the sense that in him individuality, the individual singularity, imposes itself as a value. This was previously not the case, from Saint Augustine to Rousseau. For Weintraub, this new meaning of individuality as unique, irreplaceable, and singular, and the concern with it, result from the confluence of two currents that had previously remained distinct, namely, the individualistic particularism à la Montaigne on the one hand, and the historicism of Vico and Gibbon, which emphasizes the singularity of every culture and every historical moment, on the other:

> *Dichtung und Wahrheit* thus represents the moment in the history of autobiography when the self-understanding and presentation of an individual parallels the emerging historicist mode of understanding human life. (Weintraub 1978: 368)

This happens in Germany: as an emulator of Winckelmann, Herder, and Möser, Goethe shifts the historical view from the level of collective individualities to that of "individual individualities." According to Weintraub, it is the presence of the historical or collective view that makes the full development of the notion of a singular person possible in *Poetry and Truth* by providing under the form of genetic understanding a diachronic view accompanied for the subject by the duty of self-development.

   Let us remark right away that this collective background can assist in understanding the "curvature" that brings the singular individual back to the community, and this can be seen more closely in the way Goethe depicts his youth in his autobiography. But to what extent is all of this pertinent to *Meister?* The *Apprenticeship* is earlier than *Poetry and Truth,* and we cannot pretend that it contains the complete set of ideas that animates the autobiography. Yet we have seen how Goethe's youth, later recounted in his autobiography, already resonates in *Meister* (thus the puppet theater, and especially the Beautiful Soul, Suzanne von Klettenberg). Moreover, a sort of parallelism is evident in the diachronic presentation of the two heroes. For instance, Weintraub shows how Goethe carefully detailed his own development as a series of successive encounters between subject and milieu; that is to say, Goethe presents it, in conformity with the purest doctrine of Bildung, as resulting from the intersection of the subject's own tendencies and the impacts on him of the persons with whom he has contact— corresponding to what above we called *Ausbildung* and *Anbildung.* Now, all this was already true of *Meister.* Moreover, we see there environment and subject interpenetrate all along the flow of time. In this sense, the "curvature" that appears at a given moment is new only in its form. The concern with, and the cult of, singularity almost turn it into a institution, but it is absolutely not opposed to the social totality, whereas the individualism of equality was. Well to the contrary, it is constantly associated with it under various forms; singularity is fed from the rapport with the milieu, it is therefore not surprising that it curves, when the time comes, back toward the community.

All in all, the opposition between individualism and holism is not immediately—say, in the first degree—applicable to Germany. We could be reproached here with focusing on a narrowly national artifact. But on the one hand, it is undeniably more than just that, for it has entered the common domain, perhaps mostly through politics. On the other hand, we shall never do anything else: the important point being only that the tool should be used to set forth national differences, which is precisely what we are doing in these pages.

Finally, let us come back to pietism, which seems to be as important in the autobiography, with the influence of Madame von Klettenberg on the young Goethe, as it is in *Meister*. An immediate conjunction is obvious between pietism and the cult of individuality as singular—or could we say "singularism"? A subject who, like the pietist, is limited to his inwardness inevitably perceives himself as unique and incomparable—let us recall Anton Reiser for instance—while the subject of the Enlightenment sees himself as rational and therefore universal. The contrast between the Enlightenment and pietism would therefore by itself seem to account for the opposition between the French and the German way of valuing the individual. This view is simplistic, since in actuality Germany was affected by the Enlightenment, so much so that one could speak of the intensification of pietistic individualism under the influence of the Enlightenment. We have seen, in the case of Moritz, the feeling of liberation afforded by action in the world. Overall, we can probably speak of a dominance, once established and then maintained, of singularity over universality in the individualism of the German intellectual.

CONCLUSION

In what precedes, we have reserved hitherto the exegetic challenge resulting from Kurt May's interpretation. May criticizes the traditional interpretation of *Meister*, which he sees as a misapprehension, although he does not explain how it could have arisen. If, as he maintains, Bildung is altogether absent from the book, in actuality as well as in the author's intention, how can we explain that posterity almost unanimously found Bildung in *Meister*, to the point that it was to become the *Bildungsroman* par excellence? It is true that we did not accept the thesis as such, arguing that Bildung is just as much a process, or more so, than it is a given result. Moreover, Wilhelm eventually achieves something of a development, as Schiller noted and as Roy Pascal acknowledges when he mentions the transformation of a "self-centered" individual into a "society centered" one (Pascal 1956: 21). It is true, in our discussion Bildung differs from what May envisages it to be—namely, Winckelmann's conception, about which Goethe wrote in 1805 that this extraordinary success had been confined exclusively to the ancient Greeks. The problem remains: if that kind of Bildung is not the object of the novel, how can we explain that posterity stubbornly thought it was, celebrating the work while it was in fact ignoring its real message? Let us also note that May himself seems to have failed to notice this message, nor did he realize the decisive transition between the *Theatrical Mission* and the *Apprenticeship*, i.e., the transition from the artist to the common man. It is to the common man that Goethe recommends conversion to a whole larger than himself which he shall serve: the ethical and aesthetic hierarchy of values we previously described applies to the common man.

In order to explain the misapprehension, we could begin by recalling that Goethe's thesis has not yet been made explicit in 1796 and that it is only in the *Journeyman Years* that he will—I would say that he will *dare* to—propound it fully, or should we think that in 1796 it is not explicit even to Goethe himself? Whatever the case may be, the problem has another, more interesting aspect.

We can start from an observation of Schiller's. In his letter of 28 November 1796 (number 247, Herr 1923; 2:55), Schiller notes that Wilhelm is not strictly speaking the hero of the novel, which does not have one and "has no need for one." Wilhelm is "obviously the most necessary character but not the most important one." "Everything occurs in relation to him and around him, but not properly because of him." We are touching on what we said above regarding Wilhelm's passive character. He appears not as an agent with whom the reader may identify, but rather as an object the author subjects to the reader's scrutiny. A well-read reader especially, who believes he shares in Bildung, can hardly identify with this "poor dog" whom Goethe has distanced from himself and from the reader at the same time. The novel tends to become a discussion on Bildung *concerning* Meister. We discern Goethe behind Wilhelm, and the reader can always turn back to him. This presence of the artist behind the common man, of the real model behind the feigned example, is essential. Rudolf Vierhaus says the same thing in his great encyclopedic article on Bildung:

> Goethe is undoubtedly recognized as an extraordinary genius, but at the same time, the *Gebildete,* the cultured people, see in him the unremitting effort of Bildung, which is part of the consciousness of themselves and constitutes a maxim carried to triviality of their pedagogy. (1972: 518)

Simmel too can help us grasp what happens here and how it is linked to the deep nature of Goethe's craft. In a study on Goethe's individualism, he contrasts the individuality of the characters in Shakespeare and in Goethe. The superb comparison deserves to be read in full, and we can give only a faint idea of it here:

> . . . the metaphysical element [in Shakespeare's individuals] is located between their heads and their toes, while Goethe's characters act as . . . fruits from a *single* tree . . . they are bound together as expressions of a single creative subjectivity. (Simmel 1990: 84)

> . . . in spite of all their particularity and qualitative differentiation Mephisto and Ottilie, Gretchen and Tasso, Orestes and Macarie remain within the sphere of the poet's own creative life. . . .
> . . . in *Wilhelm Meister* and in the *Elective Affinities,* the artistic style is determined throughout by the fact that we feel the presence of the narrator everywhere. (85–86)

Thus Friedrich Schlegel, in his 1798 review in the *Athenäum* (1798) pardoned, because of the genius of the author, traits he would have criticized in other writers.

Simmel sheds the final touch of light on the subject in a text on Rome, which only incidentally relates to Goethe as a greatness comparable to Rome. Like Rome, Goethe is entirely present behind each one of his expressions:

> We do not enjoy it [his expression] simply in function of its immediate content . . . we rather enrich it with everything that the association of ideas with the fact that it comes from Goethe brings to it and makes us evoke with it . . . in a word of Goethe we think necessarily more and differently than in the same word uttered by Peter or Paul. (1989: 260–61)

Can we venture to say that Meister's Bildung benefited in the eyes of posterity from having been presented under the aegis of Goethe's Bildung? The circumstance would have helped reduce the distance between the harmonious plenitude that is the aim of Winckelmann's and Humboldt's Bildung and the devotion to the community Goethe demands in the *Journeyman Years*. Moreover, the two conceptions are not opposed as absolutely in German culture as one might expect. Obviously, Germans *may* always distinguish between the two, as Goethe did in the distich on totality cited previously, but there is not, properly speaking, any incompatibility between them. We have at our disposal here a trait that is in itself a proof: Simmel defined the individual as a partial whole encompassed within a larger one, namely, society or a social sphere (1989: 282–83), that is to say, as a holon in Koestler's definition (Dumont 1986: 250–51 n. 24). Here is a structural mode of thought that completely excludes the possibility of apprehending the individual as a substance, and of opposing individual and society as substances, as we do when we speak of individualism and holism. It results from this that the opposition between individualism and holism is in all rigor inapplicable to Germany, or, in other words, that in German culture we always are under holistic dominance. This in turn helps us understand that it is possible to move easily from one type of Bildung to another, contrary to what May supposed. Therefore, thanks to Vierhaus and Simmel, we can understand how the *Apprenticeship* has been viewed as the *Bildungsroman* par excellence.

In conclusion to this study, we may now come back to what Goethe has really accomplished in the *Apprenticeship*. We concluded from reading Lukács and Simmel that he had effected a transition from the individualism of Western Enlightenment, the French one in particular, to the establishment of individuality and its development, or Bildung, as a value. This formula is located on the level of interaction between national cultures and, accordingly, has a chance of being the most general that can be given. It allows us—contrary to Lukács—to recover the continuity of German culture in its very relation to its environment and to the great event at the end of the eighteenth century. Moreover, there has emerged in our development the idea of a close relation between the view of the individual as incomparable and irreplaceable and pietist inwardness. To say this is in a way just to underscore the presence of the Beautiful Soul beside Wilhelm and the adolescent Goethe. Pietism, an outcome of the Reformation, is as important in Germany during the second half of the eighteenth century as the Declaration of the Rights of Man will be in France. These twin conceptions of individuality—the rationalistic individualism and incomparable and jealously guarded individuality—correspond to the French Revolution and to the Reformation, respectively.

As the same time, however, considered on the level of German culture itself, *Meister* represents, in our view, an echo of the great contemporary event, or more precisely, a form of adaptation of German culture to this major upheaval. We perceive the progress of the adaptation if we compare Humboldt and *Meister* serially. What May did not see is that *Meister* DE-MOCRATIZED Humboldt. Here is, to be sure, the reason for what May mistakenly assumed was the betrayal of Winckelmann's ideal. It is this generalization, or democratization, that caused Goethe so much trouble. Goethe was, on the one hand, entangled in his didacticism; on the other, contrary to what Schiller naively imagined, he could not, and possibly he felt he ought not, reveal the whole extent of his thought, which he will do in 1829. It seems safe to surmise, however, that he knew as early as 1796 that by emphasizing his difference the subject curves back toward a totality outside himself, and that to insist on *disparitas* is enough to refer back to *ordo*.[23]

23. "Ordo autem maxime videtur in disparitate consistere" (Thomas Aquinas, *Summa theo.*, Iq 96a.3; cf. Dumont, 1986: 248 n. 22).

PART FOUR

Back
to
France

] 8 [

French Political Ideology Seen in the Light of an Incipient Comparison of National Cultures

1. LEFT AND RIGHT

My main theme here is going to be the chronic division of Left versus Right in French political ideology and political life. But before coming to it, allow me to recall one or two definitions and some of the results of previous comparisons between France and Germany.[1] I call ideology a system of ideas and values current in a given social milieu, and we shall have in view here mainly the *global* ideology, the whole system of ideas and values found there. Moreover, we shall speak of a certain ideology as being *predominant* respectively here and there. What is predominant ideology? We shall here be content with stating that it is something that comes forth when two ideologies are globally compared. It is not exactly the ideology of a majority of the people, nor something stable that would be seen to underlie historical changes. It is in a way all that, or rather something that comes spontaneously to the minds of people living in a given cultural milieu, something in terms of which those people speak and think, and which is best revealed by comparison with other cultures.

Thus, there is a difference between what it means to be a Frenchman and to be a German. Let us recall the basic contrast with which this book opened. In his own idea of himself, the Frenchman is a man by nature and a Frenchman by accident, while the German feels he is first a German and then a man through his being a German. I quoted a saying of a French historian naively expressing the notion that the person is independent from his particular cultural milieu, something like "There is no cause for blushing in having been born a Frenchman, for it is a matter of chance."

The same idea figures in the "Thoughts" of Montesquieu, which he presented as "uncontrolled" (Montesquieu 1949: 974, no. 10). This dissociation of personal and collective identity is spontaneous among the French, while elsewhere, at any rate in Germany, the naive representation would

---

In English, section 1 of this chapter was first published in John A. Hall and I. C. Jarvie, eds., *Transition to Modernity: Essays on Power, Wealth and Belief.* (Cambridge: Cambridge University Press, 1986). It was dedicated to Ernest Gellner.

1. Apart from the texts present in this book, let me recall especially, regarding politics, a study that has appeared in my *Essays*, chap. 4, "Herder's *Volk* and Fichte's *Nation*" (Dumont, 1986: 113–32).

express on the contrary the *cultural* belonging, the particular collective identity. This poses a problem about the Frenchman. I think the answer is that it is essentially as a citizen that the Frenchman feels and acknowledges himself as French. His sense of belonging lies at the *political* level. The collective identity is cultural in the former case, political in the latter. (This is not to deny that politics is part of culture at large, but here we need to distinguish them.)

For our Frenchman, France means first of all democracy, the Republic. If he is somewhat educated, he will say that the French have shown the world the way of the Rights of Man and the Citizen, and he will be inclined to add that the destiny of France is to be the teacher of mankind.

After all, this is only a particular form of a feeling that is universal: people everywhere believe that their own society is superior to others. That is what is called ethnocentrism—I prefer to say sociocentrism. It would be wrong to suppose that modern societies do not harbor such feelings, under modified forms. The corresponding trait in Germany for a long time was pan-Germanism, that is to say, the belief that Germany was called to dominate the world by reason of the excellence of its culture or of its organizational powers.

Elsewhere I gave reasons to think that pan-Germanism had actually very deep and ancient roots in the Holy Roman Germanic Empire. It is thus a survival of the primitive and fundamental idea of universal sovereignty, which had not been superseded in Germany, as it was in England and France, by the essentially modern idea of territorial sovereignty—the condition and basis of the idea of the nation (see above, chap. 2). We shall come back to this point in the second part of this chapter.

Let us make the picture a little more precise on the French side. To reiterate, we are considering here the major or maximal level of the most common ideology. On that level, I maintain that only the individual human being on the one hand, and the human species on the other, are acknowledged —and nothing in between, nothing like different nations or different cultures: the French tend naively to identify their own culture with culture at large, universally considered. Anything that differs from that model is either strange or defective.

This may seem unbelievable, and at this point loud protests must be expected: isn't it clear that the French, like anybody else, recognize the existence of boundaries, distinct states, and so on? They do, of course, but this does not impinge on what is essential. This is so true that in the nineteenth century the foreign policy of the French government, under one political regime or another, was strongly influenced by the notion that the constitution of the peoples of Europe into nations in conformity with the Rights of Man would be sufficient to abolish war, the emancipation of the individual being in the last analysis the alpha and the omega of foreign policy as well as of internal politics.

No doubt the distinction I make here between a global or primary level of the ideology and other representations, which are less important, less closely bound to the deep identity of the subject, may seem a delicate matter, but only this distinction allows for a comparative grasp of cultures. If we fail to distinguish *levels* of thought, we wipe out all differences, all specific patterns; we are back to the Hegelian night where all cows are black. To sum up, for the Frenchman, the existence of boundaries, of different languages, of conflicts of interest between nations, is negligible in relation to man's essence as expressed in his watchword: Liberty, Equality, Fraternity. The basic or global French ideology is as powerful as it is simple, and devoid of concrete elements. At bottom it consists of a single principle: the human subject as universal. The creed has come down to us from the Enlightenment, of course, through the dispensation of the great Revolution that fondly marks the beginning of the establishment of truth on earth.

If this is so, then the next question one will be expected to ask is surely how has it been possible for such an ideological configuration to endure, and in particular how could it survive the numerous and bloody confrontations with the world as it really is? To answer that question, it is necessary to know more about French internal politics. Therefore we reserve the question for later consideration and we now turn to the Right-Left dichotomy.

•

Two features go to characterize France's internal political history since the 1789 revolution: one is political instability, the other an all-pervading ideological rift between Right and Left. Already in the 1830s Tocqueville was struck by the contrast between the happy implementation of democratic values in the United States and the permanent strife and chronic instability that had followed their introduction in France, and he went to America to compare the two cases more closely.

It is only in the 1870s, after the Franco-Prussian War, that a democratic regime—the Third Republic—was securely established. Until then, the nineteenth century had seen three revolutions—the Three Glorious Days of 1830, the Revolution of 1848 with the ephemeral Second Republic, and the Paris Commune in 1871—and three different kinds of monarchy. Raymond Aron graphically summed up this dramatic course of events, saying that France had been "suffering in turn under the sordid egoism of the rich, the rage of the Revolutionaries, and the despotism of one man" (1967: 18). Can we, long after Tocqueville and with a richer store of dearly bought experience, take up again the question to which he provided a first answer: how can the introduction, in one particular country, of what was thought to be rational human values have ushered in such a train of evils?

Is it only due to the resistance of entrenched privileges and vested interests, within the country and outside it? The question is rarely asked in such terms and current explanations are only partial, for it is generally presumed that no relation prevails between the predominant ideology of the period and the course of events. The same may be said about all the undesirable phenomena that have occurred in the political world at large in our own era, even the massive ones that would appear particular to it, such as world wars or totalitarianism. We believe, and always imply, that our modern ideology is good, and it follows by definition that it can have nothing to do with such scourges. Yet all this belongs to one and the same world, and if only we would admit that there are more things on earth than are dreamt of in our ideology, and that, whatever its excellence, it may have its shortcomings—that is, if we were to look at it comparatively—we would be prepared to face such questions as this: can any understandable relation be discovered between the particular form of democratic ideology inaugurated by the French Revolution and the unfortunate course of history that prevented the establishment of a stable democratic regime in France for almost a century?

Moreover, we note that even during the Third Republic all instability did not disappear. It was only transferred to a relatively minor level: cabinets changed in rapid succession until the end of the regime in 1940. It was then, moreover, with the paramountcy of Parliament over the other agencies of government, that the Right-Left division, of much older origin, became all-embracing and assumed the form under which we still know it today.

•

The distinction between Right and Left in politics has spread far and wide in the world. Nowadays it is perhaps understood everywhere, and used more or less intensively in many places. It originated in France in 1789 and it began to spread only relatively late, first in the mid-century to Italy with parliamentary democracy, and, remarkably, in the socialist movements after 1920 (Laponce 1981: 52–56). Nowhere, probably, has it acquired the pregnancy, the intensity and the scope that it has in France. Nowhere has it become the kind of Manichaeism—a twofold Manichaeism—deplored by the French on occasion as an obstacle to consensus, although it is something like the warp on which their political life is woven.

Everyone in France speaks of the Right and the Left (the words are substantivized), and yet one is hard put to say what the distinction is really about. A concrete reference is implied, for only a human body has a right and a left side. That suggests interdependence. And yet the distinction is abstract, each side being supposedly self-sufficient and excluding the other as an enemy. It is simple in comparison with the direct designation of the different political parties, but it is highly complex in regard to the issues it evokes. It appears as a stable dichotomy whereas in actual fact much water—or should we say blood?—has flowed between those two rival banks over the last two centuries.

At any given moment those two little words allow us to reduce the political nebula to a straight line, a single axis along which all qualitative differences become a mere matter of degree. One forgets that there are three distinct "Rights," as was the case around 1875, and several kinds of socialism—even revolution is but an "extreme" reform. Moreover, the distinction can be segmented at will. All parties, and even the Center, have their Right and their Left.

Although the distinction is familiar to all, it is diversely used and nuanced in different environments. For a Parisian worker of my generation, it was even more social than political. He saw himself as belonging to the Left with his trade union and the party of his choice, probably a socialist one. On the Right were the employers, the rich, and of course the Church and the Army. On the parliamentary level, one reaches the utmost sophistication, as in this formula of 1930: "A Republican of the Left is a man of the Center whom our hard times compel to sit on the Right" (Goguel and Grosser 1981: 26). We shall not grapple with such subtleties but only try and grasp what is comparatively essential.

First, let us go back to the beginning. The French Revolution broke out in 1789, when the king, for the first time after a long interruption, convened the Estates General of the realm. When Louis XVI solemnly opened the Estates General on 5 May 1789, he sat above the Assembly. Below him were first the members of his house, on his right side the Princes, the Princesses on his left. Lower down sat the Deputies: to the right the Clergy, to the left the Nobility, and further off, in between, the Third Order. Soon after, the three orders mixed in a single assembly where the Deputies began to group according to their affinities, debate after debate. The result was to polarize the Assembly from the extremes: the adepts of change were on the

Left, the supporters of tradition on the Right. Historians note that the disposition is fully established on 28 August 1789, when the vote on the royal veto is taken (Laponce 1981: 47).

We see here the origin of a reversal of values. It is generally observed that the right hand has preeminence over the left hand. The Revolutionaries, insofar as they opposed tradition and worked to change the established institutions, were compelled to assemble on the Left. The Revolution established a preeminence of the Left. Henceforth the Left would represent the Revolutionary legacy.[2] To quote a political scientist: "French politics developed in the nineteenth century in terms of a kind of Manichaeism, a permanent conflict between the adversaries and the partisans of the principles of the Revolution" (Goguel and Grosser 1981: 26). The word "principles" should be underscored, for, as we shall find again and again, everything here is a matter of principle.

In the first place, the stress on "principles" makes understandable how for two centuries the Right-versus-Left division could survive all the changes that took place on the political stage and in the objects of political debates. It is clear that at any moment the Right and the Left have something in common (beginning with a common language, including the use of the distinction itself, which allows for the integration of the *other* as an adversary). It is also clear that that common basis has significantly changed over time. In 1789 all Deputies certainly had in common something of the Enlightenment philosophy which pervaded the minds at the time and especially inspired the reformers.[3] But the Rights of Man, and even more so, popular sovereignty, were not accepted without a struggle. And yet, who today would call in question universal franchise? It is obvious that a considerable part of the initial values of the Left have become common to all. But if the themes have changed, if the locus of debate has shifted, the principle of opposition stands. It is sometimes possible to pinpoint the migration

2. Here, François Furet asks us not to forget that the opposition between adepts and adversaries of the French Revolution forms only the matrix of French political opinions and that, owing to the very course of events that constitute it, the Revolution engendered many divisions in the camp of its followers. One has only to consider our nineteenth century, when Orleanists, Republicans, Bonapartists, Jacobins, socialists, etc., confront each other. But it can also be said that in a sense these divisions reproduce the one that has been their model and their origin, inscribed in the Manichaean partition of 1789 between *aristocrates* and *patriotes*. (Personal communication).

3. There is more to it than that, according to Furet. The revolutionary culture based on political overinvestment for the regeneration of the society is common to all parties, even to those who oppose the principles of 1789, and even, a little later in the century, to those who want to oppose the progression of political and social democracy. This culture does unceasingly divide the national political space in radical confrontations. (Personal communication).

of a theme from one camp to the other. Thus we shall see that the word "nation" passed from the Left to the Right between 1792 and 1890. One could even speak of a fluctuation of ideological contents between Left and Right. Thus the Assembly of the Second Republic elected by universal suffrage in 1849 decided to return to limited franchise, with the result that Louis Napoléon, who put an end to the Republic through a coup d'état, could give himself an air of the perfect democrat by organizing a plebiscite. Even a few years ago, we have seen our socialists exchange at short notice (1981–83) a mystique of nationalizations for an apologia for the daring individual entrepreneur.

But to come back to principles. The Revolution itself was characterized by an absolute disjunction between principles on the one hand and the empirical state of things on the other. I noted earlier a remark by Condorcet which is the more interesting as he had worked with Thomas Paine (Dumont 1986: 96). Regarding the Constitution, he criticizes the Americans for having stressed identity of interests rather than equality of rights: here is the difference between an orientation toward utility and practicality, and the assertion of naked principle.

Our Left has inherited this exclusive attention to principles, to the neglect of the difficulties of their factual application, and it is still alive with us. There is no doubt that this is what characterizes France in contrast to the Anglo-American democracies, and which explains why our Right-Left opposition is as absolute, irremediable, indeed almost as inexpiable as it is.

On this point, I shall quote Emile Littré. Littré is known as the author of the most authoritative dictionary of the French language. He was also trained in medicine, and as a positivist philosopher and political analyst was a disciple of Auguste Comte. He wrote in June 1851, about the watchword Liberty, Equality, Fraternity:

> Considered in itself the Revolutionary formula reveals immediately its metaphysical origin. I mean that it does not represent how things actually are, but rather a subjective notion, an idea that came to the mind at the end of the eighteenth century of what a normal society should be. (1879: 330–31)

Littré added that the Revolutionary motto was completely unable "to represent the actual existence of any society," that it was inapplicable to the present and the future as well as to the past.

By and large, Littré was right: the "actual existence" of any society, whether past, present, or future, is not reducible to the individualistic principle. I have directly demonstrated the fact elsewhere. There are only two points on which Littré's dictum, illuminating as it is, must be corrected or modified. First, Littré's positivism misled him into thinking that the eighteenth-century ideal was becoming obsolete; it is quite alive at present in the whole world. Second, we should introduce a distinction, which Littré does not make, as to the applicability of the ideal. He is right in saying that the revolutionary principles are inapplicable *in toto* and instantly. But history shows that they have not been altogether ineffective either. The truth is that they have managed to become reality in some measure, gradually, in some respects. Only the price that had to be paid for this slow and incomplete implementation may be judged a high one. One positive result of this limited applicability is that the ideal, remaining unrealized in its perfection, may be invoked again and again as fresh as ever.

Let us recall that the positivists thought that the Revolutionary watchword had presided over a destructive, negative stage of the Revolution, and expected the Revolution to close with a second positive, constructive stage, whose motto would be "Order and Progress," and which Littré saw dawning in 1878 with the Third Republic. From 1789 until then, the country had been torn between progress without order, or rather against order, that is, Revolution, and order without or against progress, that is, reaction and conservatism. To these two terms, and in conformity with the historical record, Raymond Aron's formula adds a third one, "despotism" (quoted above). It has often been observed that it is natural to have recourse to one man to maintain unity in a deeply divided society, but the point requires analysis.

We have in our country a recent example of such a resort. I am thinking of de Gaulle in 1958. Looking back, one sees France, facing the Algerian crisis, on the brink of civil war, so much so that her savior needed a measure of Machiavellianism to avoid it. (Jean Lacouture wrote recently that the Prince had increased tensions by overdoing it, but this is perhaps not the last word in the matter.) Let me note in passing that the French intellectuals on the Left, distrusting de Gaulle as a man of the Right, were mistaken to the end about his real intention, and that today our ideological blinkers have the effect of throwing the event into oblivion, for neither side has been able to retain the lesson. To do so, we must define politics, or the political domain. The French tend to be suspicious of the State, and they have for long lent an ear to the theory that reduces politics to a secondary category dependent on economics. Fortunately things have changed in the last decades, and the political category is now better acknowledged as a fundamental one. What is the grounding principle of the political domain in relation to society at large? We shall posit that the political level appears when a society is seen as a unit facing other societies (whether empirically as in war, or ideologically). The society taken as *one* is *ipso facto* superior to the society seen in its multiplicity and legitimately commands over it. This is found even with Rousseau, who opposes the general will to the will of all, the citizen as participating in sovereignty to the subject.

Once the political category is thus defined in its very principle, we are reminded that the immediate figure of this unity is its incarnation in a person. This is true not only of the past but of the present as well, except that for contemporary nations the function is no longer generally conceived as hereditary. On this point alone—excepting the United Kingdom and a few others—history has vindicated the sarcasms Marx once directed at Hegel's justification of monarchy.

What interests us here is the case where an insoluble ideological conflict, rooted, if not in different rationalities, yet in different rationalizations, leads to the supremacy of one man. Most commonly, attention is paid exclusively to the concentration of power; I should like to draw attention to another aspect, the one for which Max Weber borrowed from theology the word, widespread today, of charisma. The word by itself obscures the matter rather than clearing it up. Actually the mere introduction of a human being reopens a world of perceptions and sentiment that had no place in the ideological debate. The citizen-subject may again feel respect, admiration, attachment, devotion, identification, and he may even feel alleviation from a tension that had been experienced as at once extreme and narrow. I am here only expressing in terms of human feelings what is called a shift from a rational to a traditional orientation, or, in Talcott Parson's terms, from universalism and specificity to particularism and diffuseness. Given the strength of universalism among the French, the change may be deemed a fall, or self-disavowal. Let us not forget that they had put to death in the person of Louis XVI the figure history had given to their particularity.

This seeming digression was intended to set the third term of Aron's dictum, "despotism," in its proper relation to the two others. Long before Aron, in 1848, Littré again, calling the period "an eternal halt between anarchy and disorder," laid bare the vicious circle of its dynamics:

> Ever again reactionary successes would in the end discredit order and
> open the way to new commotions; ever again revolutionary successes
> would in the end discredit progress and open the way to new reactions.
> (1879: 161)

The problem for us is to get out of the dilemma, to master the alternation. This Aron did not do, for in his well-balanced formula he was content with looking at the Left with the eyes of the Right, seeing "the fury of the Revolutionaries," and at the Right with the eyes of the Left, seeing "the sordid egoism of the rich." We must, on the contrary, as Littré hinted, be able to identify positive content on both sides.

It is possible to do so by finding a hierarchical relation between the two terms. To start with, we know full well that generally speaking the right hand and the left hand are never equal, and we have seen that the Revolutionaries have not abolished the hierarchical relation between the two, they have only reversed it for their own use. The problem for us is to find whether one or the other of the two opposed "preeminences" has been underwritten by history, can be taken as historically established. To this question the answer is plain, there is no place for doubt. We saw earlier that comparison delivers a picture of French *global* ideology which is by and large that of the Left. History tells us something similar, for the point of arrival is not identical with the point of departure, and all the intervening dramas that have occurred should not hide from us the final result. As we already stated in passing: *in the long run,* some of the fundamental themes of the ideology of the Left have imposed themselves, political institutions have been transformed and even in some measure social institutions. In retrospect it cannot be denied that the motive force in our history was on this side. We must conclude that the ideology of the Left has been and still is predominant as such, that is to say, on the ideological level.

In good method, this ideological predominance authorizes a hypothesis, namely, that the historical development was determined in its general shape or rhythm by the characteristic or idiosyncratic features of the ideology of the Left. Indeed we already touched on that point when we said how the divorce between the ideal and the actual made impossible a global implementation of the principles and condemned them to be translated into facts only slowly and piecemeal.

Now the theory of hierarchy prepares us to find a reversal when passing from the ideological to the empirical level: whatever is preeminent ideologically will be disadvantaged empirically. This is very much the case here. As the Left did not concede ontological status to anything that then existed and that was not in conformity with its principles, it left out all that was just actually given in the society, backed by tradition and history, except for the points or restricted domains where the legislator intervened. It is as though the Left had by its extreme one-sidedness abandoned to the care of the Right, and put at its disposal as a store of strength, most of the complex interrelations that made for the functioning of the society. Hence the proverbial figure, in this century, of the Leftist voter, who supports anti-

Church policies but goes to church for his family ceremonies. Only after they had fought side by side in the trenches of the First World War were the village curate and the state schoolteacher reconciled enough to act together in an association of veterans.

The Revolutionaries thought they were building everything anew, from scratch, while they were actually busy grafting a scion onto a live tree. That is why the Right, ideologically impotent, has been empirically powerful in the long run. Yet, if such was the balance of forces in general, we should not forget that changes have taken place. The permanence of the oversimple vocabulary of French political struggles should not mislead us into exaggerating the continuity and into surmising that the balance of forces has remained stable except for short-term oscillations. Looking at the scene today, it is obvious that the enormous increase of state power has corresponded with an increase of the relative weight of the Left through the recurring intervention of the State in economic and social life.

A clear discontinuity was marked by the establishment of the Third Republic, actually the first viable one. In the words of a historian, the word "Republic" then ceased to be "that mythical opening into Hell and Paradise that it had been ever since 1792" (Nicolet 1982: 204); it ceased to be a utopia and became something real. Its birth was slow and difficult (1870–78), it was the fruit of a series of compromises between politicians of the Right and of the Left. To accept compromises was for people of the Left an absolutely new occurrence. It was done thanks to a handful of shrewd men in whom the values of the Revolution were quite alive but who had learned from history, and probably from the recent humiliation of being defeated by the German armies, that principles are not everything.

From that time onward, the process of slow implementation of Leftist values went on more smoothly under the institutional dominance of the Left, eroding in succession the strongholds of the Right: the Army, the Church, and the power of wealth.

•

In order to size up our subject matter through two centuries of political life, we have neglected hitherto the changing contents of the ideological struggle. Let us now consider a concrete example of confrontation. We shall choose one of the deep crises the regime went through, the Dreyfus Affair. The Republic was twenty years old when Captain Dreyfus, an artillery officer born in Alsace of a Jewish family, was accused by the Intelligence Branch of the army of having passed confidential information to the military attaché of the German Embassy in Paris. First degraded and banished to Guyana for life under especially cruel confinement conditions, he was finally rehabilitated, after many years and several trials, his accusers and the army hierarchy having been convicted of forgery and complicity. This was achieved thanks to an unprecedented mobilization of public opinion where Leftist intellectuals played a decisive role, for the first time, of which the famous pamphlet by the novelist Emile Zola entitled "I accuse . . ." was the starting point and can serve as the epitome. The intensity of the strife caused by what was simply called "the Affair" can hardly be imagined, as it divided the whole country, best friends and otherwise united families. It can be conveniently studied in an excellent recent monograph, which I shall use (Bredin 1983).

A diplomat who was commissioned to attend all the sessions of the Courts and had witnessed the development of the affair from beginning to end, Maurice Paléologue, gave the most condensed definition of it. He saw it as a struggle between what he called "two sacred sentiments, the love of justice and the religion of the fatherland." We need not speak of something "sacred," but two supreme values were indeed at stake. In one camp were the high officers of the army, fearful of the German neighbor and later on committed by esprit-de-corps and raison d'état to cover up any blunder their subordinates might have committed, backed by vibrant patriots respectful of the army and more often than not sensitive to anti-Semitic propaganda. In the other camp was most of the Left, suspicious of the army as a reactionary corporation and rallying all those who cared above all for the dignity of man and for justice. Adrien Dansette expressed well that it was a matter of the paramountcy of one value or the other: he saw "on one side the principle that everything had to be judged in relation to France" (that is, nationalism, still in a nascent state after the 1870 defeat); on the other, the principle that "the Rights of Man are above any institution and any conviction." And still more clearly, Jaurès, a great Socialist leader who, as a Socialist, did not take sides immediately, soon declared: "The human individual is the measure of all things, of fatherland, family, property, humanity, or God. Here is the logic of the Revolutionary idea." And, he added, "here is Socialism" (Bredin 1983: 631), a dictum to which we shall have to come back.

This declaration of Jaurès tracing Leftist values to their ultimate principle is valuable for us insofar as the principle applies beyond the Left alone and therefore throws light upon the concrete situation of the Right. If individualism, properly defined, is the cardinal value of modern times, and especially of post-1789 France, then it is clear that its systematic development by the Left has ensured its ideological supremacy. And, furthermore, who would pretend that the adepts of what Maurice Paléologue called "the religion of the fatherland" were absolutely immune to individualism? They could only limit its application, admitting it here—say in economic matters —and excluding it there—in matters of national import. This sort of disposition explains how the Right was somehow inferior and weaker ideologically, as *encompassed* in the Left, and felt itself to be so, taking on occasion a defensive or shameful attitude and appearing insecure and self-conscious.

A strange feature of the Affair is found in the very personality of its involuntary hero. In the end he disappointed his champions as well as his enemies through his modesty, his reserve, his refusal of any affectation or rhetoric, to the point that he tended to pass for an insipid character, someone deprived of any strong conviction or courage—despite the fact that his having withstood the terrible conditions of his transportation would be enough to demonstrate the contrary. Bredin notices this, and in the last page of his book he reflects that this startling quality of Dreyfus is due, at least for a large part, to his having housed in peaceful association within himself the two ideologies that he saw so fiercely assaulting each other around him. Deeply attached to France and to its army—never distrustful of his superiors until their indignity was made clear to him—he would never separate the cult of his fatherland from that of justice and the dignity of man. For him both were but one thing, and he witnessed in incredulity and bafflement the deadly fight of which he was himself the occasion. His humility was that of a saint who did not know the reason for his martyrdom.

But let us go back to the beginning. The volunteers of Valmy in 1792 would have found as incomprehensible as did Dreyfus a conflict between "the Nation," that is, France, and the Rights of Man. The clue to Dreyfus's attitude is perhaps that, as a perfectly assimilated Jew, he was a kind of neophyte to the Republic who had not gone beyond the Valmy stage. He was blissfully ignorant of the checkered history of the intervening century, of the ever recurring struggle between the universalist ideal and the forces of conservation, that struggle which Littré, and with him Gambetta and Jules Ferry, the founders of the Third Republic, had been so intensely conscious of having inherited.

In fact, we are led to conclude that something that was united at the dawn of the Republic, in Valmy, and that remained united for Dreyfus himself, had become divided when put to the test of history in the nineteenth century. This is reflected in the vocabulary, as what Claude Nicolet has described as the migration of the word *nation* from the camp of the Left to the that of the Right (1982: 16). The proud outcry of the troop at Valmy, "Vive la nation," expressed the identity of the community (*Gemeinschaft*) with the new society of free and equal individuals (*Gesellschaft*). In other words, at that exceptional historical moment the individualism of the Revolution asserted itself as the heir which implicitly carried on the holism of the traditional society. The people of one land, one territory, gave itself over to universal values. It was this enthusiastic and paradoxical identification that would not stand the test of history. Hence a shift of the word "nation" itself. It began with the Right slowly accepting the term in the course of the century, so that it became part of the common vocabulary. Then the trauma of 1870–71 intensified the feeling, and there appeared a new phenomenon, a French nationalism. To quote Nicolet:

> This nationalism [which Renan, Taine, Fustel de Coulanges occasionally discuss] will not renounce anything of the Revolutionary patrimony but at the same time, by dissociating the nation from the transitory regimes,—especially from the Republic—, by rejecting universalist and cosmopolitan ideologies, finally by recovering the ethnic roots of the nation of the Ancien Régime [let us call it the holistic perception of the French community] . . . , it will become a Rightist, mostly anti-Republican ideology. (1982: 17–18)

Such a nationalism nourished the ephemeral popularity of General Boulanger, who seemed for a short time to represent a threat to democracy, and after the crisis the Left decidedly preferred the words "patriot," "patriotism." The shift was then complete: the word "nation" had accomplished its migration.

This shift can be seen to be the trace of an ideological fission: the particularistic holism which the 1792 Revolutionaries encompassed in their universalistic individualism asserted itself independently from and in opposition to this universalism. That is what Dreyfus was blind to.

Did nationalism become the essential content of the Rightist ideology in the days of the Boulangist crisis and the Dreyfus Affair? In the perspective adopted here, it is one fundamental element. Thus, for instance, what was in the same period in Germany the core of the global ideology was in France only a relatively minor component of the global ideology. This does not mean that the Right has a monopoly on patriotism, for the Left participates in it in some way, just as the Right does not totally escape the individualism which is at the core of the Left. It is only a question of the relative rank attributed, on either side, to the preoccupations of universal justice and national destiny, as in the formulas of Paléologue and Dansette that we quoted. In other words, the relative rank of France as a community and as a society.

The Dreyfus Affair is important in many respects. For our present concern, it confirms our analysis insofar as its final solution went according to the hierarchy of values that we have acknowledged here. The fact that the Republican regime was able to weather such a shattering storm shows the wisdom of its founders. The Constitution itself had issued from a difficult conciliation between some royalists on the one hand, some liberals and republicans on the other, and the great republican statesmen chose to govern through a union of moderate republicans and those of the conservatives who were nearer to them. Claude Nicolet underscores the role of three men. The influence of positivism was important, especially through Littré, who had lived through all the great conflicts of the century and had the courage to republish his old articles with commentaries, including some painful recantations (he died in 1881). Gambetta and Jules Ferry, despite their republican zeal, were also sages who were able to postpone their most cherished reforms—the "Separation between Church and State"—and to introduce at first only those the country was prepared to admit. It is thanks to them, and to the public education which they introduced, that a series of victories at the polls, first of the republicans and then of the radicals, secured the Republic and made possible the "Separation" at the beginning of the twentieth century.

The wisdom of a few statesmen has of course not brought to an end France's ideological dichotomy. The Republic only assuaged it and made the Parliament the arena of choice for its exercise. Very soon, for instance, the republicans were divided into "opportunists" and "radicals." The preeminence of the Left among the representatives of the nation was so marked that latter day political scientists have coined the word "sinistrism" (or *sinistrose*) to designate it. Nicolet aptly defines the phenomenon as a

> double movement: with age most Leftist parties and labels evolve toward the Center, toward the Right. . . . On the other hand formations periodically appear on their left, which play the same structural role toward them as they themselves played one generation earlier. (1982: 184)

The party called "Radical" is a case in point. Soon doubled by the "Radical-Socialists," it opposed at first, between 1875 and 1885, the opportunism of Gambetta and Ferry. Its chief figure was Clemenceau. And just as Clemenceau then opposed Ferry, so in the 1890s the Socialist Jaurès would oppose Clemenceau. The evolution of the latter was spectacular. He actually exchanged one camp for the other, being a libertarian anarchist at the beginning of the Dreyfus affair, and a minister who implacably repressed the workers' strikes in 1906—not to speak of his incarnating the war effort in the last years of the First World War and dictating the harsh conditions of the Peace of Versailles. Equally clear is the Socialist shift from intransigent opposition to participation in the government, beginning with that of Millerand in 1906, which appeared as an act of treason to the party.

The whole situation has sometimes been summed up by saying that a politician had to belong to the Left to get elected, and had to move toward the Right to attain a government post. In brief: "One gets elected on the Left, and one governs on the Right."

Nicolet admits that this "sinistrism" had deep social and ideological causes. Actually, we can show that it results from the ideology itself as analyzed here. The disjunction between principle and actuality, on which we insisted, implied, under the Third Republic, a dynamic of political life. For if the ideology cannot be implemented in its pure state, then people of the Left cannot govern without compromising with the existing order, without, that is, betraying their initial commitment. And as long as the ideology remains alive and strong, it will revive as a phoenix under the form of a new party, ever more radical than its forerunners, rising to the left of the Left: after the Radicals properly called, the Socialists, then the Communists.

It can be objected that the political ascension of socialism in the widest sense, no doubt a major ideological event of the period, introduced a new, heterogeneous element, for, as I stated elsewhere (Dumont 1986: 103), socialism does not merely continue the French Revolution, it also goes against it in some of its aspects—in varying degree in its diverse tendencies. Yet Socialists like to think of themselves as its direct heirs. Karl Polanyi saw in socialism the end product of Christian individualism (*The Great Transformation*). In France this was ideologically decisive. Thus Jaurès, in the passage quoted, identified with the individualistic principle both "the Revolutionary idea" and socialism. From 1920 onward, the supporters of the Bolshevik Revolution presented it as the sequence and the achievement of 1789. As unlikely as the thesis may look, the wide audience of the Communists in France up to the Second World War was due to their having thus managed partly to confiscate for their own purposes the Leftist ideology which was so strongly alive among the common people.

Apart from the peculiar pattern called "sinistrism," many general features of political life under the Third Republic may, we believe, be understood through the existence and the strength of the ideological configuration we

have outlined. This is true of the notorious shortcomings of the political
system. We cannot here enter into details, but only mention government
instability, the frequent ineffectiveness of policies, the weakness of the executive. With respect to the latter, it is characteristic that the dissolution of
the Chamber by the executive, although explicitly provided for in the Constitution, was not resorted to one single time. More important perhaps, the
particular path taken by the progress of legislation and political action on
the society, the fact that such and such measures—and not others—were
taken, in such and such an order, should be amenable to our analysis, but
we can here only sketch an approach. On the one hand, one can discern the
main stages that secured the foundations of the regime, and thus laid the
basis, at one remove, of the present-day political and social system. On
the other hand, it has been stated, and it is fairly obvious, that social progress has been relatively slow in comparison with other countries. Thus, it
is remarkable that Bismarck established a social security system in Germany, while France had to wait for it until after the Second World War. At
the same time Bismarck failed against the Catholic Church, where the
French succeeded. Political action in France in that period was oriented
more to ideological and political aims than to social welfare.

•

Summing up the course of this study, I think we have acquired two perceptions: the predominant ideology in France is that of the Left. It implies the
commonly held belief that whatever is easy to conceive of should be easy to
realize in practice. But in actual fact, and contrary to this belief, that ideology was so foreign to social actuality that the efforts to implement it issued
in recurring disappointments and setbacks, with the final result that a Republic based on universal suffrage—or almost so—could be really established only after a century of hardships and trials. We have thus enabled
ourselves to understand, in general terms, the kind of fatality recalled by
Raymond Aron, and also to acknowledge how the Right, though being
ideologically subordinate, has nevertheless been in charge of a part of the
common patrimony.

This latter point will come out still more clearly if we contrast individualism, in which, as Jaurès put it, "the individual is the measure of all
things," and holism as the reverse case, where the social totality, the global
society, is valued above and against the individual.

If we compare France with its neighbors regarding the respective place
of individualism and holism in the global ideology (and the institutions) of
the country, we find that France is characterized essentially by the exclusive

affirmation of the individualism inherited from the Enlightenment. In contrast, England possesses an altogether similar form of individualism, but has been able to combine with it a good deal of traditional, older, holistic inheritance. Thus it has no written constitution but relies much on precedent, in its jurisprudence and in general; it keeps a monarchy, and has a state religion, although not a national one. As for Germany, it acculturated intensely to the newest form of modernity around 1800 and built up a culture in which, in contrast with England, enlightened individualism figures as an element partly modified by a new and original combination of holism and individualism.

If now we ask where in the French configuration the holistic aspects present elsewhere are to be found, those aspects which the encompassing French values, those of the Left, ignore and without which the society could probably not exist, the political domain offers an answer: these aspects are found on the Right, mostly in a subordinate position, sometimes shamefaced or self-conscious, and reasserted now and then in unexpected and sometimes violent ways.

My aim here has been to elucidate an ideological configuration and some of its factual concomitants. If I may submit a methodological conclusion: in my view the study of such general representations requires three conditions: (1) they should be identified through comparison; (2) they should be considered in a long-range historical perspective; (3) the analysis should follow a hierarchical method, going from the global level to the local and not the reverse.

2. THE IMPACT OF WAR

We can now confront a question that we encountered earlier and preferred to put off for a while. It appeared as an objection: if the French as a people are in essentials as universalist in spirit as we claim here, how was it possible for them to engage in or connive at so many wars since 1789? Or, conversely, given the recurrent experience of war, how could the universalist ideology, which relegates national particularity to an accessory rank, maintain itself? And, secondarily, should we neglect the stereotype, widespread among their neighbors, according to which the French are by nature aggressive and quarrelsome?

In English, section 2 of this chapter was first published, in slightly different form, under the title "Modern Ideology and War: The French Case Seen in Comparison with the German," in *Literature, Culture, and Society in the Modern Age: In honor of Joseph Frank,* ed. Edward J. Brown et al., part 1, Stanford Slavic Studies, vol. 4 (Stanford, Calif.: Department of Slavic Languages and Literatures, Stanford University, 1991). The present version was translated by Christophe Robert and revised by the author.

Behind this question there looms a more general problem: we have to deal with the relations between war and ideology under a particular form. Modern ideology in general accounts poorly for the existence of war in its universe. Let us recall that war was supposed to disappear with the end of the supremacy of the martial order and the advent of the bourgeois, the merchant, and the scholar. It was widely perceived as an anachronism, a barbaric survival. Quite naturally, there was a recourse to economism, and a theory of imperialistic war arose. But here as elsewhere we can say very generally that war—and the same is true of totalitarianism—is construed as foreign to modern ideology, as a fatality imposed on democracy from without, resulting from the interplay of obscure forces. Democracy is help-less but innocent; modern ideology cannot be held responsible for war and has no inner relations to it whatsoever. For instance, the First World War is seen retrospectively as a nonsense accompanied by millions of casualties.

This is actually a deeply demoralizing view, a view opposed, after all, to the democratic spirit, for it amounts to admitting that the millions who died were deceived.

It should be obvious that a deep flaw underlies all this. War, and totali-tarianism as well, are modern phenomena, which necessarily are in a deter-mined relation with contemporary ideology. The latter skirts the debate only by recourse to its own double internal prejudice, i.e., that it is all good and cannot produce any adverse effects, and moreover that the annoyances in question arise, conversely, from material facts and their concatenations. Clearly, there is here a fault to be remedied in modern consciousness.

One may agree about the principle, but what about the means? Is not the expression "modern ideology" too vague to be of any use? By no means. The present research has begun to unravel its overall configuration.

The true difficulty here is that modern ideology assumes different forms in different countries. Hence comparison is indispensable. Just as it has previously allowed us to distinguish the modern from the nonmodern, the comparison between France and Germany should here help us establish the relations between ideology and events. It so happens that these two countries exhibit, in the end, beyond a most pronounced difference, a par-allelism that is instructive for our concern, as we shall see at the close of the study.

We shall deal mostly with France and the two wars of 1870–71 and 1914–18, but it is useful first to recall the contrasting forms of what we customarily call ethnocentrism—or, preferably, sociocentrism—in the two countries. Since 1789, and in virtue of the Declaration of the Rights of Man, the French fondly see themselves as the teachers of mankind. In Germany sociocentrism assumes a different form, apparently of much more remote origin. During the period under consideration, we witnessed (using the ethnographic present throughout, I will say we *witness*) pan-Germanism, that is, Germany's vocation to dominate other peoples. I proposed elsewhere that it be understood in terms of the survival of the idea of *universal sovereignty,* with which the Holy Roman Empire of the German people was indeed invested in medieval Christendom. As we know, universal sovereignty is a very ancient idea, widely encountered in all great civilizations. It is actually the primitive idea of sovereignty, for which it would be difficult to find another origin. The Holy Roman Empire still represented universal sovereignty during the Middle Ages, and in Germany it was not superseded by the idea of *territorial sovereignty,* as it was in France and in England, as the result of a deep transformation. The hypothesis may seem surprising. I cannot justify it here,[4] but only point out that it allows one to account for the apparently aberrant form of German sociocentrism. As for the long remanence this hypothesis supposes, we shall hereafter suggest reasons why these ideological forms are remarkably stable and enduring. The notion of universal sovereignty is a special case in the sense that once it existed, and for lack of an alternative, it could probably only maintain itself.

•

Let us now focus on France. In any case, the two countries are so closely bound to each other in the two wars we shall consider that this long digression is not irrelevant to what follows.

In our study of the impact of the defeat of 1870–71 on French ideology, we shall use as a guide Claude Digeon's *La Crise allemande de la pensée française* (1959). We shall only have to transcribe the conclusions of this work into our general conceptual framework, but let us first recall what was said previously. In the predominant ideology, the Frenchman sees himself as a man by nature and a Frenchman by accident, which is what we call individualism, while the German feels he is first a German and a man through his being a German, which corresponds to what we call holism. For the German, belonging is cultural, while for the Frenchman it is political. This represents the global level set forth by the comparison. There are

4. A somewhat more ample development is found above, in chap. 2. The emergence in France and in the United Kingdom of the political domain as we know it results from the transformation in question. The chapter 2 of my *Essays* (1986) should in principle be rewritten accordingly.

also subordinate levels, two of which are indispensable in our discussion of France: first, the global French ideology is that of the Left, and there is also an ideology of the Right which exhibits relatively explicit holistic aspects;[5] and second, we encounter what we shall call patriotism (in opposition to nationalism). The Right may appropriate patriotism as much as it pleases, while on the Left, one is French by accident: there is a deep-seated, perhaps, but usually barely conscious feeling—it can even occasionally be denied by the subject—of the *Patrie*, the fatherland. The word itself, by the way, invites reflection. The French word is feminine, it speaks of the Fathers in the feminine gender, whereas the German language says *Vaterland* and English *mother country* (or *fatherland*): is it futile to see here a sense of sentimental decency? Universalism is to the fatherland somewhat as reason is to the heart, or value to fact. What follows will show the advantage there is in taking into account the difference of levels.

At the risk of oversimplifying, we will now summarize the events of 1870–71 from the point of view of French ideology, of the division between Left and Right and the attitude vis-à-vis the outside world. The fall of the Empire, followed by the disastrous outcome of a defensive war, resulted in an unprecedented national humiliation and deeply divided the country between the "rural people" and the Assembly on the one hand, and the democrats and the people in the large cities and in Paris on the other. The former, peasants and others, accepted defeat and turned to their traditional conservative leaders, while the latter—craftsmen, industrial workers, and others—reasserted their revolutionary heritage and were ready to fight to the death for liberty and progress. In these circumstances, it is clear that the supporters of order were not steadfastly ready to fight the foreigners at any price. There is here an analogy, not to be overemphasized, with the defeat of 1940 and the call to Pétain.

Before mentioning the short-term political developments, we have to consider further the consequences of these events on French public opinion or rather, since more is involved than simply opinion, on French minds.

Our guide, like other authors, tells us that until 1870 patriotism and universalism were quietly united in France. We encountered something akin to this in the enthusiasm of the volunteers of Valmy. However, it is essential to take into account the hierarchy between these two allegiances,

5. "relatively explicit": the psychology of a man of the Left should not be supposed to be completely, monolithically subjected to individualism. In our formal opposition, it is a matter of relative predominance, and of conscious aspects only. Opposite features can coexist in various ways (different levels of consciousness, relative isolation of different domains, etc.).

since universalism is primary and prohibits any aggressive attitude toward other nations. Only then can one understand the depth and the true nature of the trauma the French underwent in 1870–71.

Let us add a note to underline how far the French were, until then, from nationalism as we understand it today. The "principle of nationalities" was in fashion, and the emperor Napoleon III himself subscribed to it: for instance, he helped the unification of northern Italy (which was rather advantageous for France) and he even looked favorably upon a limited unification of Germany. There was a widespread opinion that if only all people organized themselves as nations, the way the French had done, peace would be guaranteed thanks to the "solidarity of sister nations" (Littré; quoted in Digeon 1959: 86). Being a "nationalist" meant subscribing to this creed. The events of 1870–71, of course, put an end to these speculations.

For people who believed that their values elevated them above all differences, national and otherwise, it was a rude awakening to be confronted with the most implacable policy of power, with an enemy that was hostile not only to the fallen regime but also to the nation itself, to the point of imposing its amputation at gunpoint. In brief, the cardinal French value, the naive universalism that seemed to result immediately from the Rights of Man, was in check. Bismarck demonstrated to the French that they were simply a particular society or nation among others, and they had to reappraise their fondest beliefs to account for this fact. The shock is well expressed by Littré, who wrote at the end of 1871:

> We who brought up our children in a benevolent respect for foreign peoples! We have to change all that . . . we have to inculcate in them that they must always be ready to kill and be killed, for it is the only way to avoid the fate of Alsace and Lorraine, the saddest of misfortunes, the most poignant of pains.

And again: for the time being, we must

> reorganize militarily with unyielding determination . . . and cultivate a deep love of the fatherland in all hearts. In our rebuilding effort, let us never forget what it means to be beaten and invaded. (Quoted in Digeon 1959: 86)

"Rebuilding"—in French *reconstitution*—or more often "regeneration," were the watchwords during the following years. No doubt there were several ways to conceive of this "regeneration." The overall climate of public opinion favored views that we would today call revisionist; for a time the more moderate views of the Right were in favor. French people were admonished to turn away from their complacent universalism and their humanitarian dreams, to turn inward and to dedicate their energies to the pressing needs of the country. According to some, the noble ideal of 1789 had to be discarded and the principles of 1789 repudiated. For others, only a part of the heritage was to be rejected. And dedicated but shrewd republicans such as Edgar Quinet, who had long before foreseen Germany's evolution, were forced to set aside their fondest ideals for the time being and save them for a distant future.

The worst wound was Alsace-Lorraine. For the republicans it was the most direct demonstration that they had deluded themselves by supposing that their values, by virtue of their being universal in principle, would re-main unshakable in fact. In particular, they had believed that their own idea of the nation was the only one. And now, not only had France wit-nessed the loss of part of herself, but this exaction was being justified by eminent and respected German scholars thanks to another theory of the nation, the ethnic theory, according to which belonging was not a matter of free consensus but of inherited characteristics, such as language, culture, or race. Obviously, no Frenchman could ever subscribe to such a negation of liberty.

In this atmosphere, the development of France's internal politics is more readily understandable. Hastily planned elections had sent a majority of royalists and a minority of republicans to the Assembly, but the number of republicans steadily increased as a result of successive special elections. As one knows, there were three kinds of monarchists: traditional, constitu-tional, and "imperialist," as the supporters of the empire were then called. The latter, which were weak at the beginning, regained strength over time. Thus there existed three irreconcilable parties on the Right of the Assem-bly, or, as was sometimes said, three different Rights. The Assembly re-mained in session after the peace treaty was signed in order to draw up a new constitution, which took time. If the monarchists had not been unable to make concessions to each other, France would actually have received a royalist constitution. The traditional monarchists were naturally the least affected of all parties by the national humiliation, since they could see it as an additional confirmation of their judgment that since the Revolution, France had been heading in the wrong direction. In their view, it was now being providentially brought back to its natural leaders.

Conversely, the republicans were the most affected by the disaster. As we pointed out, they had seen the invader trample down their highest beliefs. They were now suffering, in the deepest recesses of their souls, where an unreasoned attachment to the fatherland bore the seal of the universal ideal. The most moderate and shrewdest among them sobered down to a surprising degree. The wise Littré confessed a little later that he would not have opposed the restoration of the monarchy if it had been proposed right away, since, in his words, "after the dreadful disasters that the foolish ineptness of the Empire has precipitated us into, the single most pressing issue is to reconstruct our moral and material forces" (quoted in Digeon 1959: 85). As a positivist republican, Littré was not superstitiously attached to a given form of government. His case may be extreme, but we know that he was not the only one taught by urgency to move from distress to moderation. We previously mentioned Claude Nicolet's judgment that the capacity for compromise of the moderate republicans was decisive in establishing the first stable republican regime. We are suggesting here, on the whole following Digeon, that their moderation was taught them by the torturing humiliation they had just suffered, and that it is what made the Third Republic possible. Here is a quite unexpected gift from Bismarck to France. The figure of Gambetta can in itself serve as a symbol. He was originally the most valiant champion of resistance to the invasion, but once prevented from continuing the fight, he became a most reasonable and clever politician and the best builder of the Republic, which was originally so frail.

Two facts illustrate how improbable the actual result appeared throughout. After the majority of the Assembly had agreed upon the type of monarchy to be established, the Count of Chambord was asked to accept the tricolor flag as the national emblem, but he refused in the end to abandon the dynastic white flag. This was the decisive turn. And yet the new regime did not assume the name of republic until 1875, when, indirectly, with the notorious Wallon amendment that passed with a majority of one vote, the head of state was to be elected as "president of the Republic." It was only in 1878, with the election of the new president, that the three foremost powers of the State, the presidency and the majority in the two Chambers, were in the hands of the republicans.

What was said above concerning the ideology of the French has an immediate bearing on their reaction to the loss of Alsace-Lorraine. As we saw, a Frenchman feels he is first a man, i.e., universal, and he sees his belonging to a given nation as essentially political: he is a citizen according to the Rights of Man, and thus a Frenchman. The same was true for the people of Alsace-Lorraine, as they perceived themselves and were perceived by other French people. Let us recall that in 1790 a social contract had been proclaimed throughout the nation. In Alsace, as elsewhere, people associated themselves—one said "federated" at the time—locally first, then regionally, and finally nationally in Paris for the first anniversary of the storming of the Bastille. They had sworn fidelity to the country as a whole. The Rights of Man were the cement of the unity thus established, and the tricolor flag remained the symbol of the event, in Alsace as elsewhere, as Max Weber testified later upon visiting the Colmar museum.

France was thus sooner or later bound to fight to regain its lost province. It was not simply a State matter, nor one of pure and simple national will, but a question of self-definition. No Frenchman could acquiesce to the situation imposed by Bismarck, for it would have negated the very principle of his being, the universality rooted in the unanimous will of the citizenry. On this point, we see that the war had absolutely not altered French ideology but rather had reinforced it, as patriotism and universal principle still coincided. Later on, it is only when the government of the Third Republic, absorbed in other tasks, appeared to some people to be insufficiently preoccupied with reconquering Alsace-Lorraine that the situation would feed the ephemeral popularity of General Boulanger (1886–89). Later still, it would also help establish a new nationalism. Yet, historians tell us today that the resolve to recover the lost province weakened somewhat with time, only to revive when Franco-German relations became conflictual once again at the beginning of the twentieth century.

Overall, the national upheaval of 1870–71 had two major ideological consequences. We just mentioned the first one, what Nicolet called the transition of the republican idea from utopia to reality, that is to say, the establishment of a republican regime. The second consequence is of an entirely different nature and concerns the long term. The defeat introduced in France a tendency to look up to Germany as superior and worthy of imitation in some regards. We mentioned the widely felt need for "regeneration." It was thus natural to reflect on the enemy's superiority and its causes. The vanquished would then either borrow recipes for success or, noticing some elements in their victorious neighbor that were despised or subordinate in their own ideology, they would promote them in their turn. We shall mention a few areas where this occurred, but the global phenomenon is our primary concern, for it represents a reversal of the influence between East and West when considered in a long-term perspective.

French culture and Western (English and French) Enlightenment had predominated until the end of the eighteenth century. I attempted to show elsewhere that the unprecedented development of German thought and literature between 1770 and 1830, which almost constitutes a cultural mutation, can be understood as a powerful response to the challenge Western Enlightenment and the French Revolution presented to German culture. In other words, it can be seen as the global acculturation of Germany to the influence of the West. From then onward, German culture, assured of its excellence, quietly remained centered upon itself, save for a few occasional borrowings.

France in the meantime, in spite of its political vicissitudes, remained assured of its own superiority, complacently inherited in part from the past to be sure, but also based on the assumed supremacy of universal values. In accordance with these values, intellectuals could admire without reserve the triumphs of their neighbors, especially German idealist philosophy, and the subsequent development of history and the human sciences or "sciences of the spirit" (*Geisteswissenschaften*). War abruptly shattered this self-satisfaction of the French, for it revealed that what is sometimes called the "value orientation" of German development differed from what they had complacently imagined. Their neighbor was not a sister nation devoted to the highest undertakings of the mind but a rival power bent on domination. Or were there two Germanys?

At any rate, Germany represented more than a challenge. It was a permanent threat. It had found sources of power from which one would have to draw. France had to relinquish the role of teacher and assume that of pupil, at least in some matters. Predominance had switched sides: from now on, the main current of influence would flow from East to West.

Germany's success was very widely attributed to the excellence of its science and university education. Some efforts were made in France to imitate in particular the close association between teaching and research. German universities were taken as models, and around the end of the century the most promising French students in the humanities were awarded State scholarships to perfect their formation in Germany and to familiarize themselves with the latest research. Durkheim, for instance, attended lectures by Wundt and others. Yet, foreign influence remained limited. The basic tenets of the French system of public education were not modified; it was excellent for primary and secondary education but remained weak for organizing research, which went on outside the university system.[6] Let us also add that over time the German system was more critically appreciated.

Perhaps the best expression of the changes in the French intellectual climate after 1870 was the conversion to Kant in philosophy. Kant's influence was predominant at the end of the century, and well beyond, and a phenomenon as substantial as the lengthy supremacy of neocriticism for instance would need to be studied for itself. From the present vantage point,

6. Victor Duruy had anticipated the movement by creating just before the war the Ecole Pratique des Hautes Etudes as an institution for research.

it is clear that a critical appreciation of the progress of the natural sciences, in opposition to positivism, and a stern emphasis on duty corresponded to the needs of the hour, as did the choice of a German thinker altogether closer to the Western Enlightenment than his great idealist successors.

Another form of German predominance appeared in the twentieth century with the Socialist International, dominated by the large and disciplined battalions of German socialism, and consequently by Marxist ideology.

These are notable examples of the cultural predominance of Germany at the time. We could add the supremacy of Wagner's music. In order to understand a similar but deeper process, let us recall once again our comparison between the two ideologies. We have noted how some elements that are honored and accentuated in the global German ideological framework are conversely submerged on the French side, where they are present not in the predominant model of the Left but in the subordinate model of the Right. Thus the universalistic individualism of the French excludes or subordinates the holistic perception of themselves as a particular cultural and historical community, which is usually the view of the traditionalists on the Right. It requires a fair amount of imagination to understand how, in France, praising the values of "Work, Family, Fatherland" can be seen as reactionary and antinational. These values, which are submerged on the national level, could, in the long run, only benefit from being regarded as victorious through the enemy. Here is the stumbling block for the French Right: the particularizing attachment to the fatherland which is ordinarily encompassed in universalism triumphs only in times of defeat. The Pétain episode is somewhat analogous to this.

To perceive the interplay of these values, we must turn to the opinions and the works of intellectuals, following Claude Digeon. Immediately after the defeat of 1871, doubts and critical views about the national heritage found a wide audience. Thus, famous authors such as Ernest Renan, a philologist and historian of Christianity, and Hippolyte Taine, a philosopher and historian of modernity, who had always criticized the predominant French ideology, exerted a great influence in the long run. The case of Renan is special, and may be exemplary. Having been formed as a scholar under the influence of German philology, he was a great admirer of the social constitution of Germany and of German science, and a critic of the egalitarian philosophy of the French Revolution. Yet he was also a convinced universalist, for he believed in humanistic modern science. He was therefore doubly shattered by the war, in his French patriotism and in his exclusive worship of the German mind. For him, the war was scandalous and a cause for despair, since in his eyes Germany had forfeited its universal mission by its conduct of the war. In the polemic between German and French scholars regarding Alsace, he attacked his revered predecessor D. F. Strauss, thus somewhat unexpectedly espousing the elective theory of the nation and illustrating it admirably with his definition of the nation as an "everyday plebiscite." Renan progressively isolated and repudiated the militaristic element in Germany and accepted the French republican regime. But in the meantime his critique of French ideology, and his plea in favor of the abandonment of humanitarianism and a return to traditional social forms contributed to establish, according to Claude Digeon, a new type of intellectual opposition to the Republic.

Taine, a positivist and implacable critic of Cartesian and French rationalism, had been roused to indignation by the insurrection of the Paris Commune. During the last twenty years of his life, he devoted himself to a vast historical research which was to issue into a book entitled *The Origins of Contemporary France*. The book was to demonstrate that France, throughout the last centuries, be it under the absolute monarchy, in the Revolution, or ever since, as a result of the hold of the rationalist abstraction and in the absence of the solid concrete virtues found among German and Anglo-American people, had reiterated the same fatal cycle from rise to ruin.

Even more than with Renan, we can speak here, following Digeon, of desperate patriotism, for Taine condemns what he rightly considers to be the main intellectual faculty of the French, or, in other words, a major aspect of their ideology. Despair is understandable given the circumstances, and our own studies should help us penetrate these authors better: their perception of the importance of holism in societies in general was correct— it is, by the way, a perception that we have since almost entirely lost—but they underestimated the strength of the individualistic modern ideology. Such a radical questioning of predominant French values was not immediately relevant to political life, but it was nevertheless important, for it helped the next generation develop a rightist ideology renewed around an antirepublican nationalism. A talented writer, Maurice Barrès, gave that ideology its credentials. Barrès was not simply influenced by German representations; rather, his personal evolution from a kind of cult of his own personality to a pious holism of "the land and its dead" is like an echo of German romanticism. This new nationalism, very much influenced by Germany, would later form the basis for a new protofascist monarchist party called l'Action Française. This was a long-term outcome of the defeat of

1870, which alienated the Left once and for all, if not from patriotism, at least from any pronounced accentuation of the concept of Nation.

Here is a schematic summary of the main ways in which the predominance of Germany, experienced in 1870, acted upon French ideology. In the short term, by shaking the foundations of the supreme values of the French, it prompted republicans to modesty and compromise for the first time in their history, thereby rendering the instauration of a moderate and thus durable republican regime feasible. In the longer term, as the shattered ideology progressively regained its strength—a process well illustrated by Renan's personal evolution—and as the Republic managed to establish its foundations successfully, the effects of the trauma of 1870–71 and of German influence remained circumscribed, encompassed in the whole. The most important result was the assertion, on the level of rightist values, of an ideological form unknown in France until then, I mean nationalism in the common sense of the word.

•

We have seen how the war of 1870 taught the French a hard lesson, i.e., that contrary to what they fondly believed, the Rights of Man were not the alpha and the omega of politics, and that they themselves were but a nation among others. As such, they would have to fight and be ready to die for the independence and the integrity of their country. We have also seen how, as a result of the special division of France between the two political camps of the Right and the Left, the stronger recognition of national interest had evolved into a nationalist doctrine on the Right, in conflict with the values of justice and social emancipation of the Left, which were increasingly represented by the socialist movement. Thus, two ideals that are not fundamentally incompatible in themselves were embodied by two opposite forces in the political arena.

With the progressive reassertion of the republican ideology between 1871 and 1914, and as a result of the succession of generations, a part of the population in 1914 was very far from accepting the lessons their fathers and grandfathers had learned earlier. Many people, including workers, now adhered to a form of universalism no doubt slightly different from that of preceding generations but dogmatically opposed to war. For them, the social and political reality consisted not of nations but of classes engaged in a struggle. The proletariat had its enemy within each nation and had to unite beyond boundaries, and thus make war impossible.

We know the subsequent course of events. The Socialist International collapsed. Internationalist workers, like other French soldiers, fought bravely and died in large numbers for more than four years, in a war of an unprecedented cruelty and in previously unimaginable conditions. Allow me to delineate provisionally the problem we shall investigate. Those who survived among these men, who were imbued, to begin with, with a generous but utopian universalism, had experienced more radically than anyone before them the reality of the conflict between nations. One would expect that they would have relinquished or modified their universalism following this experience, but they did not. The French veterans (or *Anciens Combattants*) were to play a considerable role in domestic politics through their numerous associations and, independently from all political tendencies, to spread their intransigent pacifism throughout the country until the Second World War, thus by the way contributing to disarm the country in the face of the rising threat of Nazism.

We note that this pacifism born from the war experience of the *Anciens Combattants* was not simply an erroneous conclusion, but represented once again a utopian manner of minimizing the difference between nations. In the last analysis, it was just a resurgence of French universalism, born from its ashes and reasserting itself, disastrously, by incorporating the terrible experience of its ruin. Can such an astounding phenomenon be understood? Should we agree that national ideologies, such as the French one here, are absolutely impervious to experience and reassert themselves as soon as possible, with minimal alterations? Aren't French citizens thinking beings who are able to alter their conception of the world when painful experiences mandate it?

Actually, this preliminary statement of the problem is not quite adequate. It will have to be modified, but this is how it first appeared to me, and I wanted to retrace briefly here the progression of the inquiry. We have at our disposal a monumental three-volume monograph by Antoine Prost entitled *Les Anciens Combattants* (1977), based on an extensive wartime literature coming mostly from the soldiers themselves, and on an exhaustive examination of the periodicals of the veterans associations.[7] On the basis of this imposing set of data, the main correction to be made to our hasty statement of the problem is to recognize that pacifism did not suddenly appear after the war, but that it was present during the war itself and inspired those who fought, as incredible as that may seem. Charles Péguy, who was to be killed soon afterward, expressed at the time of mobilization what was going to become a widely held belief: "I am leaving as a soldier of

7. See also, for the initial phase, Becker 1977, and recent notes in *L'Histoire*, no. 107 (January 1988).

the Republic for the last of all wars and for general disarmament." The war to end all wars became in popular speech "the last of the last" (*la der des ders*), a common expression later tinged with irony. Let us look at this more closely.

To begin with, how did the internationalist creed collapse? First, it was contradicted in Germany, where the powerful socialist and trade union machine actually proved to be an instrument of regimentation. Let us recall here Charles Andler, and especially his pamphlet on the political decomposition of German socialism (Andler 1919), and note in passing that, as Andler pointed out early on, socialism in fact meant two different things in France and in Germany, in virtue of its being associated with liberty in the one country and its constraining relation to the State in the other: internationalism was but a phantasm.

Second, the way the Germans conducted the war—their disregard for the law of nations, starting with the violation of Belgian neutrality, and the invasion itself—convinced the French that they were engaged in a just, defensive war. While not enjoying it, they had no recourse but to fight. In relation to the actual conditions of the war, which remained a war of the trenches for a long time, the protagonists developed a particular mentality. A German veteran reiterated the judgment of Marshall Davout that the French are warlike but not militaristic (Distelbarth 1942: 182). They disliked the army as such and chafed at its hierarchical formalism; they were distrustful of or hostile toward higher officers, who were stationed far from the front and ordered vain and murderous offensive operations. There were local mutinies, often triggered by irresponsible orders, and the high command had to become more sparing of human lives. The defense of Verdun reorganized by Pétain is a model of the conduct of the war on the French side (Prost 1977). Under a deluge of shells that endlessly altered the ground surface, Verdun held, thanks to a fast rotation of troops Pétain called a *noria,* which successively brought to the front most of the units of the French army. Verdun was a national battle if there ever was one. The horror of war and its inescapable nature promoted a feeling of resignation. As Pétain was able to recognize, the men were doing their duty, sinister as it was. Experience condemned the bragging nationalism of the Right as well as the internationalism of the extreme Left. Antoine Prost notes that this nationalism will find no echo among the veterans until 1934. Hence a kind of amnesia; the soldiers forgot Déroulède and Barrès, as if no one in France had ever wished for war.

Another trait of the soldiers' mentality was their emotional distance from "those back home." Going on leave was somewhat demoralizing, in the first years of the war at least, as seems to have been the case in Germany also. In large towns life went on as before, and this was incomprehensible and even scandalous to the soldiers, who bitterly mocked the heroic feats that these *embusqués* (dodgers) attributed to those on the battlefront.

Finally, their experience brought the fighters closer to the enemies facing them, while moving them away from their fellow countrymen, officers or civilians. We should probably not exaggerate the importance of localized episodes of fraternization.[8] More significant is the fact that proximity made it possible to see the German soldiers as trapped in the same situation, as fellow victims of a war that was forced upon them. Since, according to the French soldiers, responsibility rested with the German side, they reserved the blame for the German higher officers, who were also removed from the front lines, and, not undeservedly, for the emperor and his general staff, who had wanted the war and chosen a strategy that flouted international law.

On this, French soldiers were closer than they thought to the official view and the propaganda of their country, which focused on the defense of the rule of law and of humanity. At any rate, this narrow attribution of responsibility allowed French soldiers to believe that after the elimination of the guilty military clique, war would be abolished by the unanimous will of peoples. Many said that this belief sustained them during their nightmarish experience, and we cannot question their testimony. For instance, Henri Barbusse, who later published a famous book on the war, *Le Feu*, and became one of the leaders of the antifascist movement, wrote in 1917:

> Some assure that in order to walk to one's death and sacrifice one's life, it is necessary to be stimulated by a narrow patriotism or inebriated by hatred for a given race. No, it is rather the lofty promise of final progress which leads the true men to give their blood. We, who fought as Frenchmen, and above all as men, can say proudly that we are living proof of this. (Quoted in Prost 1977, 3:84)

Barbusse's "lofty promise of final progress" is obviously the end of all wars, as is Péguy's "general disarmament." We should stress the passage "we, who fought as Frenchmen, and *above all as men*," which is a full expression of the predominant French ideology: patriotism is sanctioned by its coinci-

8. Local episodes of fraternization often took place at Christmas. In Germany the two Christmas days are a sacred moment lifted out of time, and the Frenchmen did not understand that the fight would be taken up the next, third, day as if nothing had happened. *L'Histoire*, no. 107 (1988): 77 ff.

dence with the supreme belonging to humanity. It is clear that the ideology itself was not questioned but rather confirmed by the very experience of war, probably thanks to a resurgence of the idea, widespread in the modern era, that war is outdated and a simple relic of the past on the verge of being abolished forever.

Barbusse's words, after those of Péguy, express the thought of many of those men, and we should stop to examine it. Is it possible that these people, the better part of a nation, upon seeing their brothers fall one after the other, have crossed the ordeal by so to speak turning their heads from its horror? Many parallels come to mind. For instance, beyond the Stoics, how could we not think of the detachment Krishna teaches Arjuna in the *Bhagavad Gita:* he who accomplishes the duty of his rank for the love of God does not sin. A further question is: were these men entirely mistaken when they thus justified their sublime conduct? I believe they were not. It is true that they did not abolish war, but they must have felt that the German claim to world domination, which, as they were well aware, did indeed exist, was not tolerable in the modern world. In this they were right. It is beyond our power to put an end to war, contrary to the naive hopes that arose following the destruction of the old order of things, but we must fight all claims to tyranny, be they external or internal.

Such were the convictions of the soldiers. The idea that the First World War had been in vain and meaningless spread only afterward, with the development of the pacifist movement.

After the war, the French veterans joined forces in an incredible number of federated associations, constituted on very diverse bases, either locally, or by service, unit, or corps, etc. Beyond their fight for pensions and collective rights, veterans had the extremely strong feeling that they had shared a common experience, which had set them apart from the rest of the nation and invested them with a sacred mandate and a national mission, as survivors and implicit representatives for those who had died. This ideology was remarkably homogeneous, and in conformity with it, they avoided, although barely at first, the pitfalls of the traditional French political divisions. There were various political tendencies among the veterans, but they were careful to keep them in check. Most striking is the fact that this feeling of collective unity helped them supersede the division between Right and Left. Antoine Prost sheds light on an important point, namely, that the antagonisms that had shaken the Third Republic were all transcended in the unity of the veteran movement. Experience had discredited nationalism, so that nothing remained of the conflict between the nationalism of the anti-

Dreyfus faction and the naive internationalism of the socialists. Even the curate and the schoolteacher, who on the eve of the war had clashed violently on the issue of the separation of Church and State, were reconciled as veterans, as they were on the battlefront.

What prevailed here is a strong feeling of the unity of the country, arising from the terrible confrontation with the enemy and supported by the fraternal pride of these men. It transcended all the divisions that social life, and especially political ideology, could have caused or sustained. This was a holistic perception, opposed to the individualistic framework that usually governs French ideology and political life in peacetime.

At this level, the veterans saw themselves as a moral elite attempting to unite the forces of the nation around itself. Their ambition was to develop a political program, and they did in fact propose several reforms to strengthen the executive against the Parliament, which they perceived as inefficient and divisive. They proposed in particular the election of the president of the Republic by universal suffrage rather than indirectly. It is only much later, but with similar intentions, that de Gaulle would introduce this provision into the Constitution, which is no doubt a useful rectification. What we should notice above all is that the veterans never questioned the republican regime, even though Parliament was rather unpopular among them. Their holistic inspiration was thus limited and contained within the individualistic framework that has predominated in French politics since the Revolution.

Moreover, in order to situate this holistic perception within their ideological framework, we must consider their views not only on the internal life of the nation but also on foreign relations, which were perfectly simple and could be summarized in one word, pacifism. War belonged to the past, and from now on the Society of Nations would outlaw and prevent all war. Aristide Briand translated the veterans' yearnings into political proposals.

Now, as we said at the beginning, this pacifism was essentially a modified version of the congenital universalism of the French. Overall, the holistic sentiment the veterans had brought back from the battlefront was clearly confined within their pacifist universalism and their attachment to the republican regime. They remained faithful to the universalistic individualism of the French Revolution, tempered only by a few realistic political reforms designed to counterbalance in practice some of the excesses of the French democratic system. Until the Second World War, the movement never strayed from this republican and pacifist course. Efforts made from 1934 onward to lure the veterans into protofascist "leagues" failed.

•

It will be instructive to complete our comparative perspective by examining briefly the impact on Germany of the defeat of 1918. In the initial stages, the similarities with what occurred in analogous circumstances in France, in 1871 and in 1940, are striking. In both cases, the main short-term reaction was the pure and simple refusal to accept the facts. Defeat was at first attributed to treason: the people themselves had not been defeated, but the nation or the army had been the victim of a treacherous conspiracy. According to this view, the German army was still undefeated in 1918, as indicated by the fact that it was on enemy territory when the armistice was signed: it had succumbed because it had been "stabbed in the back," the morale of the rear having been ruined by the enemy and its accomplices. This belief was extremely strong and durable, and was later part of Nazi propaganda. Similarly, in France in 1940, men who on the eve of the conflict had positively stated their refusal to join the fight later attributed the collapse to the conspiracy of a "fifth column" under the orders of "Fascism."[9] The unfolding of events was more complicated in 1871; yet the Communards were supported in their desperate attempt by the belief that Thiers and a majority of the Assembly were traitors.

We note also that in these three cases—1871, 1918, and 1940—public opinion focused responsibility on State leaders. There was also a change in the political regime, thus further dissociating the people themselves from the defeat. It is true that in 1919, as in 1940, the new regime had the sanction of the victors, which would contribute to its unpopularity. Overall, it seems clear that these modern peoples, once mobilized in more or less total wars, find themselves unable to openly accept the hard reality of defeat.

Their collective identity undergoes a trauma whose effects become evident in subsequent ideological changes. We shall here leave aside the case of France after 1940, because of the subsequent complications. In France, after 1871, ideas and values adjusted in a way to the changing situation. In the long run, the basic ideological principle of universalism slowly reasserted itself. In sum, the process set in motion by defeat finally resulted in the reaffirmation of collective identity and its fundamental ideology through *minimal ideological modifications.*

The same is true for the German evolution after 1918. In this case, the basic ideological principle was shattered just as deeply as it had been in France in 1871. To a people that had very widely believed in its voca-

9. Author's testimony.

tion to world domination, and had put all its energies to maximum use for four long years of war, history demonstrated that its pretensions were untenable.

After the failure of socialist revolutionary attempts, the Germans were forced to accept a republican regime agreeable to an enemy who simultaneously imposed a vengeful peace and heavy war reparations. Moreover, there was a direct ideological reason for the unpopularity of the Weimar Republic, i.e., the fact that the German people with its strong holistic bent was not prepared for democratic individualism. The Republic survived somehow or other until 1933, while the real problem was being debated, not in Parliament, but in a nebula of splinter groups and agitators groping for a revolution that would restore a State worthy of the German tradition, that is to say, a State in accordance with German ideology. Here we need to keep in mind that what ideology demanded after the defeat, as it had before, was a holistic State that would assume the vocation of domination and refuse altogether the transition to a democratic spirit, both within the State and between States. Given the circumstances, the task could obviously not be carried out in broad daylight, but a specific party and a leader who had found a way out of the impasse emerged. The solution consisted in basing the claim for domination no longer on the State itself but on race instead, by subordinating the State to the racist principle, and correlatively by submitting all legitimacy to brute force. This was not clear upon Hitler's accession to the chancellorship in 1933, but it is clear retrospectively when we look at subsequent developments in the light of the fundamental ideological principle concerning the State and politics.

Thus, we can say that the ideology of domination was finally preserved in Germany thanks to a modification. This modification had disastrous and abominable consequences, yet it allowed the collective identity of the German people to reassert itself without relinquishing its fundamental article concerning relations with other peoples. There is a continuity between the First and the Second World Wars, which most often remains masked by the exceptional characteristics of the Nazi regime, but which we have to restore if we want to understand better than is usually the case the true nature of the Nazi regime in connection with the German people as a whole.

Let us now compare the ideological evolution in France and in Germany until 1939. France had reasserted its basic universalism after the defeat of 1870–71. After the experience of the First World War, it transformed it into a pacifism that engulfed the country and paralyzed belated efforts to mobilize forces against the imminent threat. This pacifism is symbolized by the visit the leader of the main federation of French veterans paid to Hitler in the hope of finding common ground with a man who had himself experienced war in the trenches.

In Germany, also, a way had been found to overcome the ideological impact of the defeat of 1918. The German vocation of domination was reasserted, as universalism had been in France. Could we imagine a more striking instance of similarity within difference?

That these two countries, each bound to its idiosyncrasy, are impervious to that of their neighbor should not cause surprise. But is it not somewhat pathetic to see each of them neutralize its own experience in order to salvage the ideological framework in terms of which the country had been wont to think of itself and the world over a great length of time?

Works Cited

Aarsleff, Hans. 1982. *From Locke to Saussure: Essays on the Study of Language and Intellectual History.* London.

Andler, Charles. 1919. *La Décomposition politique du socialisme allemand.* Paris.

———, ed. 1917. *Le Pangermanisme philosophique (1800 à 1914).* Textes traduits de l'Allemand. Paris: Conard.

Aron, Raymond. 1967. *Les Etapes de la pensée sociologique.* Paris: Gallimard.

Becker, Jean-Jacques. 1977. *1914: Comment les Français sont entrés dans la guerre.* Paris.

Besançon, Alain. 1977. *Les Origines intellectuelles du Léninisme.* Paris: Gallimard.

Béteille, André. 1986. "Individualism and Equality." *Current Anthropology* 27 (April): 121–34.

Blackall, Eric A. 1976. *Goethe and the Novel.* Ithaca, N.Y.: Cornell University Press.

Blake, William. 1927. *Premiers livres prophétiques.* Translated by Berger. Paris: Rieder.

Bredin, Jean-Denis. 1983. *L'Affaire.* Paris: Julliard.

Brown, Jane. 1983. "The Theatrical Mission of the *Lehrjahre.*" In William J. Lillyman, ed., *Goethe's Narrative Fiction: The Irvine Goethe Symposium.* Berlin and New York.

Bruford, Walter H. 1933. "Wilhelm Meister as a Picture and a Criticism of Society." *Publications of the English Goethe Society* 9: 69–84.

———. 1959. "The Idea of 'Bildung' in Wilhelm von Humboldt's Letters." In *The Era of Goethe: Essays presented to James Boyd.* Oxford.

———. 1962. "The Idea of 'Bildung' in Wilhelm von Humboldt's *Briefen an eine Freundin.*" In Albert Fuchs and Helmut Motekat, eds., *Stoffe, Formen, Strukturen: Studien zur deutschen Literatur,* 261–73. Munich.

———. 1975. *The German Tradition of Self-Cultivation: "Bildung" from Humboldt to Thomas Mann.* Cambridge: Cambridge University Press.

Brügeman, Fritz. 1976. *Die Ironie als entwicklungs-geschichtliches Element.* Darmstadt. (Originally published 1909.)

Butler, Eliza Merran. 1935. *The Tyranny of Greece over Germany.* Cambridge.

Cassirer, Ernst. 1922. *Freiheit und Form: Studien zur deutschen Geistesgeschichte.* Berlin.

Caussat, Pierre. 1974. "Introduction du traducteur." In Humboldt 1974: 9–28.

Charbonnel, Nanine. 1987. *L'Impossible Pensée de l'éducation: Sur le* Wilhelm Meister *de Goethe.* Cousset, Switzerland.

Cowan, Marianne, ed. and trans. 1963. *Humanist without Portfolio: An Anthology of the Writings of Wilhelm von Humboldt.* Detroit.

Croce, Benedetto. 1915. *What Is Living and What Is Dead in the Philosophy of Hegel.* Translated by D. Ainslie. London: Macmillan.

Digeon, Claude. 1959. *La Crise allemande de la pensée française, 1870–1914.* Paris.

Distelbarth, Paul. 1942. *La Personne France.* Paris. (Originally published 1937.)

Dumont, Louis. 1971. "Religion, Politics and Society in the Individualistic Universe." *Proceedings of the Royal Anthropological Institute for 1970,* 31–41. London.

———. 1976. "The British in India." In *History of Mankind: Cultural and Scientific Development,* vol. 5, *The Nineteenth Century,* ed. C. Morazé. London: Allen & Unwin.

———. 1977. *From Mandeville to Marx: The Genesis and Triumph of Economic Ideology.* Chicago: University of Chicago Press.

———. 1980. *Homo Hierarchicus: The Caste System and Its Implications.* Complete English Edition, Revised. Chicago: University of Chicago Press. (Originally published in French, Paris, 1966.)

———. 1981. "On Value." *Proceedings of the British Academy* 66: 207–41.

———. 1983. *Affinity as a Value.* Chicago: University of Chicago Press.

———. 1983. *Essais sur l'individualisme: Une perspective anthropologique sur l'idéologie moderne.* Paris: Le Seuil. (English version, Dumont 1986.)

———. 1986. *Essays on Individualism: Modern Ideology in Anthropological Perspective.* Chicago: University of Chicago Press.

———. 1987. "Individualism and Equality." A rejoinder to André Béteille. *Current Anthropology* 28/5: 669–72.

———. 1988. "Les Malentendus d'un référendum." *Esprit* 12: 5–7.

Enright, D. S. 1983. "The Abyss of German-ness." *Times Literary Supplement,* 5 August, 825.

Erikson, Erik. 1958. *Young Man Luther: A Study in Psychoanalysis and History.* New York: Norton.

Ferry, Luc, J. P. Pesron, and Alain Renaut, eds. 1979. *Philosophies de l'Université: L'idéalisme allemand et la question de l'Université.* Texts by Schelling, Fichte, Schleiermacher, Humboldt, and Hegel. Paris.

Gierke, O. 1957. *Natural Law and Theory of Society, 1500 to 1800.* Translated by E. Barker. 2 vols. Cambridge: Cambridge University Press, 1934; 1-vol. repr., Boston: Beacon Press.

Goethe, J. W. von. 1924. *La Vocation théâtrale de Wilhelm Meister.* Translated by F. Halévy. Introduction by M. Arnault. Paris.

———. 1930. *Entretiens avec le chancellier F. de Müller.* Translated by A. Béguin. Paris.

———. 1941. *Souvenirs de ma vie. Poésie et Vérité.* Translated by Pierre du Colombier. Paris: Aubier.

———. 1947. *Hermann et Dorothée.* Bilingual edition. Translated by H. Loiseau. Paris.

———. 1951–82. *Poésies.* Bilingual edition. Translated by R. Ayrault. 2 vols. Paris.

———. 1954. *Romans.* Translated by B. Groethuysen, P. du Colombier, and B. Briod. Bibliothèque de la Pléiade. Paris: Gallimard.

———. 1962. *Wilhelm Meisters Wanderjahre.* 2 vols. Munich: Deutscher Taschenbuch Verlag.

———. 1973. *Wilhelm Meisters Lehrjahre.* 2 vols. Munich: W. Goldmann Verlag (Goldmann Klassiker, 1578–9).

———. 1974. *Aus meinem Leben: Dichtung u. Wahrheit.* In *Werke,* Hamburg Ausgabe, vols. 9–10.

———. 1987. *From My Life: Poetry and Truth.* Parts 1–3. Translated by Robert Heiner. Introduction and notes by Thomas P. Saine. New York: Suhrkamp.

———. 1988. *Théâtre complet.* Edited by P. Grappin, in collaboration with E. Henkel. Paris.

———. 1989a. *Wilhelm Meister's Apprenticeship.* Edited and translated by Eric A. Blackall, in cooperation with Victor Lane. New York.

———. 1989b. *Wilhelm Meister's Journeyman Years.* Translated by Krishna Winston, edited by Jane K. Brown. New York.

Goguel, François, and Alfred Grosser. 1981. *La Politique en France.* Paris: Armand Colin.

Grillparzer, Franz. 1916. *Werke.* Tagebücher II.

Gundolf, Friedrich. 1922. *Goethe.* Berlin.

Hadot, Pierre. 1981. *Exercices spirituels et philosophie antique.* Paris.

Hamilton, N. 1978. *The Brothers Mann: The Lives of Heinrich and Thomas Mann 1871–1950 and 1875–1955.* London: Secker & Warburg.

Hegel, G. W. F. 1964. "The German Constitution." In *Hegel's Political Writings,* translated by T. M. Knox, with an introductory essay by Z. A. Pelczynski. Oxford: Oxford University Press.

———. 1979. *Esthétique.* Translated by S. Jankelevitch. 4 vols. Paris: Flammarion.

Heidegger, Martin. 1977. *Schelling: Le Traité de 1809 sur l'essence de la liberté humaine.* Paris: Gallimard. (French translation of *Schellings Abhandlung über das Wesen der menschlichen Freiheit* [1809], Tübingen: Max Niemeyer, 1971.)

Heine, Heinrich. 1979. *De l'Allemagne* (1855). 2 vols. Paris: Slatkine Reprints.

Heller, Erich. 1958. *The Ironic German.* London.

———. 1961. *The Disinherited Mind.* London. (Originally published 1952.)

Henrich, D. 1975. *Hegel in Kontext.* Frankfurt: Suhrkamp.

Herr, Lucien, trans. and ed. 1923. *Correspondance entre Schiller et Goethe, 1794–1805.* 4 vols. Paris.

Herzfeld, M. von, and C. A. M. Sym, trans. *Letters from Goethe.* Introduction by W. H. Bruford. New York.

L'Histoire. No. 107. January 1988.

Humboldt, Wilhelm von. 1903–36. *W. von Humboldt: Gesammelte Schriften.* Edited by A. Leitzmann et al. 17 vols. Berlin.

———. 1956. *Schriften zur Anthropologie und Bildungslehre.* Edited by A. Flitner. Düsseldorf.

———. 1974. *Introduction à l'oeuvre sur le Kavi et autres essais.* Translated and edited by Pierre Caussat. Paris.

———. 1985. *La Tâche de l'historien.* Introduction by J. Quillien. Lille.

———. 1986. "Août 1789: Journal de voyage à Paris." Translated and with a postscript by Marianne Schaub. *Nouveau Commerce* 64: 101–31.

Kaehler, Siegfried. 1927. *Wilhelm von Humboldt und der Staat.* Göttingen.

Kaiser, Gerhard. 1973. *Pietismus und Patriotismus im literarischen Deutschland.* Frankfurt. (Originally published 1961.)

Kant, Immanuel. 1965. *Politische Schriften.* Cologne: Westdeutscher Verlag.

Kantorowicz, E. 1957. *The King's Two Bodies*. Princeton: Princeton University Press.

Koestler, Arthur. 1967. *The Ghost in the Machine*. New York.

Korff, Hermann August. 1957. *Geist der Goethezeit*. 5 vols. Leipzig. (Originally published 1923.)

Koselleck, Reinhardt. 1972. "Fortschritt." *Geschichtliche Grundbegriffe* 2: 351–423.

Koyré, Alexandre. 1976. *La Philosophie et le problème national en Russie au début du XIXe siècle* (1929). Paris: Gallimard.

Laponce, J. A. 1981. *Left and Right: The Topology of Political Perceptions*. Toronto: University of Toronto Press.

Lefeuvre, Martine. 1988. "Le Devoir d'excision." *Revue du Mauss* 1: 65–95.

Leitzmann, Albert. 1935. "Politische Jugendbriefe W. von Humboldts an Gentz." *Historische Zeitschrift* 152: 48–89.

———. 1936. *Georg u. Theresa Forster und die Brüder Humboldt*. Bonn.

Leroux, Robert. 1932. *Guillaume de Humboldt: La formation de sa pensée jusqu'en 1794*. Paris.

———. 1945. "La Métaphysique 'sexuée' de Guillaume de Humboldt." *Mélanges 1945: Études historiques* 3: 23–51.

———. 1948. "L'Esthétique sexuée de Guillaume de Humboldt." *Études germaniques*, 3d year, 261–73.

———. 1958. *L'Anthropologie comparée de Guillaume de Humboldt*. Paris.

Littré, Émile. 1879. *Conservation, révolution, positivisme*. 2d ed. Paris. (Originally published 1852.)

Lukács, Georg. 1947. *Goethe und seine Zeit*. Bern: A. Franke. (Originally published 1936.)

———. 1955. *Die Zerstörung der Vernunft: Der Weg des Irrationalismus von Schelling zu Hitler*. 2 vols. Berlin: Aufbau-Verlag.

———. 1964. *Essays on Thomas Mann*. Translated by S. Mitchell. London: Merlin. (Originally published in German, 1963.)

Lyotard, Jean-François. 1982. "Réponse à la question: Qu'est-ce que la postmodernité?" *Critique* 419 (April): 357–67.

———. 1985. "Histoire universelle et différences culturelles." *Critique* 456 (May): 559–68.

Maine, Sir Henry Sumner. 1887. *Ancient Law*. London.

Malia, Martin. 1961. *Alexander Herzen and the Birth of Russian Socialism, 1812–1855*. Cambridge, Mass.

Mann, Klaus. 1984. *Le Tournant: Histoire d'une vie*. Translated from the German. Malakoff: Solin.

Mann, Thomas. 1922. *Betrachtungen eines Unpolitischen*. Berlin: G. Fischer Verlag. (Originally published 1918; English version, Mann 1983.)

———. 1965. *Reden und Aufsätze*. Berlin: G. Fischer Verlag.

———. 1976. *Les Exigences du Jour*. Grasset.

———. 1983. *Reflections of a Nonpolitical Man*. Translated by W. D. Morris. New York.

Marquard, O. 1981. "L'Homme accusé et l'homme disculpé." *Critique* 413 (October): 1015–37.

Marrou, Henri-Irénée. 1956. *A History of Education in Antiquity.* Translated by George Lamb. London and New York.

Masaryk, Tomas G. 1967. *The Spirit of Russia* (1919). 3 vols. London: Allen & Unwin.

Mauss, Marcel. 1968–69. *Oeuvres.* Edited by V. Karady. 3 vols. Paris.

May, Kurt. 1957. "Wilhelm Meisters Lehrjahre, ein Bildungsroman?" *Deutsche Vierteljahrsschrift für Literatur, Wissenschaft und Geistesgeschichte* 23: 1–37.

Meinecke, Friedrich. 1965. *Die Entstehung des Historismus.* Munich. (Originally published 1936.)

Millett, Kate. 1969. *Sexual Politics.* New York.

Minder, Robert. 1936. *Die religiöse Entwicklung von Karl Philipp Moritz auf Grund seiner autobiographischen Schriften: Formen der Mystik und des Pietismus im "Reiser" und Hartknopf.* Berlin.

———. 1962. "Deutsche und französische Literatur." In Minder 1962a.

———. 1962a. *Kultur und Literatur in Deutschland und Frankreich: Fünf Essays.* Frankfurt-am-Main.

Montesquieu. 1949. "Mes Pensées." In *Oeuvres complètes,* edited by Roger Caillois, 1: 975–1574. 2 vols. Bibliothèque de la Pléiade. Paris: Gallimard.

Moritz, Karl Philipp. 1962. *Schriften zur Aesthetik und Poetik: Kritische Ausgabe.* Edited by H. J. Schrimpf. Tübingen.

———. 1977. *Anton Reiser: A Psychological Novel.* Translated by P. E. Matheson. Westport, Conn.

———. 1986. *Anton Reiser.* French trans. Paris.

Muhlack, Ulrich. 1967. *Das zeitgenössische Frankreich in der Politik Humboldts.* Lübeck.

Neue Brockhaus, Der. 1938. 4 vols. and an atlas. Leipzig: F. A. Brockhaus.

Nicolet, Claude. 1982. *L'Idée républicaine en France: Essai d'histoire critique.* Paris: Gallimard.

Novalis. n.d. *Henri d'Ofterdingen.* Bilingual edition. Paris.

Pascal, Roy. 1956. *The German Novel.* Toronto: University of Toronto Press.

Pinson, Koppels. 1934. *Pietism as a Factor in the Rise of German Nationalism.* (Reprinted New York, 1968.)

Plass, Ewald. 1969. *What Luther Said or Says.* St. Louis.

Plessner, H. 1969. *Die verspätete Nation.* Stuttgart: Kohlammer.

Prost, Antoine. 1977. *Les Anciens Combattants, 1914–1940.* 3 vols. Paris.

———. 1986. "Verdun." In Pierre Nora, ed., *Les Lieux de mémoire,* vol. 2: *La Nation,* 111–41. Paris.

Quillien, Jean. 1983. *Guillaume de Humboldt et la Grèce: Modèle et Histoire.* Lille.

Rorty, Richard. 1984. "Habermas, Lyotard et la post-modernité." *Critique* 442 (March): 181–97.

———. 1985. "Le Cosmopolitisme sans émancipation: Réponse à J.-F. Lyotard." *Critique* 456 (May): 569–80.

Ryan, Lawrence. 1962. *Friedrich Hölderlin.* Stuttgart.

Schiller, Friedrich, and C. G. Körner. 1973. *Briefwechsel zwischen Schiller und Körner.* Edited by K. L. Berhahn. Munich.

Schlegel, Friedrich. 1970. "Ueber Goethes Meister." In *Schriften zur Literatur: Deutsche Taschenbuch Verlag*, 260–78.

Schopenhauer, Arthur. 1963. "Ueber die Universitäts-Philosophie." In *Sämtliche Werke*, 4: 173–242. Parerga und Paralipomena, 1. Stuttgart: Cotta.

Seidel, Siegfried, ed. 1962. *Der Briefwechsel zwischen Friedrich Schiller und Wilhelm von Humboldt*. 2 vols. Berlin.

Shils, Edward. 1982. *Tradition*. London: Faber.

Simmel, Georg. 1971. *On Individuality and Social Forms*. Edited with an introduction by D. N. Levine. Chicago: University of Chicago Press.

———. 1981. "Questions fondamentales de la sociologie." In *Sociologie et épistémologie*, translated by L. Gasparini, 83–160. Paris. (In German, *Grundfragen der Soziologie*, 1970, Berlin.)

———. 1989. "L'individualisme," "L'individu et la liberté." In *Philosophie de la modernité*, translated by Jean-Louis Vieillard-Baron, 1: 281–304. Paris. (In German, *Brücke und Tür*, Stuttgart, Koehler 1957: 251–69.)

———. 1990. "L'individualisme de Goethe." In *Philosophie de la modernité*, translated by Jean-Louis Vieillard-Baron, 2: 69–104. Paris.

Singer, Milton. 1968. "The Concept of Culture." In *International Encyclopedia of the Social Sciences* 3: 527–41. New York.

Spranger, E. 1909. *Wilhelm von Humboldt und die Humanitätsidee*. Berlin.

Stahl, Ernst Ludwig. 1934. *Die religiöse und die humanitätsphilosophische Bildungsidee und die Entstehung des deutschen Bildungsromans im 18ten Jahrhundert*. Bern.

Staiger, Émile, ed. 1966. *Der Briefwechsel zwischen Schiller und Goethe*. Frankfurt.

Steinthal, Heymann. 1883. *Die sprachwissenschaftliche Werke Wilhelm von Humboldts*. Berlin.

Stern, Fritz. 1965. *The Politics of Cultural Despair: A Study in the Rise of the Germanic Ideology*. New York: Anchor Books. (Originally published Berkeley, 1961.)

Sweet, Paul R. 1973. "Young Wilhelm von Humboldt's Writings (1789–1793) Reconsidered." *Journal of the History of Ideas* 34: 469–82.

———. 1978–80. *Wilhelm von Humboldt: A Biography*. 2 vols. Columbus: Ohio State University Press.

Taylor, Charles. 1975. *Hegel*. Cambridge: Cambridge University Press.

Todorov, Tzvetan. 1977. *Les Théories du symbole*. Paris: Le Seuil.

Toennies, Ferdinand. 1971. *Ferdinand Toennies on Sociology: Pure, Applied, and Empirical*. Selected writings, edited and with an introduction by Werner J. Cahnman and Rudolph Heberle. Chicago: University of Chicago Press.

Troeltsch, Ernst. 1922. *Die Soziallehren der christlichen Kirchen und Gruppen*. Vol. 1 of *Gesammelte Schriften*. Tübingen. (Originally published 1911. Translated by O. Wyon as *The Social Teaching of the Christian Churches and Groups*, 2 vols., New York, 1960.)

———. 1923. *Naturrecht und Humanität in der Weltpolitik*. Vortrag von Ernst Troeltsch bei der zweiten Jahresfeier der Deutschen Hochschule für Politik. Berlin: Verlag für Politik und Wirtschaft. (Also in *Weltwirtschaftlicher Archiv*, 18-3, translated by E. Barker in Gierke 1957, 201–22.)

———. 1925*a*. *Deutscher Geist und Westeuropa*. Tübingen. (Reprinted Aalen, 1966.)

———. 1925*b*. Review of *Freiheit und Form*. In *Gesammelte Schriften,* vol. 4. Tübingen.

Tucker, R. C. 1972. *Philosophy and Myth in Karl Marx*. 2d ed. Cambridge: Cambridge University Press.

Varenne, Hervé. 1984. "Collective Representation in American Anthropological Conversation." *Current Anthropology* 25: 281–99.

Veblen, Thorstein. 1915. *Imperial Germany and the Industrial Revolution*. London and New York: Macmillan.

Vierhaus, Rudolf. 1972. "Bildung." In *Geschichtliche Grundbegriffe* 1: 508–51.

Walicki, Andrej. 1981. *A History of Russian Thought*. Oxford: Oxford University Press.

Walzel, O. F. 1922. "Zwei Möglichkeiten deutscher Form." In *Vom Geistesleban alter und neuer Zeit*. Leipzig: Insel.

Weintraub, Karl Joachim. 1978. *The Value of the Individual: Self and Circumstance in Autobiography*. Chicago: University of Chicago Press.

Wundt, Max. 1932. *Goethes Wilhelm Meister und die Entwicklung des modernen Lebensideals*. Berlin. (Originally published 1913.)

Index

Aarsleff, H., 86, 137n, 141

Acculturation, viii, ix, 6, 41; German, 10, 17, 18, 20, 21, 58; global process of, 27, 29; Russian, 12, 14

Action Française, 226

Activity: in Humboldt, 102; in Moritz, 77, 78; utmost enjoyment in, 101

Alsace-Lorraine, 11, 221, 223, 226; French reaction to the loss of, 222. *See also* War of 1870–71

Andler, C., 36, 229

Anschauung: in Kant, 30

Antiquity, 10; spiritual liberty in, 43

Aquinas, T., 188, 195

Aron, R., 201, 215; on despotism, 206, 207

Aufhebung: in Hegel, 75

Augustine, Saint, 73, 74, 166; and individuality, 190

Author: distance between reader and, 31–32; friendships between authors, 31; Goethe as, 31; as mediator, 28, 45, 46

Barbarossa, F., 22

Barbusse, H., 230, 231

Barrès, M., 226, 229

Beethoven, L., 29, 46

Belonging: cultural and sociopolitical modes of, 44–45

Besançon, A., 11n, 13, 27n

Bildung: and *Bildungsroman,* 145; as counterpoint to the French Revolution, 95–96; defined by Humboldt, 93–95; differs in Humboldt and Goethe, 100; as ideal found in ancient Greece, 92; as an institution in Germany, 145; internalizes individual liberty, 97; and notion of totality, 100; and philosophy, 132; place of writing in, 105–6; as process directed toward the ideal, 102; state remains subordinate to, 97–98. *See also* Goethe; Humboldt, W.

Bismarck, 23, 51n, 215, 220, 223

Blake, W., 101

Brahms, J., 63

Brown, J., 156n, 157, 161n, 184

Bruford, W. H., 19n, 54, 77n, 85, 88, 90, 92, 169; *The German Tradition of Self-*

Cultivation, 145; on Humboldt as representative of Bildung, 86

Bruno, G., 83

Calvin, J., 118

Carlyle, T., 70

Cassirer, E., 65, 70, 81

Caussat, P., 109, 138

Charbonnel, N., 155, 174n

Civic education, 134

Clemenceau, G. B., 213, 214

Clitoridectomy, 125n

Collective identity, 3, 36; German, 28, 59; in France and Germany, 3, 15; varying strength of, 27

Comte, A., 205

Condillac, E. B. de, 141

Condorcet, 205

Contradiction: and contrariety as tokens of truth, 25–26; as remnant of hierarchy, 26

Cosmopolitan humanitarianism, 58

Croce, B., 43

Cultural borrowings, 92–93

Cultural identity, 10, 14, 20

Culture: definition of, 4–5; diversity of cultures, 4, 9; and environment, 28; and idea of truth, 34; interaction of cultures, 4, 5, 6, 9; as a living being, 5; rivalry between, 31, 33; and society in American anthropology, 142; universal, 31; world culture and national traditions, 35

Dalberg, K. T., 96, 106

Dansette, A., 210, 212

de Gaulle, C., 206, 232

Descartes, R., 35

Diede, C., 115

Digeon, C., 218, 225, 226

Dilthey, W., 57, 145, 147

Dostoevsky, F. M., 59, 61

Dreyfus Affair, 209, 211, 212, 213, 214. *See also* War of 1870–71

Durkheim, E., 224

Duruy, V., 224n

Eckermann, J. P., 153

Economic liberalism, 8